A New Theory of Industrial Relations

T0330854

Most existing theoretical approaches to industrial relations and human resources management (IR/HRM) build their analyses and policy prescriptions on one of two foundational assumptions. They assume either that conflict between workers and employers is the natural and inevitable state of affairs; or that under normal circumstances, cooperation is what employers can and should expect from workers. By contrast, *A New Theory of Industrial Relations: People, Markets and Organizations after Neoliberalism* proposes a theoretical framework for IR/HRM that treats the existence of conflict or cooperation at work as an outcome that needs to be explained rather than an initial presupposition. By identifying the social and organizational roots of reasoned, positively chosen cooperation at work, this framework shows what is needed to construct a genuinely consensual form of capitalism.

In broader terms, the book offers a critical theory of the governance of work under capitalism. 'The governance of work' refers to the structures of incentives and sanctions, authority, accountability and direct and representative participation within and beyond the workplace by which decisions about the content, conditions and remuneration of work are made, applied, challenged and revised. The most basic proposition made in the book is that work will be consensual—and, hence, that employees will actively and willingly cooperate with the implementation of organizational plans and strategies—when the governance of work is *substantively* legitimate. Although stable configurations of economic and organizational structures are possible in the context of a bare procedural legitimacy, it is only where work relationships are recognized as right and just that positive forms of cooperation will occur.

The analytic purpose of the theory is to specify the conditions under which substantive legitimacy will arise. Drawing in particular on the work of Alan Fox, Robert Cox and Jürgen Habermas, the book argues that whether workers fight against, tolerate or willingly accept the web of relationships that constitutes the organization depends on the interplay between three empirically variable factors: the objective day-to-day experience of incentives, constraints and obligations at work; the subjective understanding of work as a social relationship; and the formal institutional structure of policies, rules and practices by which relationships at work are governed.

Conor Cradden is an independent researcher and consultant.

Routledge Research in Employment Relations

Series editors:
Rick Delbridge and Edmund Heery
Cardiff Business School, UK.

For a full list of titles in this series, please visit www.routledge.com

Aspects of the employment relationship are central to numerous courses at both undergraduate and postgraduate level.

Drawing from insights from industrial relations, human resource management and industrial sociology, this series provides an alternative source of research-based materials and texts, reviewing key developments in employment research.

Books published in this series are works of high academic merit, drawn from a wide range of academic studies in the social sciences.

35 **Gender Equality and Work-Life Balance**
Glass Handcuffs and Working Men in the U.S.
Sarah Blithe

36 **Board-Level Employee Representation in Europe**
Power and Articulation
Jeremy Waddington and Aline Conchon

37 **Employment Relations under Coalition Government**
The UK Experience, 2010–2015
Edited by Steve Williams and Peter Scott

38 **Work-Life Balance in Times of Recession, Austerity and Beyond**
Edited by Suzan Lewis, Deirdre Anderson, Clare Lyonette, Nicola Payne and Stephen Wood

39 **Trade Unions and Arab Revolutions**
The Tunisian Case of UGTT
Hèla Yousfi

40 **A New Theory of Industrial Relations**
People, Markets and Organizations after Neoliberalism
Conor Cradden

A New Theory of Industrial Relations

People, Markets and Organizations after Neoliberalism

Conor Cradden

Routledge
Taylor & Francis Group

LONDON AND NEW YORK

First published 2018 by Routledge

2 Park Square, Milton Park, Abingdon, Oxfordshire OX14 4RN
52 Vanderbilt Avenue, New York, NY 10017

Routledge is an imprint of the Taylor & Francis Group, an informa business

First issued in paperback 2019

Library of Congress Cataloging-in-Publication Data
A catalog record for this book has been requested

ISBN: 978-1-138-12461-5 (hbk)
ISBN: 978-0-367-87584-8 (pbk)

Typeset in Sabon
by Apex CoVantage, LLC

This book is dedicated to all of the extraordinarily brave, determined, committed, articulate, clear-headed, friendly, generous and welcoming developing world trade unionists I have been fortunate enough to meet over the last few years.

Contents

List of Figures and Tables   viii
Preface   ix

1 Can Industrial Relations Save the World?   1

2 Industrial Relations Policy: Conflict & Cooperation in the
   Governance of Work   17

3 Industrial Relations Theory: From Industrial Democracy to the
   Web of Rules and Back Again   49

4 System, Lifeworld and Points in Between   93

5 Frames of Reference   118

6 A New Theory of Industrial Relations   141

7 What Can We Do with NTIR? Implications for Research
   and Policy   167

Appendix: Outline of a Q Study of the Frames of Reference   188
Bibliography   195
Index   203

Figures and Tables

Figures

3.1 Cox's 'Dimensions of a Mode of Social Relations of
     Production'   83
6.1 The Relationship Between the Objective, Subjective and
     Institutional Aspects of the IR System   148

Tables

3.1 Cox's Modes of the Social Relations of Production   84
5.1 The Frames of Reference   133
5.2 Mapping Fox's Frames of Reference onto NTIR Categories   133
6.1 The Characteristics of the Stable Frames of Reference   161

Preface

What a book is called is obviously less important than what it says, but titles do speak to the intent of a work. A title and subtitle together are like an elevator pitch for the elevator pitch, compressing the point of the whole exercise into ten or fifteen words. These words are inevitably highly coded, signalling to potential readers something of the content and, more especially, the analytic approach of the book. And of course, in contested areas like business and management studies, the analytic approach is itself a kind of code for the author's politics. I am not quite sure what the title of this book will say to its intended audience. There are not enough theories of industrial relations around to have a clear idea of what gaps there are in the market or what a new theory could potentially bring to the table. Even the idea of newness is quite difficult to get a grip on. Worse still, I suspect the subtitle might indicate a worrying corporate orientation to some readers.

Just to pin my colours to the mast, then, I want to say clearly that I believe that capitalism in its current form is an unalloyed human and environmental disaster, and without radical action to reform it we are doomed. I do not mean that to be remotely funny or ironic. We are doomed not only to climate change and the destruction of biodiversity, but to being trapped in the sociocultural cage created by capitalism and reinforced by the algorithms of big data. Adorno's 'administered world' is looming. The situation is far too serious for ironic distancing and playfulness. Something needs to be done and it needs to be big enough to change the world. We know that the planned economy is not the answer. We know that individual liberty, the freedom to live, love and speak as we please, is critical—to the extent, of course, that what we choose to do with our liberty is compatible with the same freedom for everyone else. Above all, we know that as things stand, corporations will not spontaneously choose genuinely sustainable modes of production. This is not the conclusion of a complex research project but is a simple observation. If they were going to do it, they would have done it by now.

The reason I think we need a new theory of industrial relations is that we do *not* know the full range of organizational forms and decision-making structures that could be alternatives to what we are currently stuck with. Experiments on the radical fringes of capitalism and in the social and solidarity economy give us hints of the democratic and participatory models that might be viable, but the full force of human ingenuity has never been unleashed on the organization of production.

Carrying on in the spirit of full political disclosure, I have to admit to believing that the objections of the labour movement to worker participation in management are one important reason why positive forms of industrial democracy remain marginal. I also believe that these objections are seriously mistaken. Trade unions are extraordinary and essential vehicles for the pursuit of basic human rights and industrial justice, but collective bargaining is not the best available way to organise the routine participation of workers in the governance of work—not because it brings too much democracy to the workplace, but because it does not bring enough.

The inadequacy of collective bargaining as a means of decision-making was the starting point for the thinking that eventually led to this book. As a trade unionist in the UK in the 1990s, I was frequently frustrated by the inability or unwillingness of my union comrades to engage with the self-serving nonsense that managers tend to use in place of actual argument. At the same time, if unions made actual arguments in return—and as a union researcher I saw it as my job to come up with these—they were simply shrugged off by managers with a 'well you would say that, wouldn't you?' Maybe all that this means is that I was never cut out to be a union negotiator. Still, I felt that the continued degradation of the employment conditions of workers, especially in the public sector where I worked, would not have been happening if decision-making had been based on substantive argument rather than the degree to which a contingent balance of power allowed managers to pursue their own agendas.

This was the era of the 'Celtic Tiger', the wave of rapid growth and development of the Irish economy that had started in the late 1980s. Perhaps the most interesting aspect of the period was the structure of national 'social pact' collective bargaining that seemed to be making an important contribution to this unexpected boom. I learnt a lot about what was going on from my father, Terry Cradden, an industrial relations academic and former trade unionist who had a particular interest in the Irish labour movement and was a great advocate of partnership forms of trade unionism. He was well aware of the shift in thinking that had led at least some parts of the Irish labour movement away from its traditional distributive focus towards a willingness to talk seriously about giving workers a voice in strategic and operational decision-making. Having taken a close look at the policies and politics behind Irish social partnership myself, I ended up seeing it as the great 'might-have-been' of the governance of work. The national level process was much more than just tripartite bargaining. Rather, it was a genuinely new type of engagement between different actors in which actual argument played an essential role and in which participants were aware that—contrary to what many of them will have had hammered into their heads in a lifetime of negotiating—getting to 'yes' was not all that mattered.

Yet, as many readers will know, the Irish partnership experiment never took root at the enterprise level and the national process did not survive the crash of 2008. Nevertheless, as far as I could see, the ideas that were at the heart of it were sound. It seemed to me that two things were missing that would have been needed for partnership to become securely embedded in practice. The first was a robust, settled conceptualization of what partnership was and how it was different from both conventional collective industrial relations and managerially driven forms of high performance management. Without this, no one was sure exactly what commitments they were making and what options for action might be cut off in the future. The second missing piece was a set of rules to guarantee that partnership would happen. The decision to leave the existing institutional structure of industrial relations unchanged meant it was too easy for both unions and businesses to say 'this is too much of a risk; let's stick with what we know'.

Although I only address the Irish case in passing, one of the things that this book does is show how these gaps might be filled. A whole theory of industrial relations may seem like a hammer to crack a nut in this context, but the intellectual territory of work and labour is complex, existing theoretical approaches are fragmented and, as I explain in the opening chapter, the stakes are higher than just the future of the economy of Ireland.

What I am offering here is a synthesis of existing thinking about industrial relations with the addition of a new underlying structure drawn from the work of Jürgen Habermas. The result is a single theory that gives coherence and unity to the field of industrial relations and that opens up new perspectives for research and policy development.

This claim having been made, I have to admit to having had little opportunity to discuss the theory with those best qualified to provide feedback. For this reason, this book is something like the new British Leyland car models of the 1970s, whose final development towards roadworthiness notoriously tended to take place after they were put on sale rather than before. Like British Leyland, I will have to rely on the complaints of early adopters to iron out the many problems that remain.

I have two acknowledgements to make. Over the last five years I have spent a lot of time working on industrial relations in the developing world in a variety of capacities. During that time, I have had the pleasure and privilege of talking to many trade unionists from countries as diverse as Brazil and Myanmar. Apart from their consistent generosity with their time and their knowledge, what was most striking about these men and women was their clear-headed determination to fight on behalf of workers regardless of the personal cost. We in the global policy community owe them the opportunity to take part in a much more serious conversation about the future of work than any that is currently taking place. I hope this book is a step in that direction.

My second debt is to my former colleagues at the ILO: Susan Hayter, Chris Land-Kaslauskas and Verena Schmidt. I learned a great deal from them, and I am grateful for their continuing friendship. Although it is perhaps a forlorn hope that this book will make their very difficult jobs a little easier, I hope it nevertheless. Needless to say, none of this should be read as suggesting that they agree with or bear any responsibility for the arguments presented here.

1 Can Industrial Relations Save the World?

Introduction

Industrial relations is potentially much more significant a discipline than its rather marginal academic status might suggest. Granted, someone writing a book offering a new theory of industrial relations (IR) does have an interest in saying that, but the claim is made very seriously. Although its theoretical tradition is fragmented, IR remains the discipline that has engaged most consistently with the question of how actors in organizations navigate a passage between individual and collective interests, between utilitarian and deontological ethics, between material incentives and social norms. It has resisted the temptation to focus exclusively either on the macro or micro level and continues to try to connect the perspectives of different individual and collective actors with the functioning and impacts of social and economic structures.

The contemporary significance of these achievements is bound up with the impasse in which progressive politics currently finds itself. As I write this in the spring of 2017, the USA is enduring the chaotic early months of the Trump presidency. In the UK, government and opposition alike are struggling with Brexit, the consequence of a colossal political mistake made by a prime minister under threat from right-wing populists. In France and the Netherlands, although they failed to take power, extreme right anti-system parties have made significant electoral gains. Across the developed world, social market politics is under attack from economic nationalists who argue that global capitalism has nothing to offer ordinary people. Mainstream left-of-centre parties, which built their historical base of support on the proposition that capitalism and social progress are compatible, have successfully been portrayed as part of a metropolitan elite whose interests are tightly bound up with the maintenance of international free trade and its counterpart, the free movement of labour. The multicultural social liberalism that, in the absence of any distinctive economic policies, has become the badge of the left is derided as at best an irrelevance and at worst an attempt to suppress the 'native' cultures of the developed world.

It may not be immediately obvious that IR has anything to contribute here, but a moment's reflection should be enough to see that the epicentre of the political earthquakes that progressives are currently failing to withstand is *work*. Work is critical not only for the satisfaction of our basic material needs but also for the construction of individual and collective identities. The critical policy issue, then, is *control* over work: Who gets work, who gives it and who takes it away? What is it worth and who profits from it? Who says what it is and what it is not, what it must be and what it cannot be?

The 'old' left promised at least a negative kind of control in the shape of strong unions able to negotiate improvements to pay, conditions and job security on the basis of their capacity to disrupt production and veto management-driven change to work organization. The defining feature of the 'new' left that emerged in the 1990s was its willingness to accept that the freedom to organise and remunerate work exactly as we wish is a luxury we cannot afford. Mainstream socialist parties bought into the technocratic logic of management, accepting the argument that there are narrow technical limits to effective business and economic decision-making. To this extent, they slipped back into what Beatrice and Sidney Webb—writing in 1897—thought was the rather ludicrous and old-fashioned idea that the "conditions of social life" cannot be "a matter of human arrangement" and that the possibility and desirability of deliberately altering these conditions is to be "regarded as unscientific, if not as impious" (Webb and Webb, 1902, p. 559). The Webbs mocked the idea that intentional change to societies is somehow artificial, "it being apparently supposed that changes unintentionally produced are more 'natural' than others, and more likely to result in the ends we desire" (Ibid.). They argued that the goal not just of trade unionism but of civilisation itself is precisely to create social types different from those which "the free play of social forces would have produced" (p. 560).

120 years on, though, this foundational article of social democratic faith has been all but abandoned. Its scope of application has been so narrowed that there seems to be barely any room left for 'human arrangement'. When it comes to pursuing social and political goals, the position of the contemporary mainstream left is that our margin for manoeuvre in policymaking is only whatever remains once the demands of an impersonal, uncontrolled and uncontrollable market have been met. In trying to move past the old left's grudging and limited accommodation of the market to a more serious and forward-looking engagement with capitalism, the new left rejected the social veto power that was the lynchpin of traditional labour politics, but failed to replace it with any plausible *positive* conception of social control over the economy (Cradden, 2014).

This failure goes a long way to explaining why the radical right has been able to colonise a niche in the political ecosystem that the traditional parties of the left could previously count on having to themselves. That we can and should 'fight back' against a system that limits the pursuit of non-economic social and political values is no longer exclusively a trope of the radical left.

The populist right too now argues that we should reject the narratives of the possible handed down by the corporate establishment and the conventional parties of government.

The argument that a wide range of decision-making prerogatives that ought to belong to the people have been handed over to the anonymous and unaccountable functionaries of 'the system' clearly has some resonance with the public. What is not so clear is why the right is currently having so much more success with this argument than the left. One possible explanation is that the values the right proposes to pursue once 'the system' has been relegated to its proper place in the socio-economic order are the permanent and immutable values handed down by national tradition. Precisely what these values and priorities are is less important than the supposed link between policy choices and the permanence of blood and soil. For the *Front National* in France, for example, policy should be guided by 'economic patriotism'. Former Trump administration adviser Steve Bannon has called the new US government approach 'economic nationalism'. Those who campaigned for a 'leave' vote in the UK's referendum on its membership of the European Union emphasised the impossibility of governing in the national interest while remaining within the EU. The logical sleight of hand here is the implication that national values and interests are not only permanent but well defined and well understood. On this reckoning, there is no shadowy cabal of technocrats that gets to determine the content of policy according to the narrow political and economic exigencies of the moment. It is not the outcome of behind-the-scenes wrangling and under-the-table deals but is determined by simple, common sense extrapolation of our national interest. The values pursued are not just uncontroversial, then, but add up to a set of goals and priorities that *demand* our adhesion in the name of our shared history and culture and can brook no change or disagreement—least of all from those groups who draw on other, potentially competing sources of ethno-national identity.

In the face of this competition for the anti-system vote, mainstream socialists and social democrats continue to struggle to find enough scope to develop convincing policies within the very limited terrain on which they allow themselves to operate. Their more radical comrades, whether traditional eurocommunists, newer movements like *Die Linke* in Germany and *Podemos* in Spain, or the revived radical left currents within mainstream parties like the UK's Labour Party, have in some cases adopted genuinely innovative policies like universal basic income. They are also careful to stress the need for environmental protection alongside industrial and agricultural development. Nevertheless, their main focus is on Keynesian macroeconomic management, indicative industrial planning, public ownership and strengthened individual and collective rights for workers. Aside from the emphasis on sustainability, there is little in the manifestoes of Europe's contemporary radical left that would have looked out of place in the programmes of the Labour Party or the *Parti Socialiste* of the 1970s.

Regardless of any assessment of the likely effectiveness of this kind of approach in practice—and there is a lot to be said in its favour—it poses exactly the same problem that it has always posed and that the new left tried and failed to correct. This is that the typical radical left programme contains vanishingly little that looks likely to open up a new space for positive popular control over the economy. Instead, it simply proposes to shore up an existing anti-system political force, the labour movement, which is viewed by many as at least as inaccessible and unaccountable as the economic system it opposes. Even where it manages to escape identification with the infamous metropolitan elite, the question of why the labour movement can save us when it has had such little success in resisting neoliberalism up to now is still difficult to answer.

The project of the contemporary radical left is problematic because it involves (re)institutionalising a permanent social opposition to the existing market economic system rather than presenting a positive conception of a socio-economic structure we can all unequivocally support. The recognition of the need for such a positive conception is exactly what brought the 'new' left into being in the 1990s. Parties like the UK's 'New Labour' offered a vision of a political community at ease with its economy, where business was a force for the good of all and not just the few. Justice, fairness and sustainability was to be built into decision-making from the outset rather than tacked on at the end when the major parameters of action were already fixed. From an electoral perspective, this vision had some success. In practice, however, the policies of the pro-business left have tended simply to carry on a slightly attenuated version of the neoliberal project of reducing the capacity of workers and unions to oppose management and of government abstention from intervention in the market. Decisions about the level of justice and fairness that is compatible with business success and about the degree of market regulation that is appropriate have simply been handed over to 'business leaders'. The contemporary radical left is certainly proposing to roll this strategy back, thereby increasing social oversight of economic activity, but its approach remains external to business decision-making. There is no suggestion that either the process or logic of decision-making *within* business enterprises should be changed. As French sociologist Danièle Linhart recently put it, the organization of work was and remains something unthinkable ('*un impensé*') for the left. Rather than trying to improve or at least to prevent the further degradation of the quality of working life, she argues that the reaction of the CGT, the historically dominant French union federation, has simply been to negotiate some kind of compensation, a process she describes as the "monetization of the deterioration of the condition of the manual worker" (Jami and Achin, 2017, p. 169; my translation). Although Linhart's comments were directed at the French trade unions, they would be equally valid for most other labour movements. Occasional counter-movements like the Institute for Workers' Control in the UK or the '*autogestionnaire*' (self-management) movement in France have remained marginal.

This brings us back to industrial relations and the reason for this book. The proposition of the populist right is both hateful and fraudulent, but its success shows that voters respond to the idea that there is a set of social norms, values and conventions that will in the end take priority over policies that merely reflect the strategic calculations of those who hold the reins of the economy. The relative failure of the radical left alternative, a political project based on reinforcing an existing social capacity to resist the owners and managers of capital, shows that mere opposition to capitalism without a positive vision of what the economy is for is a poor substitute for even so transparently dubious a project as the pursuit of 'national values'. The implication to be drawn here is that the future of progressive politics depends on being able to offer the public a convincing vision of a capitalist economy that works for everyone because it is under social control *from the inside*. Rather than some mechanism that allows us to step in to limit the damage once business strategies have already been formulated and critical decisions already taken, the vision needs to involve the integration of moral and ethical criteria into organizational processes from the outset.

A basic premise of the book is that this kind of social control is actually possible; that there is nothing inevitable or given about the structure of social relationships within business organizations nor about the substantive choices that businesses make. This is not to say that the market in the sense of the actual or potential demand for particular products and services at specific prices has no influence on what businesses decide to do. Clearly it does. However, it does not by itself determine organizational action. More importantly, neither does it dictate how decisions are made nor the systems of coordination and control by which they are translated into action. Markets do not design production systems or determine the content of jobs. Markets do not decide what conditions workers will accept or when they should go on strike. Markets do not decide on the length of the working day or whether workers should wear uniforms. For all that the decisions by which organizations are animated are subject to certain constraints, they are ultimately the result of choices made by real living people.[1] My concern is with how these choices are made, and how they might be made differently.

In addressing these questions, I am not proposing to consider the potential of revolutionary reorganisations of production: those that would entirely overturn the fundamental principles of private ownership of the means of production, production for profit and exchange via markets. This is to some extent a pragmatic choice made to limit the scope of the book, but it also reflects a conviction that the possibilities for the radical reform of capitalism are far from exhausted. While there is much that is wrong with what we have, there are also many aspects of the system that are valuable. We do not have to stray too far into Burkean conservatism to recognise that, for the moment at least, revolution is a counsel of despair.

This book, then, is about making capitalism better by changing the organizations we already have. It does not envisage any alternative system of production, supposing instead that economic and social justice is possible *within* capitalist societies. It assumes that justice is a question of the structures of social relationships that are the fabric of every organization, but that the nature of these structures does not depend solely or even mainly on the ownership of capital.

What Is a Theory of Industrial Relations About and What Is It For? Normative and Analytic Orientations

The theory proposed here is aligned with the larger project of critical theory which, in Bohman's words, aims to "transform contemporary capitalism into a consensual form of social life" (Bohman, 2016, p. 3). A consensual capitalism would be one in which we possess the social control over the economy that currently seems to be out of our reach. In pursuing this goal, critical theory aims to be

> explanatory, practical, and normative, all at the same time. That is, it . . . explain[s] what is wrong with current social reality, identif[ies] the actors to change it, and provide[s] both clear norms for criticism and achievable practical goals for social transformation.
>
> (Bohman, 2016, p. 2)

If capitalism is to be consensual, the single most important thing that needs to change about our societies is work. As Ackers puts it, "nothing is more central to the reconstitution of community and civil society than rethinking work, which consumes so much of our daylight hours, confers income and status, and shapes life-chances in so many ways" (2002, p. 15). To the extent that the transformation of capitalism demands the transformation of work, the critical theory of industrial relations I want to construct is intended to provide analytic resources for those involved in pursuing that transformation.

The first broad concept we need to address is what it would mean for work to represent a consensual form of social life. By definition, a consensual social relation can only exist if those involved have chosen it. At this early stage in the argument I want to make a hopefully uncontroversial theoretical assumption, which is that human beings will not freely choose to spend their lives in any of the astonishing range of miserable situations that the world of work has to offer. If they are in misery it is because they have no choice about it. They can see no alternative way to support themselves and their families. The empirical fact of widespread misery, therefore, must mean that the availability of choice—the most vaunted characteristic of the market economy—is for most workers entirely illusory.

This is hardly a novel observation. In volume one of *Capital*, Marx observes with biting sarcasm that labour power is bought and sold in the sphere of the market, which is a very Eden of the innate rights of man. There alone rule Freedom, Equality, Property and Bentham. Freedom, because both buyer and seller of a commodity, say of labour power, are constrained only by their own free will. They contract as free agents, and the agreement they come to is but the form in which they give legal expression to their common will. Equality, because each enters into relation with the other, as with a simple owner of commodities, and they exchange equivalent for equivalent. Property, because each disposes only of what is his own. And Bentham, because each looks only to himself . . . no one troubles himself about the rest, and just because they do so, do they all, in accordance with the pre-established harmony of things, or under the auspices of an allshrewd providence, work together to their mutual advantage, for the common weal and in the interest of all.

(Marx and Engels, 2010, p. 186)

There are two elements to the illusion. First, there is the simple truth that, as Korpi reminds us, capital can be accumulated but labour cannot (Korpi, 2006). This means that capital and labour do not confront each other in the labour market as equals despite the nominal equality of employers and workers as legal persons. Second, but no less important, labour *power* is not what employers actually need. Rather, they need *labour*. In order to get it, Marx argues, labour power has to be consumed in "the hidden abode of production" (ibid.). The potential and the promise to work has to be transformed into actual productive labour. The capitalist illusion that Marx recognised, then, works both by focusing exclusively on the moment of exchange and by conceiving it as free of power. Work itself and the social relationships by which it is stitched together into production are nowhere to be seen.

Any analytic approach intended to support the effort to transform work into a consensual social relation has to deal with this illusion. Mainstream labour economics wilfully fails to take up the challenge at all, simply refusing to recognise either the power imbalance in the labour market or the labour process that is required to transform labour power into productive work. Labour economics deals in labour power, not labour, treating it as undifferentiated and substitutable (Kaufman, 2010). It ignores the "inherent uncertainty of the transformation of labour power into labour" (Bellofiore and Taylor, 2004, p. 109), simply assuming away the internal processes of organizations and guaranteeing that the empirical impact of different types of labour process on workers and on production is treated as exogenous to any theoretical models of the labour market that might be constructed.

As Linhart's arguments suggest, the analysis underpinning the policies typical of most labour movements is better, but still inadequate. For trade unions and social democratic political parties, the critical factor is the power imbalance between labour and capital in the moment of exchange. Their demand is that the exchange of labour power for money be negotiated not between each individual worker and the employer but between the employer and labour reconceived as a collective actor. The idea is to institute a kind of structural equivalent of the capacity of capital to accumulate. The collective power of workers can then be used to leverage a better deal by increasing the price that employers pay for labour power and, in some circumstances, by narrowing the limits within which employers are at liberty to direct the concrete efforts of workers.

Although addressing the power imbalance in the labour market can undoubtedly have positive results in terms of reducing poverty and increasing aggregate demand in economies, the mere monetisation of misery—to paraphrase Linhart—hardly responds to the profound concerns about our lack of control over the economy that have contributed to recent political developments. The transformation of work surely demands not only that the distribution of the rewards of production between different participants be agreed and not imposed, but also that production itself be a consensual form of life, from the most basic decision-making about what is to be produced and where, all the way through to the finest detail of the labour process.

It is tempting to go down the path of trying to define what an objectively 'good' production system or employment relationship would look like. This would involve focusing research and analysis on the substantive questions of what practices and forms of relationship are simultaneously ethically defensible and economically viable. Once we know what these are, we know what employers ought to be doing and can check to see that they are doing it. We can also assume that workers within good production systems will be content with their lot and that any conflict is simply a mistake that can be corrected with better communication and similar practices. Employers, for their part, can set up management systems to ensure that their workplace practices remain within the realms of the acceptable but are otherwise able to organise production as they see fit. This is the logic of the current wave of private forms of regulation of global supply chains: define good practice in consultation with 'stakeholders' and with reference to international human rights and other normative and technical standards (living wages, safety standards, working time limits etc.); organise an auditing system; certify organizations that are meeting the agreed requirements and call it social control (Cradden and Graz, 2016; Meardi and Marginson, 2014).

This approach is appealing because it seems to provide a welcome degree of clarity to work relationships by putting normative limits on economically motivated action. It offers a kind of presumptive consensuality by placing universal standards ahead of partial, private interests. In this sense it is very similar to the populist nationalism I discussed above. Replace 'national values' with 'international labour standards' and the argument is pretty much the same. Like national values, international standards are—supposedly—objective and transcendent, their claim on us cutting across the base motivations of politics and the economy. As such, they can be presented as consensual even in the absence of any real participation by citizens or workers in their definition.[2] This, of course, is deeply problematic since the definition and interpretation of international standards, just like that of national values, is anything but uncontroversial. Indeed, existing research into private labour regulation has shown that institutions of market governance based on supposedly universal international standards are in fact locally situated, socially constructed and politically contested (Cradden et al., 2015). The claim that the values and standards that supposedly limit or frame economic action in these cases are universally valid is almost impossible to sustain.

One of the many reasons why the Anglo-American IR tradition is in the end the best starting point for developing the analytic framework needed to support the transformation of work is precisely that it avoids these problems via its firm emphasis on procedure; on the means by which the rules governing work are made rather than their content. As a practice-oriented discipline, IR has rarely if ever proposed substantive standards or attempted to define in concrete terms what an acceptable employment relationship would involve. Rather, it has focused on the formal and informal rules that govern individual and collective employment relationships and on the cultural, socio-political and economic processes by which these rules come to be agreed and applied. As Cox argued, the *content* of decisions about work processes and the distribution of rewards has been of interest only "in so far as they throw light on the power relations among the actors" (1971, p. 3).

The broadening of IR's focus of attention in recent decades from formal workplace rules to the 'governance of the employment relationship' maintains the emphasis on procedure while allowing a more realistic and nuanced view of how social relations at work constrain and direct behaviour. As Ackers put it, "the employment relationship has become the master concept of a British 'industrial relations perspective' on contemporary employment and management" (2014, p. 2610). The employment relationship is conceived as "a structured set of rules or regimes of regulation" (Kaufman, 2014, p. 23), while rules are in turn conceived as "complex social institution[s]" that include "beliefs, ideologies and taken-for-granted assumptions" (Edwards, cited in Sisson, 2008, p. 32). Along with rules and rule-making processes, Sisson also proposes that IR deals with "the institutions involved in governing the employment relationship [and] the people and organizations that make and administer them" (2007, p. 59).

The only point on which I would diverge from the current consensus around the analytic focus of IR is in describing its subject matter as the 'governance of work' rather than the 'governance of the employment relationship'. Although for me the distinction is largely about getting away from the conceptual association of the employment relationship with hierarchical forms of coordination (discussed further below), taking the governance of *work* as our focus also has the advantage of expanding the territory of IR to include all forms of dependent employment and forms of the coordination of work that reach beyond the boundaries of firms.

In the rest of this book I use the phrase 'governance of work' to refer to the to the structures of incentives and sanctions, authority, accountability and direct and representative participation within and beyond the workplace by which decisions about the content, conditions and remuneration of work are made, applied, challenged and revised. This definition is intended to encompass all the formal and informal social processes by which the actions of those involved in production are coordinated, and to include all types of work relationship, whether formal, informal, standard, nonstandard, direct or indirect.

Specifying an analytic focus for our theory clarifies what it is *about* but not what it is *for*. A negative answer to the question is implied in the focus on procedure. The point of a theory of industrial relations is *not* to produce hypotheses about the kinds of work and working conditions that are or are likely to be recognised as fair, personally fulfilling, socially useful, dignified, safe, healthy and so on, still less the degree to which any of these characteristics is compatible with some definition of economic success. Instead, IR theory should help us to understand how to organise production so that work and the normative framework within which it takes place is freely chosen by all involved. The aim is not simply for work to have the kind of positive characteristics I listed a moment ago, but for it to have them *because* the actors involved have agreed a vision of what it should be and are able to conduct their social relations in a way that ensures both that the vision can be realised and that any trade-offs between competing objectives are made consciously and on the basis of complete information.

From a more strictly analytic perspective, this translates into a theory of industrial relations that *specifies the different possible conditions under which the governance of work will be substantively legitimate.* I say 'substantively legitimate' to distinguish clearly between the kind of legitimacy I want to talk about and the merely procedural or legal legitimacy that is a frequent topic in classical organization theory.[3] Substantive legitimacy is what you get when rules, social relations and institutions are consensual. It is a summative evaluation of the normative character of coordinated social action made from the perspective of the actors involved in it. Where the governance of work is substantively legitimate, actors will recognise the broad *rightness* of the social relations in which they are implicated at work. Despite any potential for legally-sanctioned or other forms of coercion that exists within those social relations, the participation of the actor in coordinated action is not coerced but is rationally motivated in Weber's sense of value-rationality: it is quite simply the right thing to do.

There is nothing innovative about this focus on legitimacy, of course, dating as it does since at least Max Weber and picked up by classical organization theorists like Blau and Scott (1962). What is different about my use of the concept is that I want to make achieving it the central purpose of the governance of work; our goal should be substantively legitimate governance and the aim of government policy on industrial relations should be to ensure that law and practice support the achievement of this goal. If the economic system is to be consensual, workers cannot be constantly constrained to accept governance decisions they would not otherwise accept solely because of material need. This is why legitimacy itself must be the aim rather than specific goals like a certain set of 'fair' working conditions, improved organizational performance or even industrial peace. The evidence of supply chain monitoring systems shows that even very detailed checklists of 'good practice' can leave serious abuses in place and either of the latter two objectives could be pursued at the price of overruling workers' objections to some business strategy or decision. While I firmly believe that substantively legitimate governance of work is the best route to high performance and stable and productive employment relations, legitimacy should not be treated merely as one possible means to these ends.

Abandoning the Authority Assumption

Making legitimacy our goal does involve one major assumption, though, which is that the governance of work *can* be substantively legitimate; that there are always courses of action available to organizations that are normatively defensible from the perspective of all their members and from that of the communities within which they exist. This assumption runs directly counter to the rhetoric of tough choices and cruel-to-be-kind 'responsible' economic management to which we have spent so much of the last 40 years listening. Between the pro-business left and the neoliberal right we are assured that the choices that we—the people and the workers—would probably reject if given the opportunity are precisely those that we ought to be making since they are necessary for growth and since everything depends on growth. This is why we cannot be allowed to make these choices for ourselves. Indeed, making unpopular but 'responsible' economic choices on behalf of a reluctant electorate—or ensuring that managers are able to make those choices—has become part of what is understood to be the burden of contemporary political leadership.

Yet, organizational hierarchy is in itself a large part of what makes it difficult to accept that substantively legitimate governance is always possible. Built into the bedrock of most existing approaches to industrial or employment relations, human resource management and labour law is the presumption, whether tacit or openly stated, that the procedural rules applying to the employment relationship are mainly about defining the scope and limits of an employer's 'residual control rights' over a worker's work (Marsden, 2004; Sisson, 2008). The very existence of management decision-making structures and the associated disciplinary mechanisms implies that there is some reason why organizations cannot or should not be democratic. Nevertheless, there seems to be no fundamental reason why the governance of work necessarily involves the delimitation of a sphere of action—the production or labour process—within which a worker is obliged to participate in work practices and relationships she has had no part in designing or risk being unilaterally excluded from the organization.

By contrast, there are a number of very good reasons *not* to build a theory of IR on the assumption that the governance of work is necessarily characterised by the formal or effective authority of employers over workers. Perhaps the most obvious of these is simply that it immediately limits the scope and ambition of the theory. There are many different forms that consensual work relationships could take and it seems bizarre to start by excluding those not characterised by the ultimate ability of one class of organizational actors to impose their will on another.

Rather more importantly, putting authority relations at the centre of IR has very significant consequences for theory development. If the employment relationship is necessarily an authority relationship, actors must be divided into governors and governed; into those who have legal authority to develop plans and strategies and issue orders and those who are, as a consequence, obliged to comply. There have to be employees on one side and an 'employer' on the other. Making this assumption as a first step in theory building has at least four unfortunate consequences.

First, the focus on the employer-employee relationship draws attention away from other important relationships like those between workers and other workers or managers and other managers, between employees of all types and their families, between the employer and its customers and suppliers and so on. As a number of commentators have recently noted (Ackers, 2002; Kaufman, 2008; Piore and Safford, 2006), all of these relationships may have a significant bearing on the employment relationship but are generally excluded from the purview of IR.

Second, if managers necessarily have legal authority, then we have to think in terms of a sphere of management prerogative within which workers are obliged to comply. The authority of management cannot be absolute since its authority is based on contract rather than status. But if IR is mainly about how the limits of employers' residual control rights are defined, it is also about delimiting the territory within which employers are not obliged to pay any heed to the consequences of their plans and strategies for workers. Logically, though, it is very difficult to identify any management decision that will not, sooner or later, have consequences for workers. If we assume that a line *must* be drawn somewhere, then we are limiting the potential extent of the transformation of work before we even start.

Third, the very idea of the 'employer' glosses over the distinction between ownership and control. It involves the assumption of an approximate identity between the interests of capital and the actions of managers. There is a fusion of two distinct structural roles in a single fictitious person. This is at least as questionable as the idea that the ownership and control of business have been definitively separated. It makes it much more difficult to understand the complex and overlapping relationships between labour and capital, between workers and the organizations in which they work and between beneficial owners and workers and managers in organizations. The argument that the authority of management derives from private property is no solution. I follow Dahrendorf in believing that Marx was mistaken when he proposed that authority and power are a consequence of private property. Dahrendorf argues that since property is simply the permission to exclude others from control over an object, it is simply one of the many forms of legal authority:

> The specific type of change of social structures caused by social classes and their conflicts is ultimately the result of the *differential distribution of positions of authority* in societies and their institutional orders. Control over the means of production is but a special case of authority, and the connection of control with legal property an incidental phenomenon of the industrializing societies of Europe and the United States.
>
> (Dahrendorf, 1959, pp. 136–7; emphasis added)

The fourth consequence of the assumption that the employment relationship is an authority relationship also arises from the conflation of management and capital in the person of 'the employer'. If managerial authority is exercised with a view to pursuing the interests of capital and if the interests of capital are bound up with responding appropriately to the imperatives of the market, then one's view of the nature of the employment relationship will be predetermined by one's view of the nature of the market. The basic character of the labour process itself will be prejudged.

Views of the market tend to be located somewhere on a continuum between two extremes. At one end, there is the Marxian view that the market should be understood as a force based on "a logic of accumulation that compels capital to constantly revolutionize the production of goods and services. This arises from competition between capitalists and between capital and labor" (Thompson and Newsome, 2004, p. 145). The revolutionisation of production in response to the pressure of competition is a very effective means of increasing the wealth of the owners of capital but is anything but an unmitigated social good. The increase in productivity

> is expressed in an increased burden of work for those with jobs, alongside a growing 'reserve army of labour' who have been made redundant and are condemned to idleness. The depreciation of machinery in the course of accumulation is matched by the throwing of workers onto the scrap heap. The more rapid is 'progress' the more rapidly is work dehumanized and workers degraded, exploited and cast aside.
>
> (Clarke, 1995, p. 4)

The polar opposite of the Marxian conception of markets is that typical of the Austrian school of economics, particularly von Mises and his acolytes. On this reading, a market can be understood as a system of price signals that allows the coordination of the actions of otherwise unconnected individuals. As such it is a simply a useful mechanism for dealing with social complexity that permits levels of economic growth that would otherwise not be available. As Hayek put it,

> the basic foundation of our civilization and our wealth is a system of signals which informs us, however imperfectly, of the effects of millions of events which occur in the world, to which we have to adapt ourselves and about which we may have no direct information.
>
> (1986, p. 143)

We can distil these positions into a simple opposition: market imperatives are either an expression of the private interests of the owners of capital or they provide information about how to optimize the efficiency of material reproduction. If the former, they are normatively loaded and cannot represent a universally valid guide to action. If the latter, they are normatively neutral, objectively necessary requirements for the optimisation of the gains of economic activity.

From the perspective of the 'interests of capital' conception of markets, there appears to be a real possibility that management direction will put workers in opposition to their own well-being, whether physical, psychological or material. The contradiction between the legal authority of management (*procedural* legitimacy) and the interests of workers will sooner or later lead to conflict. As Fox delicately put it, "management sometimes feels constrained to govern contrary to the interests of employees as they themselves see them" (1971, p. 62). This means that consistently consensual workplace relations are either impossible or can only arise on the basis of some process of interest compensation or harmonisation. We can call this the conflict assumption.

From the 'price signals' perspective, on the other hand, creating a consensual capitalism does not appear to be a normative question. Management direction represents the pursuit of goals that are shared by definition and, as long as some purely technical standard of organizational effectiveness is met, it is to be expected that workers will respond to that direction in a basically cooperative way. *By definition* there is no contradiction between workers' substantive material interests and the legal authority to which they are subject in their capacity as employees; no distinction, in other words, between procedural and substantive legitimacy. If workers do not cooperate with managers then something is wrong with the relationship. To cite Fox again, this is the idea that "management's role in this process is that of disinterested mediator concerned only with some criterion of the social good" (ibid.). We can call this the cooperation assumption.

A Manifesto for a Theory of Industrial Relations

I started this chapter by arguing that the absence of any realistic prospect of establishing social control over work and production *from the inside* has contributed to support for nationalist populism and the project of limiting the excesses of globalised capitalism by integrating 'national values' into business choices. The alternatives that are on offer are clearly insufficiently convincing—on the one hand, that there is simply no need for social control at all and, on the other, that the only possible form of control is an external, post hoc restriction on capital's room for manoeuvre.

To me it is self-evident that if we want to work through the possibilities for developing consensual forms of capitalism, then we have to avoid starting our analysis having already taken a position on what is likely to be possible; having made a foundational assumption about the likely outcome of the relationship between workers and organizations. The vast majority of existing approaches to IR and closely related fields like human resource management do exactly this, deciding at the outset that either conflict or cooperation is the normal state of affairs. Having done so, they have trouble taking seriously any evidence that contradicts their foundational assumptions. Marxists and industrial relations pluralists distrust cooperative workplace relationships, seeking ways to explain them away as illusory or the result of strictly temporary configurations of economic forces. Advocates of progressive approaches to personnel or human resource management tend to see workplace conflict in purely human or psychological terms and have difficulty accepting that the most effective resolution may involve a change in the distribution of rewards or a rebalancing of power between labour and capital.

I want to propose a theoretical framework that avoids both the conflict and cooperation assumptions. I want to get away not only from the focus on workers' responses to managerial direction but also from the idea that managerial direction must be understood as a reflection of the partial interests of the beneficial owners of the organization. Instead, I will assume that whether there are or are not good reasons for workers to oppose the demands their organizations make of them—however these are determined—is purely contingent. Industrial conflict is not necessarily either some kind of moral failing or simply a mistake, but it might easily be either or both of these things. In some circumstances, enthusiastic and unlimited cooperation within organizations may be fully warranted, just as under other conditions it may be wrong for one individual or group to accept the lead of another. What is more, I assume that actors in organizations may or may not be right about what kind of attitude is appropriate.

In short, then, we need to think differently about what it is we are studying. First, a theory of industrial relations should be concerned not just with the exchange of labour power for money but also with the labour process: it should be concerned with the entire relationship between workers and organizations and not just one moment of it. We can call this the governance of work. Second, from an IR perspective, the goal of transforming capitalism into a consensual form of life can be rendered as seeking to ensure that the governance of work is substantively and not merely procedurally legitimate. Third, IR is not about either the humanisation of work or increasing the efficiency and effectiveness of production. It is about the procedural means by which the substantive legitimacy of the governance of work can be guaranteed. Fourth, we should not treat as foundational the assumption that a certain category of employee acting on behalf of and accountable only to the beneficial owners of the organization will have permanent legal authority to direct the work of other employees. Any structures of authority that exist within organizations are part of what has to be justified if the governance of work is to be legitimate. Fifth, if we abandon the presumption of hierarchical social relations, we can also abandon any a priori expectation that the governance of work will be characterised by either conflict or cooperation.

Notes

1 The Webbs cite J.S. Mill on this subject: "Demand and supply are not physical agencies which thrust a given amount of wages into the laborer's hand without the participation of his own will and actions. The market rate is not fixed for him by some self-acting instrument, but is the result of bargaining between human beings—of what Adam Smith calls 'the higgling of the market.'" J. S. Mill, Principles of Political Economy, Book V. ch. x. sec. 5. (Webb and Webb, 1902, p. 649).

2 In this connection it is interesting to note that research into private labour standards systems has found that freedom of association and collective bargaining rights in these systems are both weak and weakly enforced (Anner, 2012; Barrientos and Smith, 2007; Cradden et al., 2015; Egels-Zandén and Merk, 2014; Fransen, 2013).

3 As Besson points out (2005), the distinction between substantive and procedural legitimacy is in fact a complex and difficult area. We will discuss it in greater depth in Chapter 4.

2   Industrial Relations Policy

Conflict & Cooperation in the Governance of Work

Industrial relations policy is the ensemble of ideas, beliefs and goals that underpin and justify the structures of rules by which work and working relationships are governed. These rules in turn make up the substance of national and international labour law as well as the internal regulation and employment practices of organizations. In this chapter I want to look at how policy approaches to the question have developed since trade unionism first became widely accepted as legitimate towards the end of the 19th century. In discussing the various possibilities for IR policy I am not aiming to give a detailed account of the historical evolution of this or that idea, but to shed some light on the underlying logic of the positions taken by governments, businesses, workers' organizations and other actors. What matters is how the different ways of thinking about IR fit together or contradict each other and what insights about IR theory we can take away from how the interaction between competing policy ideas and approaches has played out over the last century.

In particular, I want to consider how the conflict and cooperation assumptions that we discussed in chapter one have structured policy-making, especially at the international level. This involves a particular focus on the International Labour Organization (ILO). The ILO is the sole international governmental organization concerned directly with policy on work and employment, and is the originator and guardian of international labour standards. It has also played a critical role in the propagation of the reformist model of collective industrial relations that has had an enormous impact on the political economy of the industrialised world, whether as a model to be copied or, since the 1980s, avoided.

Post-Traditional Forms of Authority at Work

The need for a governance of work distinct from traditional structures of social control arose as a consequence of modernisation. According to Jürgen Habermas among others (1987), the development of modern capitalist societies involved the gradual stripping away of traditional social, political and cultural influences from the design of methods of production, forms of organization and ways of doing business. Trade and commerce have existed since the dawn of time, but until relatively recently the profit motive was only one among a number of other, equally important reasons for the exchange of goods. These other reasons, bound up with cultural and religious beliefs and practices, arguably had much more influence over production and exchange than the mere value of the goods involved. The way in which artisanal production was organised, for example, was based on a conception of the techniques of a trade as valuable in themselves. The rigid organizational hierarchy of master, journeyman and apprentice was derived from this conception of technique as an end rather than—or, at least, as well as—a means. Similarly, traditional European forms of dependent employment were based on the idea that the duty of a 'servant' to obey his or her 'master' is a question of the relative social status of employer and employee rather than being a purely hypothetical imperative that depends on the continued individual interest of both sides in the maintenance of a contractual relationship. This is why disobedience or defiance of one's master, whether individual or collective, was so often counted as a criminal offence.

From a contemporary perspective, it can be difficult to grasp the extent to which these kinds of conception governed ways of thinking. Yet, for most of recorded history, changing the way things were done simply because there were better or more effective or more just ways of achieving the same end was quite literally unthinkable. The socio-cultural *means* of doing things was indistinguishable from the *end* for which these things were done.

Habermas characterises the gradual freeing of the economic sphere from traditional forms of social control as a process of the differentiation of means and ends.[1] However, as well as liberating economic activity from the dead hand of church and state, this process also had the effect of dissolving the existing normative grounding for the domination of those who owned the means of production over property-less workers. The contradiction between emerging democratic political rights and the concentration of power and control in the hands of private businesses that stood outside traditional structures of authority and accountability was brought into sharp focus. The clearer it became that social class distinctions based on heredity and ecclesiastical authority were an unacceptable basis for the distribution of decision-making authority in society in general, the more obvious it became that the subordination of workers within the sphere of production was based on nothing more than their material need. The recognition that *traditional* forms of subordination were no longer acceptable simply highlighted the lack of legitimacy of *economic* subordination. A Japanese worker delegate to an early conference of the International Labour Organization captured this idea very well:

> The feudal system was abolished in Japan more than half a century ago, but the ideas of that system still prevail in wide circles and the capitalists of today are still nursing the ambition of playing the role of

the feudal lords of earlier days. These conservative circles always refer to the inherited Japanese virtue that the worker, depending on his master, should devote his soul and body to the interests and benefit of his master. These modern feudal lords do not hesitate to take advantage of the working people and their inherited virtues, and condemn new ideas, pretending that they are importations from the western countries and tend to menace these old Japanese virtues.

(ILO, 1924, p. 152)

So, capitalist modernisation gave rise to a legitimacy crisis in the sense that there was no stable, widely accepted justification for the dominance of capital in the economic sphere. By the late 19th century the violent consequences of this crisis were increasingly difficult to ignore. The strategies of those who wanted to address it can be divided into two broad categories depending on the understanding of markets that informed the proposed solutions. One group of solutions arose from 'the conflict assumption'. As I argued in Chapter 1, this is the belief that the orientation or direction that markets give to organizational action reflects the partial interests of the owners of capital rather than a shared interest of all the organization's stakeholders. It follows that if the governance of work is based exclusively on the pursuit of market goals this will inevitably lead to conflict between workers and organizations. By contrast, 'the cooperation assumption' involves the idea that the market represents an objective, normatively neutral guide to the necessary parameters of material reproduction. Management is no more than a technical interpretation of what this means for organizational action. It follows that employment relationships ought normally to be cooperative. Since everyone shares an interest in a thriving economy, there is no fundamental reason why workers should not accept expert managerial direction.

The conflict assumption gives rise to two basic types of IR policy.[2] The first of these is simply communism: the abolition of the private ownership of the means of production. Communists believe that there is no possibility that industrial governance can be legitimate as long as businesses are the property of private individuals who have the right to dispose of that property as they see fit. For them the only possible solution is to take property into public ownership, by force if necessary. Once this has been done, decisions about production and distribution can be made on the basis of the democratically-expressed will of the people. The economic sphere would thus cease to be separate from the rest of society, and material reproduction would be subject to the same democratic control as other social processes.

The second, and ultimately more significant, policy position that can arise from the conflict assumption is collective industrial relations (CIR). Reformists (for want of a better term) share the radical analysis that business and the economy are undemocratic because the means of production is in private hands, but take the view that there is no need to go to the extreme of collectivizing private property to get a measure of economic democracy. As

Cox put it, there is "a recognition that class struggle is a continuing feature of the production process, but that it can be regulated and moderated by collective bargaining and similar procedures" (1996, p. 440). Reformists argue that it is mistaken to believe that economic activity can or should embody some kind of general interest and that the pursuit of this general interest represents the common goal of all involved. Rather, the owners of capital and those who possess nothing but their labour should be thought of simply as different interest groups within a plural society. The property rights of the owners of capital should be recognised—argue the reformists—but at the same time it has to be accepted that working people have the same kind of property rights over their own labour. Thus capital and labour are separate but mutually dependent groups of individuals pursuing their own interests within an economic arena that in itself is the creature of neither one side nor the other.

There are both economic and political aspects to this position. The economic aspect is that the optimisation of economic performance claimed to be the consequence of unilateral control by expert managers is in practice illusory. Workers will obviously resist any attempt to force them into actions that are against their own interest and the subsequent conflict will negate any theoretical advantage of absolute managerial control. Once the reality of the social force of organised labour has been recognised, it becomes clear that maximising firm performance involves an optimisation along two dimensions rather than just one. Integrating the satisfaction of workers' interests into decision-making as an objective on an equal footing with the satisfaction of employer interests will in practice improve business performance rather than damaging it.[3]

The political aspect to CIR is that it brings democracy to the workplace. Democracy, or something like it, exists when there is no longer any unilateral control, when each side is able to freely negotiate the terms of its own engagement in any joint activity. In concrete terms, policy is focused on ensuring that independent collective worker organization and action is possible, on the construction or improvement of institutions for conflict resolution and on involving workers' and employers' representatives in those public decision-making processes that have implications for the employment relationship. This means conceiving the enterprise not as a monolithic entity pursuing a single shared goal but an arena for the pursuit of separate but equally legitimate goals.

The contrasting policy position built on the cooperation assumption can be called 'control-oriented people management' or COPM. COPM involves a heavy emphasis on management as morally and politically neutral *technique*. Democracy is simply not an appropriate concept because the only appropriate and relevant criteria for decision-making are economic. There is only one dimension of optimisation for economic performance. Policies derived from this way of thinking run the gamut from outlawing or restricting worker organization and collective bargaining—on the grounds that it introduces non-economic motives into decision-making and hence potentially represents a brake on economic growth and development—through to measures to shore up the perceived legitimacy of management by encouraging cooperative modes of working in ways that have no impact on its legal authority to demand compliance. The unifying factors are an emphasis on the capacity of managers to maintain unilateral control over their organizations and the subjection of all policy measures to the test of the 'business case'. To the extent that policy promotes the involvement of workers in decision-making this is not thought of as a means of ensuring that their particular interests are represented but as a means of improving business performance by taking account of additional information and different perspectives, especially with respect to the implementation of management plans and strategies.

Revolution and Reform

It would obviously be wrong to argue that a fully-developed version of the CIR policy position was at the root of the wave of legalisation of worker collective organization and action that rippled across Europe from the 1870s until the outbreak of the First World War. The transformation of trade unionism from a subversive political movement into an integral part of the industrial landscape was a gradual process that was interwoven with the evolution of the ideas that justified it (Cradden, 2014). The tentative legislative and political steps that made trade unions at least technically legal were certainly not taken with a view to creating what would now be recognised as fully-fledged systems of collective industrial relations. Rather, the aim of legislators was simply to defuse industrial conflict that could no longer be suppressed and to pull the rug from under the feet of those who saw labour movements as a vehicle for revolution rather than reform.[4] Certainly there were those who saw in independent worker organization and collective bargaining a rational means to improve the condition of the working classes, as well as others who thought the development of orderly, mutualist forms of working class association would better integrate workers into industrial society without posing a threat to the existing order (Barbet, 1991; Fox, 1986). Nevertheless, it would hardly be too cynical to argue that fending off the threat of revolutionary insurrection was near the top of the list of priorities, as shown by attempts to restrict overtly 'political' or 'socialist' trade unionism—for example the anti-socialist laws enacted in 1878 in Germany (Weiss and Schmidt, 2008) or the limitation of French trade union activity to 'professional' matters (Barbet, 1991).

For the trade unions themselves, essentially the same set of basic policy concerns presented themselves. As Hyman argues, labour movements in Europe can be divided into those that seek to advance class interests via anti-capitalist mobilisation, those that see trade unionism as "a vehicle for social integration" and those that try to avoid ideological entanglements in favour of an economistic business unionism (Hyman, 2001a, pp. 2–3).

Almost every trade union movement in Europe has at some point split over the issue of revolution versus reform, while reformist unions vacillate between opportunist bargaining and more normatively-oriented approaches to worker representation.

The foundation of the International Labour Organization (ILO) in 1919 as part of the Treaty of Versailles marked a critical juncture in the history of industrial relations policy in the sense that it was the point at which the reformist position crystallised into a permanent international institutional form and was confirmed as a mainstream policy position in the industrialised world. Perhaps even more importantly, the ILO—eventually—established as a matter of international law that workers have the *right* to organise and to demand that their organizations are recognised by businesses for the purposes of collective bargaining.

It had been clear since early on in the First World War that any eventual peace settlement would have to address the 'labour question'. The surge of labour unrest and revolutionary activity towards the end of the war only increased the urgency of finding some compromise that would preserve the existing world order while accommodating enough of the demands of organised labour to defuse the potential for serious conflict (Phelan, 1949). Sure enough, once the Paris Peace Conference was convened to negotiate the terms of the post-World War I political and social order, one of its earliest acts was the establishment of a Commission on International Labour Legislation, commonly known as the Labour Commission. It was this Commission, chaired by Samuel Gompers of the American Federation of Labor, that was responsible for drafting the proposal to establish an International Labour Organization.

As Maupin has argued (2009), the ILO's constitution reflects both the pragmatic political value of compromise between capital and labour and more substantive normative ambitions. The preamble to the constitution is in effect a justification for the establishment of the ILO that rests on two major pillars: not only the moral duty to promote social justice, but also the need to address the empirical threat to peace and harmony arising from the continuing absence of justice (Maupain, 2009, p. 832). These concerns were to be dealt with via institutional machinery designed to ensure that neither capital nor labour were in a position permanently to dominate the other. On the workers' side this involved a tacit abandonment of any ambition to end capitalism, but it also included the acceptance at an international level of the legitimacy of workers using their collective power against employers. The Treaty of Versailles not only enshrined a symbolic equality between workers and employers within the governance structure of the ILO, it explicitly recognised workers' right of association. Both at the time and in subsequent judicial interpretations this has been held to include workers' right to use their collective power to pursue their common interests.

In the first decades of the ILO, the conflict assumption did not go uncontested, and was challenged most notably by the fascist regimes in Italy and later Germany.[5] However, by the outbreak of the second world war there was little open opposition in the democratic parts of the industrialised world to the idea that labour and capital each had their own interests that they were entitled to pursue freely and independently by any reasonable means. In the 1937 ruling that finally confirmed the constitutionality of the National Labor Relations Act, the US Supreme Court stated the case as well as it has ever been stated:

> Long ago we stated the reason for labor organizations. We said that they were organized out of the necessities of the situation; that a single employee was helpless in dealing with an employer; that he was dependent ordinarily on his daily wage for the maintenance of himself and family; that, if the employer refused to pay him the wages that he thought fair, he was nevertheless unable to leave the employ and resist arbitrary and unfair treatment; that union was essential to give laborers opportunity to deal on an equality with their employer.
> (NLRB vs. Jones & Laughlin Steel Corp., 301 U.S. 1 (1937), s.33)

Meanwhile, Back on the Shop Floor . . .

While employer representatives, trade unions and governments were working their way towards the uneasy peace of the collective industrial relations policy programme, thinking about management and industrial relations based on the cooperation assumption continued to develop. Unlike collective industrial relations or indeed communism, control-oriented people management was at this stage rarely articulated as a political programme. Instead, it was somewhere between a manifesto and a technique for managers. While the period from the turn of the twentieth century to the outbreak of the Second World War was an enormously fertile time for management research and education, I want to mention only three streams: scientific management and classical management theory; welfare capitalism; and human relations.

Frederick Taylor's scientific management, together with Henri Fayol's work on planning and administration, formed the foundations of an approach to organization whose adherents saw themselves above all as technical professionals. While Taylor's focus was on the detailed design of work activities and Fayol's on higher-level processes of organization and control, they and their successors were united in adopting a set of assumptions that Burrell and Morgan (1979) locate in what they call "the most objectivist region of the functionalist paradigm" (p. 127). For the classical management theorists—Burrell and Morgan continue—

> The world of organizations is treated as if it were the world of natural phenomena, characterized by a hard concrete reality which can be systematically investigated in a way which reveals its underlying regularities. Above all else it is a world of cause and effect
> (pp. 127–8)

From this perspective, there is no room for the imputation of political motives to one actor or another. The organization is a norm-free zone whose concrete reality is empirically demonstrable and whose laws of motion can be proven. There is no place or need for mutual distrust between workers and management. It is simply a question of understanding the nature of the organization and of the techniques that can be used to maximise efficiency for the benefit of all involved. Taylor famously referred to this as the 'mental revolution' required of both workers and managers if scientific management was to become a reality. Once both sides understand that there is one best way to do a job and run an organization and that technically competent managers can and will find that way, the need for discipline—and resistance—evaporates in the light of pragmatic or economistic rationality.

Welfare capitalism, as promoted by US employers like Kodak and Sears (Jacoby, 1998), was built on a somewhat different conception of the logic of cooperation. Rather than cooperation being a rational response to effective techniques in the context of the shared overall objective of economic efficiency, welfare capitalism sees cooperation through an essentially political lens. The emphasis is on the choice of goals that represent shared interests rather than on the means by which they are obtained. Welfare capitalism aims for the active *creation* of a unity of interest between workers and employers where it might not otherwise have existed. As Commons put it, the idea is to create "the conviction in every man in that industry that this is *his* industry, that the future of that concern is *his* future" (Cited in Kaufman, 2003, p. 16). Although the techniques of work design and organizational planning and administration used by welfare capitalists were for the most part difficult to distinguish from scientific management, what differed was the association of these techniques with elaborate systems of social protection designed to insulate workers from the moral and physical risks of industrial society. Commons and other institutional economists also noted that welfare capitalism also brought a certain 'constitutionalisation' of organizational governance in the shape of employee representation systems and procedural guarantees that placed some limits on the potentially arbitrary authority of management (Kaufman, 2003). Jacoby argues that welfare capitalism was good for workers for the all the obvious reasons of decent wages and access to healthcare and other benefits, but was also seen as "an efficient alternative to market individualism" that had the added advantage of being a "defence of freedom against laborism and statism" (Jacoby, 1998, p. 4). Both Jacoby and Kaufman also note, however, that the commitment of most US welfare capitalists to finding mutually beneficial modes of organization did not survive the depression. It seemed that when times were hard and a unity of interest more difficult to maintain, managers simply reverted to their role as the agents and protectors of the interests of capital alone.

The third policy approach arising from the cooperation assumption is human relations. As opposed to the technical rationalism of Taylorism and the political rationalism of welfare capitalism, the human relations approach does not seek the conscious assent of workers to management. Rather, it treats workers themselves as the objects of technical knowledge. Although there seems to be some dispute about precisely what kind of knowledge is involved—Burrell and Morgan emphasise the Durkheimian sociology that informed Elton Mayo's approach (1979, p. 139), while Bruce and Nyland argue that Mayo sought to develop psychological techniques of control (2011, p. 385)—what is not in doubt is that human relations is based on the idea that managers have the right and the duty to determine the activities of workers in any way they see fit and, more importantly, that the use of human relations techniques will effectively guarantee the spontaneous coop-eration of workers with management plans and strategies, whatever these may be. Given the underlying assumption that compliance with the impera-tives of the market and competition is the only rational goal for a business organization, the absence of cooperation can only arise from non-logical sources. The action of managers is therefore more akin to a therapeutic intervention than it is to political exchange or the engineering of production systems. Their role is to "to transform the subjectivity of the worker from an obstacle to an ally in the quest for productivity and profit" (Deetz, cited in Bruce and Nyland, 2011, p. 387).

The factor that unifies these three approaches is the assumption that worker cooperation with management in the sense of a positive willing-ness to comply is always potentially available without there being a need to cede any decision-making power to workers. Policy interventions are about ensuring that there are no unnecessary obstacles to the maintenance of man-agerial control over work. Independent worker organization only makes any sense from these perspectives to the extent that it enhances rather than reduces managerial control. The welfare capitalist approach leaves more room for this possibility than either Taylorism or Human Relations.

The Golden Age of Collective Industrial Relations?

The Second World War had a significant impact on thinking about IR pol-icy. The experience of wartime production confirmed that the trade unions of the allied powers could be trusted to participate in the governance of work without fomenting any truly serious opposition to management, at least in the presence of clear and undisputable national industrial priorities. Those remaining elements within the various labour movements concerned that favoured class war appeared to be marginal. However, the stakes of the game had radically increased with the expansion of the effective power of the Soviet Union into the eastern half of Europe. For all that communist influence within most trade unions was marginal, that did not mean that it did not look dangerous, particularly in France and Italy as well as those large swathes of the world in which political power was up for grabs with the prospect of decolonisation.

The US experience of the depression, and in particular the deception of workers who had trusted that their welfare capitalist employers would keep faith in the bad times as in the good, had already shifted the policy balance in the USA towards collective industrial relations. The pre-war question of unionisation versus non-union forms of management had largely been answered. Post-war, the global policy cleavage was between the revolutionary and reformist models arising from the conflict assumption. Approaches arising from the cooperation assumption were generally viewed with suspicion.[6] As Gross puts it, "for many years, it was presumed that employer hostility and resistance to unionisation and collective bargaining came from ideologues at the margins of business and industry" (1994, p. 50).

The political advantages of the CIR policy model were obvious. It provided for an apparently legitimate form of industrial governance without dispossessing capital of its most important prerogatives. It was widely thought to be an effective weapon for combating the influence of the communist bloc in the international trade union movement. Employers were willing to tolerate it because it gave them a way of dealing with what they were obliged to concede were legitimate worker concerns without this having a major impact on their freedom to run their businesses the way they wanted to. Trade unions, at least those not dominated by communists, were also happy because they were extended a kind of institutional security— a degree of respect and an official place in the governing framework of society—that they generally had not enjoyed before the war; because the system gave them at least a limited capacity to say 'no' to employers, and because they remained on the outside of the capitalist decision-making process and remained free to criticise and oppose management whenever it was opportune to do so (Gourevitch et al., 1985).

For the most part then, democratic governments in the western world abandoned any lingering doubts they might have had about collective industrial relations, placing it at the centre of economic and industrial policy. Workers' rights to freedom of association were explicitly included in the new German and Italian constitutions, for example, as well as being enshrined in ILO Convention No. 87 in 1947. Collective bargaining was widely promoted as *the* essential means to the end of economic progress in democratic market economies and workers' rights to collective bargaining were formalised in international law in ILO Convention No. 98 in 1949.

Beyond the industrialised world, CIR was heavily promoted as an integral part of the development process. Again, this was to some extent a question of supporting the 'free' trade unions thought to be a bulwark against communist influence,[7] but, as we will see in more detail in Chapter 3, it was also linked to the 'industrialisation' thesis. This is the idea that development from a traditional pre-industrial society into a modern industrial society is a process with a series of necessary stages that follow an immanent logic of industrialisation. The use of certain industrial and organizational technologies is an inevitable part of the development process. Development is independent of the historical specificities of any given situation and tends towards a convergence on a single model which, of course, involves the joint determination by workers and employers of the web of rules that maintain order in the workplace. While there may be some variation in IR systems, and while there may be different roads to the ultimate destination of mature CIR, it was thought to be simply in the nature of the beast that industrial development points in a single direction. From this perspective, the ILO's role is that of coach and midwife, helping the social partners in each industrialising state not only to develop an appropriate body of labour law, but also to construct IR institutions and to help government, employers and unions develop the technical capacity to play their pre-assigned roles within them.

The Return of COPM

As readers of this book are likely to know all too well, the postwar policy consensus around collective industrial relations did not prove to be durable. Indeed, the period during which it remained largely uncontested only lasted about 30 years. Since the late 1970s, the model has faced a sustained challenge from a coalition of business interests, right-wing governments and the international financial institutions. Even where the letter of the legal rights of workers and trade unions to take industrial action has not been significantly eroded—as it has been in many of the industrialised common law countries—the political acceptability of unionised employment relationships has declined, and the aims and motivations of labour movements have been called into question.[8] With a handful of exceptions, trade union membership and collective bargaining coverage in the private sector have fallen and in certain economies simply collapsed. Although globally competitive economies with high union membership and, more importantly, high collective bargaining coverage still exist, these increasingly appear to be northern European exceptions to the rule. No emerging economies currently look likely to develop anything even approaching the kind of high bargaining coverage IR system that in the 1950s and 1960s was thought to be the inevitable end-point of industrial development.

Fully accounting for the decline of collective industrial relations would take a book in itself, and I cannot hope to do justice to the subject here. It would have to address the conjuncture of economic, social, cultural and technological change, the mutation of political parties, movements and arguments, global political events including most especially the end of the Cold War, the changing nature of 'management' as a profession, the emergence of a global epistemic community of business policy makers, advisers and consultants (Haas, 2015), the evolution of social science and its relationship to policy-making, representations of business in the media, the nature of popular protest, contestation and representation . . . the list of potentially relevant factors could go on for pages. All I can do here is to try to characterise the broad outlines of the arguments used to justify the re-emergence of control-oriented people management as a respectable public policy orientation.

Before doing that, though, I want to recognise that CIR has frequently been subject to attack for purely political reasons. CIR gives trade unions a formal institutional role and an influence over public policy and business decision-making that many business executives, capital owners and their allies in government would rather they did not have. Korpi's point that employers do not *choose* collective industrial relations so much as accept it when they have no choice is telling here (Korpi, 2006). Beatrice and Sidney Webb also argued that the substantive ends of trade union action, like higher wages, were likely to be a lot less distasteful to authoritarian governments than their democratic methods.[9] Any attempt to reduce the influence of trade unions, then, regardless of its on-paper policy justification, is likely to be welcome in certain quarters. However, the arguments used to justify the IR policy reversal of the 1980s cannot be written off merely as window-dressing for the right's exploitation of a dip in the political fortunes of organised labour. Rather, they were the outcome of the re-emergence of the cooperation assumption in a new and harder form. In contrast to the firm-centred versions of the assumption typical of the interwar period, the new justification for compliance was centred on the inescapable demands of the market.

There is a long tradition of justifying restrictions on trade union action (a) to ensure that they do not stray out of some legitimate sphere of purely economic action. and (b) to ensure that their influence does not become in some sense disproportionate; that they do not become 'too powerful'. Nevertheless, these arguments are in practice supplementary to a more basic claim that that the conflict assumption is mistaken. This claim is rooted in (something like) the Austrian School conception of markets as systems of price signals that represent a guide to the optimisation of the returns on economic action and, as a result, the most efficient allocation of capital. Although—the argument goes—there is a certain leeway for businesses in responding to these signals, straying too far from the direction they give because of a misguided concern for worker welfare will inevitably lead to sub-optimal economic outcomes. Once the optimisation of economic outcomes along the single dimension of competitiveness has been accepted as an overarching policy priority, it looks like worker collective action only makes sense to the extent that it does not force businesses too far from the courses of action indicated by the price signals of the market. Problems like low growth, inflation, high levels of unemployment and high levels of industrial action can be explained by reference to the inability of businesses to respond to market signals because of industrial action or the threat of action.

This argument is reflected in the IR policy adopted by many governments starting from the end of the 1970s. In the USA, for example, the decisions of the National Labour Relations Board under its Reagan-appointed chair Donald Dotson were strongly oriented towards "maximising employers' ability to compete in domestic and foreign markets by deregulating the management end of labor-management relations. Dotson's NLRB subordinated collective bargaining to the economic interests of employers" (Gross, 1994, p. 48). Comstock and Fox (1994, p. 91) argue that by the end of Reagan's presidency, the emphasis in US labour relations was on preventing or getting rid of collective bargaining, that firing striking workers had become an acceptable practice, and advising businesses on how to block or break unions had become a growth industry.

In the UK, the IR policy adopted by the Conservative government of Margaret Thatcher also reflected a new priority for the interests of employers in the guise of an emphasis on the need to ensure that collective bargaining was 'realistic' and 'responsible'. A Conservative Party strategy document argued that "Those who negotiate around the table must understand and be aware of the constraints within which they are operating, and must have a responsible attitude to those realities" (Howe et al., 1977, p. 7). Those 'realities' were the price signals of the market, which Howe and his colleagues argued we ignore at our economic peril. Taking industrial action to prevent management action to deal with them was painted as at best Canute-like and at worst a kind of industrial terrorism. This approach was closely linked to the adoption of supply-side or monetarist economics. Inspired principally by the work of Milton Friedman, monetarism reversed the long-established Keynesian policy consensus to focus on the supply side of the economy rather than on the management of demand. In particular, it was thought that inflation could be controlled by controlling the money supply, which was in turn achieved by controlling interest rates and by altering levels of taxation and government spending. Previous attempts to control inflation had focused on prices and incomes policies, which in the context of high union density and collective bargaining coverage demanded the cooperation of the trade unions. Regardless of the effectiveness of the monetarist approach, then, it had the enormous collateral advantage of removing any political need to get union assent to government policy.

On the international level, the neoclassical economic paradigm rapidly displaced older approaches to development economics, particularly the 'international dependence' models of the 1970s that emphasised the need to close down or at least carefully control economic relationships with a global economy dominated by the industrialised economies at the expense of those with low levels of development. The new thinking was, again, principally inspired by the idea that the market was a normatively neutral system of price signals that pointed to the most efficient international allocation of capital. Opening up economies and allowing capital to flow in from abroad was thought to be the most effective, indeed the only path to rapid growth. In this light, the CIR model was suspect for two reasons. First, from the perspective of developing world governments, too strong an emphasis on collective industrial relations might deter international investors. Second, from the perspective of the neoclassical economic models that came to dominate the research and policy work of the Bretton Woods institutions, collective bargaining was by definition an obstacle to growth because it replaced flexible market wage rates with rigid rates bargained on the basis of the monopoly power of trade unions. A thriving labour movement would also have implications for the distribution of political power, something that evidently made the technical experts of the international institutions uncomfortable at best.[10] The result was that the World Bank and the International Monetary Fund—the international financial institutions or IFIs—increasingly resorted to loan conditionality that demanded structural reforms of labour markets to increase flexibility as well as "weigh[ing] in on the advisability of labor law reform in the form of technocratic advice, research studies and policy reports" (Finkin and Mundlak, 2015, p. 89).

International IR Policy in the Context of Neoliberalism: CIR in a COPM World

By the mid-1990s, what had emerged on the international level was a kind of policy stalemate. On the one hand, the pursuit of growth via international trade and the integration of emerging industrial capacity into global production networks had taken on the status of an unchallengeable policy priority for the developing world. Particularly within the international financial instititions (IFIs), rights to unionisation, collective bargaining and employment protection were seen at best as luxuries that needed to wait for a late stage of economic development and at worst as obstacles to growth on the same plane as cumbersome licencing requirements or corrupt planning permission processes.[11] On the other hand, the institutional legacy of the post-war policy consensus on CIR remained: workers' rights to freedom of association and collective bargaining were firmly established in international law in the shape of ILO conventions 87 and 98. The tension between the ILO and IFI approaches was and remains palpable. As Rittich remarks, there are

> two labor agendas simultaneously in play on the international plane: core labor rights and labor market flexibility. They represent quite distinct normative visions with respect to the structure and operation of labor markets and the location of authority and control in the workplace
> (2003, p. 161)

This coexistence of fundamentally opposed policy positions means that the ILO has been obliged to spend a great deal of time and energy actively defending the CIR model, something that was largely unnecessary between the end of World War 2 and the 1980s. This task has been significantly complicated by the fact that the terms of the policy debate are now largely dictated by the COPM policy model, whose most basic assumption is that there is no reason why there should be conflict between employers and workers since economically optimal outcomes (a) represent a shared interest and (b) can be achieved on the basis of technically appropriate management decision-making.

At the same time as having to fight a rearguard action in defence of labour regulation in the face of the hegemony of the neoliberal model, the ILO has come under pressure from those who believe that it does too little to ensure that the existing international labour standards are implemented. The model of optional ratification of conventions and enforcement exclusively via the bully pulpit has been widely criticized for its weakness.[12]

In this and the next two sections, I want to look at what the ILO has tried to do to defend itself and the CIR model from critics on both sides. In the remainder of this section I will look at arguments for change and reform that have taken place inside the ILO. In the two following sections I will discuss what I call the unfinished project of collective worker representation: first, the question of the normative logic that underpins the ILO approach to collective representation rights and, second, the attempt to construct an 'evidence-based' case for collective representation, which is to say a case that starts from the logic of COPM.

The main policy question the ILO faced in the early- to mid-1990s was how to put some kind of floor on labour rights that would address the most flagrant employer abuses without opening ILO to the accusations of growth-destroying regulatory over-reach that were so much in vogue at the time. Since the second half of the 1980s, pressure had been growing for action to prevent the 'race to the bottom' that appeared to be the inevitable consequence of the integration of the global economy on the basis of neoliberal policy priorities. The tension between the partisans of growth and the defenders of regulation was thrown into sharp relief during a debate sparked by the 1994 agreement to create a World Trade Organization to replace the General Agreement on Tariffs and Trade. The prospect of a new international organization with the power to authorise economic sanctions against states in retaliation for unfair trade practices became the focus of an argument about whether that new organization should integrate a 'social clause' into its trade rules. This would have been a provision saying that the violation of certain basic labour and environmental standards will count as giving states an unfair commercial advantage and as such would represent grounds for a trade dispute.

The social clause was discussed at the ILO's annual decision-making conference in 1994 (ILO, 1995). It was widely criticised by employers' representatives and the governments of the developing world, not only as something likely to be damaging to their economies but also as hypocrisy by the developed economies. The criticism echoed the international financial institutions' conception of neoliberal industrialisation in which the optimisation of the performance of industry has only one, strictly economic dimension and in which social policies that have any impact at all on the freedom of managers to respond to market imperatives as they see fit are considered to be guilty of slowing growth until proven innocent. What is more, since the developed economies would have little difficulty meeting any labour standards that might be included in a social clause, the inclusion of the clause in trade agreements, far from combatting unfair competition, would itself be a disguised form of protectionism.

The Singaporean minister of labour captured the thrust of many of the arguments made at the conference:

> In a recent OECD report on work and employment, rigid labour laws and inflexible labour policies, in addition to other factors, were identi-fied as important causes of the unemployment crisis in the industrialized countries . . . The . . . attempt to introduce social clauses in international trade agreements . . . is seen by the developing countries as a disguised form of protectionism, aimed at eroding their comparative advantages and blunting their competitiveness. If rigid labour laws and policies are indeed the causes of serious economic woes and unemployment crises in the industrialized countries, why should social clauses based on such laws and policies be imposed on the developing countries? What is the real intention behind such a proposal? Beginning with basic workers' rights, it will soon lead to the imposition of other standards and practices based on the values and norms set by the western industrialized countries.
>
> (ibid., p. 143)

In response, most workers' representatives and many developed world gov-ernments argued that all that was at issue was the effective implementa-tion of flexible minimum standards that would level the playing field for international trade and reduce the danger of socially damaging competition on labour costs. This is quite a long way from the post-war version of the conflict assumption in which bargained accommodations between labour and management are the very fabric of industrial governance. The primary focus is on the substantive issue of respect for basic human rights, with the procedural questions relating to worker participation in decision-making relegated firmly to second place. One influential workers' representative,[13] for example, described collective bargaining as a rational mechanism that responded to the need to set wages and conditions at a level that would meet basic needs in each different country: "The cost of . . . basic needs varies between countries, and the wages needed to meet them should be deter-mined by the time-honoured means of collective bargaining" (ILO, 1995, p. 6/31). Collective bargaining is here not defended as a valuable institution in itself, but simply as a means to ensure that certain substantive conditions are met. There is nothing in this argument that says some technical calcula-tion of the level of wages required to meet basic needs would not be just as good a means of proceeding.

In the end, the issue of what attitude ILO should take to a social clause was rendered moot by the G-77 group of developing states' success in keeping the issue off the agenda at the WTO's first ministerial meeting in Singapore in 1996 (Rodgers et al., 2009, p. 216). The WTO's members instead simply confirmed that they recognised the competence of the ILO in the field of international labour standards. With the ball back in the ILO's court, the new big idea for tackling the problem of how to ensure wider respect for minimum standards was to focus on principles rather than regulation. According to Rodgers and his colleagues (ibid., p. 221), the idea that the ILO should move away from its exclusive emphasis on conventions with specific legal obligations and towards a more flexible approach based on the promotion of certain underlying principles had been brewing among employer representatives for some time. Obviously, employer representatives saw any kind of regulation as a burden on businesses, but they insisted that employers *would* respond to encouragement and technical assistance.

The 1998 *Declaration on Fundamental Principles and Rights at Work* identified 8 ILO conventions as 'fundamental' and deemed it to be the duty of all ILO member states to respect these conventions, regardless of whether they had been formally ratified. Among these fundamental conventions were, of course, those protecting freedom of association and collective bargaining. The others were the more substantive conventions outlawing child labour, forced labour and discrimination in the workplace.

In making respect for a series of conventions effectively a condition of membership of the ILO, the Declaration was a radical departure from the Organization's long-established practice. However, the potential impact of what appears to be a momentous decision was severely limited by the political price that had to be paid for its having been taken. The fundamental conventions would not be enforced in member states that had not ratified them using the ILO's existing supervisory machinery. Nor would the interpretation of what compliance with the conventions means in practice draw on the existing jurisprudence of the ILO as established in the decisions of its two independent adjudication bodies, the Committee of Experts on the Application of Conventions and Recommendations (CEACR) and the Committee on Freedom of Association (CFA).

Alston (2004, p. 494) quotes Edward Potter, a US employers' delegate to the International Labour Conference and vice-chair of the 1998 Declaration's drafting committee:

> One thing that was unambiguously clear to every person who negotiated the ILO Declaration . . . [is that its] obligations are not the detailed legal requirements of the eight fundamental ILO conventions but rather the failure to achieve the policies underlying them.

So, the same constitutional innovation that introduced the idea of fundamental or 'core' international labour standards in the first place also broke the connection between the core conventions and what Alston (2004) calls the 'jurisprudential acquis' of the ILO. Alston's reading of Potter's claim (2004, pp. 494–5) is that the Declaration brackets off the content of the conventions as this has been interpreted over the years in favour of a focus on the 'policies underlying them'. However, beyond the very spare text of the conventions themselves, those policies have never been definitively or authoritatively formulated. In terms of interpretation, the decisions of the ILO's supervisory bodies represent the sole source of precedent. Thus, with respect to the core conventions and in the context of the Declaration, "[t]he discipline, or the acquis, of the conventions has been escaped, and individual governments and employers are now empowered to determine for themselves what the ILO really meant in adopting the standards in question" (Alston, 2004, p. 495).

The predictable result of this delinking of conventions and ILO jurisprudence has been an expansion of reference to ILO core conventions, but a reduction in clarity about what they mean. The situation might be less fluid if the ILO had been able to respond to the demands of employers and NGOs who, even before the Declaration, were already asking for guidance on how to apply conventions in corporate social responsibility and social labelling initiatives. In a report to the ILO's Governing Body, Director General Guy Ryder commented that

> It is striking that the ILO has been largely passive in the face of the exponential growth of corporate social responsibility initiatives over the last decade. That is despite the fact that many such initiatives make explicit reference to ILO standards, particularly those relating to fundamental rights.
>
> (ILO, 2013, p. 23)

What Ryder did not say, but what many of those to whom his report was addressed will have known, is that this passivity has not been accidental. On the contrary, it was the result of opposition within the Governing Body to the programme of work on enterprise codes of conduct and social labelling initiatives that had been started on the initiative of Hansenne (Rodgers et al., 2009, pp. 221–2). Hansenne's vision was precisely that of a global labour governance regime involving multiple public and private actors but centred on ILO standards and put into effect via a proactive programme of technical advice and assistance to NGOs and business enterprises. His report to the 1997 International Labour Conference (ILO, 1997) makes it clear that he saw market incentives for standards compliance at firm level as a critical part of this project. In the wake of the agreement of the Declaration, work carried out by ILO staff confirmed there was a need for ILO to step in to ensure that the operational definition of fundamental principles and rights at work used in private standards systems was both consistent across different systems and not subject to dilution for the convenience of participants

(ILO, 1998). While Rodgers et al. do not offer any explanation for the opposition of the Governing Body to this kind of outreach work, the idea that the ILO should attempt to align interpretations of the 'policies underlying' the core conventions with the existing decisions of the supervisory system—the only possibility for outreach work of the kind proposed—is clearly inconsistent with the logic of the arguments made by Edward Potter.

In short, then, the ILO's 1998 declaration did not achieve any resolution of the contradiction between the conflict and cooperation assumptions. Rather, it was a largely political reform that simply cleared a space for different actors to interpret the core labour standards in whatever way suited them, ensuring that the organization was not forced to address the contradiction between CIR and COPM.

The tension between competing visions does not exist simply between the ILO and other international organizations but within the ILO itself. Since at least the early 1990s, employers' representatives and their professional secretariat within the ILO, the Bureau for Employers' Activities, have been carrying on a concerted battle against the basic principles underpinning collective bargaining. The employers have long argued that the right to strike is not protected by the conventions on freedom of association and collective bargaining and that the legal treatment of industrial action is strictly a matter for national governments. The argument was frequently to be heard during the debate on the social clause, for example (ILO, 1995).

Nevertheless, it was only in 2012 that active steps were taken to try to establish the employers' interpretation of the conventions as more than a minority position. To cut a long institutional story very short, the International Labour Conference is supposed to discuss each year's worst instances of labour standards violations. Whether or not some law or government action counts as a violation is evaluated by the CEACR. There are always too many violations to deal with in the time available, so a committee of the ILC called the Conference Committee on the Application of Standards (CCAS) chooses about 25 cases to be discussed in the full session of the conference. Unlike the CEACR, the CCAS is a political committee in the sense that it is made up of representatives of employers, workers and governments. This committee has always involved a degree of horse-trading to make sure that all involved get their issues-of-the-moment on the agenda, but within this process of negotiation what has certainly never been part of the give and take is the judgement of the members of the Committee of Experts itself. The CCAS's choice of cases to forward to the ILC traditionally carries no implication of a validation or rejection of CEACR opinion. In 2012, however, the employer members of the CCAS decided that they would veto the discussion of any case where the issue was a violation of the right to strike. Their stated reason for this was that they did not agree with the CEACR that the right to strike—nowhere mentioned explicitly in any ILO convention—could be implied on the basis of Conventions 87 and 98 on freedom of association and collective bargaining, despite the longstanding and widely-accepted view that the rights enshrined in these conventions are meaningless in the absence of a right to strike. The employers argued that they had never accepted that this was an acceptable interpretation, and that the right to strike was a matter for a purely national decision. In effect, they were arguing that the ILO has no right to call states to order for restricting the right to strike.

There are two things that we need to highlight here: one a question of procedure and the other of substance. First of all, not only did the employers question the validity of the interpretation of the CEACR, but they also actually tried to argue that whether or not a labour standards violation has occurred is a political question rather than one of legal interpretation (ILO, 2012a, paragraph 82).

Second, the employers' substantive position on the right to strike makes a mockery of the whole concept of freedom of association—as the arguments of the CEACR show very clearly (ILO, 2012b, paragraphs 117–128). While the employers do not go so far as to claim that workers should not have the right to strike, they argue that it is up to each state to decide for itself whether to permit strikes and in what circumstances. The obvious implication of this, of course, is that outlawing strikes is a legitimate state choice. This is the ultimate repudiation of the conflict assumption in the sense that it deems any collective worker action taken to change a decision of management, including decisions on terms and conditions of employment, to be an unlawful act. In effect, banning strikes says that workers do not and cannot have legitimate collective interests that are different from what employers say that they are.

Although workers' representatives declared themselves ready to go the International Court of Justice to seek a definitive ruling on whether the right to strike is implied in conventions 87 and 98, in the end the issue was settled by a deal that involved no real concessions on the issue of principle on either side. In a textbook example of empty diplomatic language, the communiqué from the meeting called to resolve the issue stated: "The right to take industrial action by workers and employers in support of their legitimate industrial interests is recognized by the constituents of the International Labour Organization" (ILO, 2015, p. 1). This leaves the employers able to say not only that they are merely recognising the fact that the right to strike exists in many jurisdictions, but also that the ILO itself has not recognised it. The communiqué is not the ILO speaking *ex cathedra* but merely the voices of its constituents speaking in their separate and hence non-authoritative capacities. Extraordinary as it may seem, the ILO's position on the right to strike action remains ambivalent.

The Unfinished Project of Collective Worker Representation Part I: The Weak Institutionalisation of the Conflict Assumption

For all that even the most enthusiastically neoliberal of employers and governments have not challenged the principles of freedom of association and collective bargaining rights head on, their various attempts to water down or get around these rights have highlighted the fact that the common law/ILO policy model actually accommodates *both* the conflict and cooperation assumptions. That it is possible for these competing foundational assumptions to coexist within a single institutional structure is a consequence of the way in which the law typically deals with collective worker representation.

The conflict assumption can be written into the law in strong and weak forms. In certain IR systems like those of France, Germany, Spain and Italy, the conflict assumption is understood in the strong sense of demanding collective worker representation under all circumstances. It is not left to employees to make an individual decision about whether the governance of work is being carried out in their interest. The rights to the collective representation, consultation and action that enable workers to 'deal on an equality with their employer' belong to workers (dependent employees), regardless of whether they are union members. Trade unions have a representative function, but they operate more like political parties within a democracy, competing for the votes of workers (who may or may not be members) in elections to works councils, personnel committees and so on. In this sense, workers are pre-defined or deemed permanently to exist as a collective actor. While trade unions have to meet certain representativity criteria before they can negotiate on behalf of workers, the concept of trade union *recognition* in the sense of the employer's formal acceptance that its employees exist as a collective body is completely alien to these systems.

However, in many, perhaps a majority of industrial relations systems—including all of the common law countries and most emerging economies regardless of their legal tradition—the conflict assumption is treated in law less as an established basic fact than as a *possibility*. It is left up to workers to decide where their interest lies in the sense that they have the right to choose whether or not to constitute themselves as a collective actor and to seek recognition from employers. In these systems, the right to take collective action belongs not to workers (dependent employees) but to trade union members. The possibility of exercising that right is limited by the need to demonstrate that there is an authentic collective will among workers to exercise it. Collective bargaining and consultation only take place once employers have recognised a demand from their employees to move to collectively rather than individually negotiated contracts on the basis of some kind of demonstration of democratic will. This could be an election on the US model or—more frequently in practice—passing a membership threshold, typically 50% of the workers in a proposed bargaining unit. In these types of IR system, the principle of collective worker representation is not absolute but has to be balanced against the rights of those workers who believe that maintaining an *individually*-negotiated employment relationship is in their interest. This does not quite amount to a right *not* to be represented, as in most systems individual workers are ultimately obliged to accept the will of the majority, but it does mean that rights to representation are highly conditional and can only be exercised where the workers who wish to exercise them have the collective capacity to do so.[14] This capacity depends as a minimum on being able to convince a majority of workers in a workplace to join a trade union or vote in favour of unionisation. In many cases it will also depend on being able to mobilise union members to take industrial action to press their employer directly for recognition or to support legal action to enforce a duty to bargain.

Depending on the IR system, even once these tests have been passed an employer may not be under a legal duty to engage in collective bargaining. In both Ireland and India, for example, even where every employee is a trade union member, an employer is not required to recognise and bargain with the union. The union can take lawful strike action against the employer to win recognition, but if the employer wishes to resist it is entitled to do so. Even where recognition is compulsory once a certain membership threshold has been passed, employers will frequently try to resist engaging in collective bargaining. This may also be recognised in the law. For instance, in Kenya, even though union recognition is compulsory once 50% of workers have joined a union, the law explicitly states that industrial action in pursuit of recognition can be lawful.

Once a union has been recognised, whether voluntarily or compulsorily, collective bargaining can begin. However, the credible threat of industrial action must be in place if bargaining is to be meaningful.[15] Being able to take lawful industrial action requires that the union clear a further series of hurdles intended to establish the authenticity and reasonableness of the bargaining goals it is pursuing. As a minimum, it will have to demonstrate via a successful strike ballot that the proposed action has a legitimate objective arising from the interests of its members. In many cases it will also have to meet other requirements like showing that all other avenues for the resolution of conflict have been explored, or demonstrating that the proposed action is related to a substantive dispute with an employer as opposed to some 'political' goal, or that it does not endanger public safety or cause serious damage to the public interest.

While unlawful industrial action almost always exposes workers to the threat of dismissal, in those IR systems where the conflict assumption is weakly institutionalised, even lawful strike action can be a lawful reason for firing workers. In common law systems, striking is a breach of contract unless the law specifically says otherwise. Although a range of different protections for striking workers do exist in different systems, employers may ultimately have the right to dismiss them. In the UK, for example, employers can lawfully dismiss striking workers after 12 weeks as long as dismissals are not selective.

In short, where the conflict assumption is weakly institutionalised, workers are obliged to prove not only that they want collective representation but also that the use they make of that representation is reasonable. Depending on established socio-cultural practice and on the law and its interpretation, this task of *achieving* collective representation may be anywhere from very easy to immensely difficult. In Sweden, for example, the conflict assumption is weak in law but strong in practice. Union membership and collective bargaining are deeply rooted in industrial and organizational culture and levels of membership have remained among the highest in the world, despite the prevailing winds of neoliberal ideology. As I write this, the government is led by a former president of the largest trade union federation and has recently launched a global effort to promote collective industrial relations. The incidence of anti-union behaviour by businesses is very low and the idea that a trade union in Sweden would have to take legal or industrial action to win recognition from an employer is little short of laughable.

However, even in circumstances where unionisation and collective bargaining have a firm grounding in socio-cultural practice, the lack of formal legal and institutional anchoring of the conflict assumption means that it can be relatively easy for determined employers to resist unionisation or for governments to withdraw support for the CIR model. Where the conflict assumption is weakly institutionalised, the default assumption is that workers accept the unilateral managerial definition of the employment relationship: they have no rights to collective representation unless they take action to seek such rights. Representation rights are not absolute but depend on a positive demonstration of majority worker support that in effect is a proxy for a judicial test of reasonableness. In these circumstances, the focus of IR policy is not the institutionalisation of joint regulation and the resolution of conflict as is commonly supposed, but the institutionalisation of the means by which the *existence* of a legitimate conflict is legally recognised. The assumption of a conflict of interests is not *made*, but is merely *accommodated* as long as enough workers are willing to accept that it is appropriate.

ILO jurisprudence relating to the conventions on freedom of association and the right to collective bargaining has not only held that a weak institutionalisation of the conflict assumption is sufficient to bring national law into line with international labour standards, but it is also the case that the standard interpretation within the ILO is that an obligation to implement a strong institutionalisation of the conflict assumption on the German or French model could not be defended. While the right to freedom of association is very clearly established, the ILO's conventions make no reference to any right to collective representation. Workers have the right to *demand* collective representation and to take industrial action to pressure employers into conceding it, but they have no right to actually get it.[16] Arguably, in fact, the international labour standards regime is caught between its commitment to the principle of free and voluntary negotiations and its commitment to "the effective recognition of the right to collective bargaining". In giving technical advice on labour law the ILO cannot insist that *workers* should have the right to collective representation in the sense of negotiating their terms and conditions of employment on a collective rather than an individual basis because this right does not exist in its conventions. Although 'duty to bargain' provisions as well as strong institutionalisations of the conflict assumption on the continental European model have been held to be consistent with international labour standards, they are not required by any convention. All that the ILO can do as things stand is simply appeal to employers not to resist the recognition of unions. As the Director General Guy Ryder said in his 2013 report to the ILC:

> where laws or practice prevent the free exercise of the right to organize, tripartism and dialogue become a dead letter. Yet people join organizations for a purpose, and in the world of work that purpose is, above all, the collective representation of interests through collective bargaining— which the ILO has a constitutional obligation to promote—and social dialogue. It follows that the strength and legitimacy of tripartism and its actors depend on mutual recognition and respect of rights and roles. Refusal by any party to engage in social dialogue at national level can only be detrimental to that legitimacy. Equally, non-recognition of representative organizations for purposes of collective bargaining erodes the representational function of organizations, regardless of the voluntarist character of the exercise. In that light, the idea that individual contract arrangements could be an equal and equivalent alternative to collective bargaining between representative organizations cannot easily be squared with the ILO's 'unique advantage' of tripartism and social dialogue.
>
> (ILO, 2013, paragraph 94)

The Unfinished Project of Collective Worker Representation Part II: The Tyranny of the Business Case

The neoliberal drift in policy-making that began in the second half of the 1970s involved a much-increased reliance on the cooperation assumption in policy-making. Policies derived from the cooperation assumption may be relatively anodyne measures to encourage employers to communicate and consult with workers. They may even give new rights to non-unionised workers, such as the right to be consulted in the case of collective redundancies, or the right to be represented in workplace health and safety governance structures. Measures of this kind are often resisted by trade unions because they have a tendency to undermine the logic of voluntary collective action, but in truth as long as these new rights have no impact on the ultimate right of management to decide what is to be done and how, they have little effect on the governance of work.

The true significance of the cooperation assumption in policy-making over the last 30 years has been twofold. First, it has been the foundation of arguments used to justify specific regulatory measures aimed at rolling back worker and trade union rights. This in itself has undoubtedly led to a decline in collective representation (union membership and collective bargaining coverage) but this effect has been supplemented by the second significant impact of the cooperation assumption, which has been on the kinds of evidence that are accepted as relevant within the policy argument.

From the perspective of the conflict assumption, the defensibility of policy measures to support CIR needs no justification. Employers and workers have different interests by definition and giving employers carte blanche to pursue their interests with no concern for those of workers is a recipe for permanent conflict. The most important implication of the cooperation assumption, on the other hand, is that businesses have a single set of goals. In the context of the market economy, the obvious candidate for a unifying, overarching aim is the maintenance and improvement of competitiveness. From this perspective, whether any policy measures should be taken with respect to trade unionism and collective bargaining depends on the extent to which they contribute to business performance. To put it another way, policy depends on the *business case* for encouraging or discouraging collective industrial relations.

Although in principle there are many ways in which a case of this kind could be made and many different kinds of evidence on which it could be based, there is a heavy bias in the international policy debate towards positivist social science models based on quantitative data. The idea that decision-making should be based on social scientific 'laws' establishing hypotheses about causal relationships that can be tested using statistical analysis has deep roots in many policy communities, best symbolised perhaps by the repeated appeal to develop policies that are 'evidence-based' or to put aside arbitrary political preferences in favour of 'what works'.[17] All ideological preferences aside, this approach has a particular appeal on the international level where the need to find 'non-political' arguments in the search for policy consensus is acute. I will have more to say about positivist social science in Chapter 4, but for the moment I simply want to use the quest for a business case for collective IR to illustrate how the projection of the cooperation assumption onto an institutional structure based on a weak version of the conflict assumption has distorted the terms of the debate and the framing of policy questions.

I was for a short time an official of the ILO, where I worked as a technical specialist on industrial relations. A regular request from the upper ranks of the organization was for a summary of empirical evidence about the impact of collective bargaining on business performance. What the requestors actually wanted was to be able to make an 'evidence-based' argument that setting the terms and conditions of employment via collective bargaining has a positive effect on firm performance. For senior officials of the ILO, the holy grail of empirical evidence to use in interaction with organizations like the World Bank, the OECD and the G20 would be a clear answer to the question of whether, having controlled for the characteristics of firms and for differences in the cultural and regulatory context, there is a statistically significant difference in some relevant, quantifiable performance outcome between those firms that engage in collective bargaining and those that do not. As we saw a moment ago, this is the kind of evidence that the World Bank believed was required before it could make any policy recommendation on whether all of the core labour standards in the ILO's (1998) Declaration could be unreservedly supported.[18]

In truth, the question about the performance impact of collective bargaining was asked more in a kind of desperate hope than in the expectation that a truly adequate answer could be supplied. Most senior ILO staff are perfectly aware that unequivocal evidence of this kind does not exist and that the best they could expect was a summary of the most relevant studies that could be presented as evidence in favour of collective bargaining without the positive spin being too obvious. Nevertheless, the fact that we cannot currently give a clear answer to the question does not necessarily mean that it would be impossible to gather the data required.[19] On the other hand, thinking through what would be required to gather it highlights the staggering technical complexity of the task.

The question implies that there is some consistent, universal causal effect of collective bargaining on (say) labour productivity. An experimental research design based on a randomised controlled trial in which one group of businesses introduces collective negotiation of pay and conditions while another does not is just about conceivable. However, it is likely to be extraordinarily difficult to implement in practice, not to mention getting us mixed up in ethical problems like offering collective representation to some workers but not others. Let us say, then, that we have to attempt an observational study. The basic principle of such a study would be to compare a group of unionised businesses with a group of non-unionised businesses and to try to isolate the causal impact of collective bargaining on appropriate performance outcomes.

The first step would be to decide what we mean when we say 'collective bargaining'. The simple observation that employer and worker representatives have sat down in a room together and come to some kind of agreement and that they call this collective bargaining tells us virtually nothing about the substance of the actual social process that is going on. We would therefore need to come up with an operational definition of what precise procedural characteristics will count as bargaining, and how to assess whether they exist. We would need to decide whether we would expect bargaining systems with narrow scope and limited content to have a different impact on productivity from those with impacts on a wide array of different aspects of the employment relationship. We would need to take a view on whether to gather data about what the participants in bargaining believe they are doing and the attitude with which they approached the conduct of the relationship (adversarial, integrative?). This implies looking not just at managers within the firm but at local trade unions and the national labour movements of which they are a part. We would need to decide whether to think of bargaining as a binary or a scalar variable: whether we say that bargaining is either present or is not, or allow that it may be on a scale from no collective relationship through a series of intermediate states up to some conception of full scale bargaining.

If we manage to settle these issues—and those mentioned above undoubtedly do not amount to an exhaustive list—we then have to decide what firm characteristics beyond the bargaining system are relevant to the impact of bargaining and what might have an independent effect on the outcome variable. These could include size, industrial sector, products and target markets, capital to labour ratios, technology employed, workforce demographic characteristics, ownership type, age of the business, contracting relationships and so on. It would be reasonable to argue that they also include management policy and practices, so these would also have to be categorised. Then we would have to find some way of characterising relevant aspects of different national contexts, which would require a judgement to be made about the elements of national law, history, culture and practice that might be relevant to the impact of collective bargaining. In short, we have to gather enough data to capture the differences between, say, a shoe factory in Addis Ababa producing for the domestic market and owned by a local tycoon and an information technology services business owned by an international consortium of tech companies and based in Helsinki.

But even if we manage to settle on answers to all of these questions and to gather the data we have decided is relevant, there would still be enormous doubt about what the eventual results of the analysis would tell us. When we observe what appear to be consistent relationships between action and outcome, the question we need to answer is why they have arisen, and that question in turn needs to be answered from the perspective of those involved in that action.

If we want to say that collective bargaining has a positive impact on labour productivity, then we have to able to guarantee that the social practice (bargaining) taking place in all of the different workplaces we look at is *the same* social practice; that its subjective meaning to those involved is consistent from context to context. But the idea that an information scientist in Helsinki and a production line worker in Addis Ababa negotiating with their employers about maternity leave are in any meaningful sense *doing the same thing* is exceptionally difficult to sustain. In the Finnish case the interaction is taking place in a context in which trade unions are stable and deeply-rooted socio-economic institutions that have played an important role in national life for many decades. Collective bargaining is an entirely routine and uncontroversial activity. Both the trade union and employer representatives will have a high level of education and a firm grasp of the legal and institutional structures and processes within which bargaining takes place. These structures and processes will for the most part be clear and well-established, giving rise to precisely defined rights and duties for the different actors involved. In terms of the substance of negotiations, that pregnant workers and their partners should have extensive rights to leave and to re-engagement after that leave is already accepted by both sides as entirely right and proper. It is likely that what is at issue are marginal improvements and adjustments to the existing situation. In Ethiopia, by contrast, trade union density is exceptionally low and the trade union movement is struggling to create a role for itself as something other than the industrial manifestation of a Marxist ruling party that it was until relatively recently. Collective bargaining is rare, the potential benefits of independent worker organization and action are not well understood and there is a lack of legal clarity about the rights of workers and trade unions. The employer representative is much more likely than the production worker to be educated to secondary or university level. The owner of the business may have ties to the ruling party and/or be from a different ethnic group to most of the workers. The situation in the shoe factory is already exceptional by virtue of collective bargaining taking place at all and the roles of the participants will be poorly defined. The subject matter of negotiation, if it is even substantive,[20] is likely to be the right of women workers who have just given birth to any period of leave at all.

Thinking in this way leads us rapidly to the point at which the very idea that there is something called 'collective bargaining' that might have a consistent causal effect on a measurable outcome like labour productivity starts to look absurd. Even if we manage to come up with an answer to our original question, the chances are very high that that answer will be nothing more than the net difference between the outcomes of a range of different types of social action carried out in two sets of circumstances (nominal presence of bargaining vs. nominal absence of bargaining) that are not, in fact, systematically different from each other. Yet, the form of the question implies that an answer is required before certain policy decisions can be taken: if we have no evidence about the impact of collective bargaining on firm performance, then policy measures to encourage it carry an unquantified level of economic risk. If we accept the terms of the positivist debate, then we also have to accept that we can do nothing until the question has been answered, no matter how little sense the idea of there even *being* an answer makes. As a consequence, we are either forced to conduct research in the full knowledge that it is likely to be inadequate, or we have to accept that those who claim that CIR has a damaging effect on the economy cannot be shown to be wrong.

Conclusions: The Reasonableness of Conflict

Despite the historical significance of the conflict assumption, its institutionalisation in common law IR systems and in the ILO's predominantly Anglo-American approach to IR remains weak. This reflects an unhappy compromise between a pragmatic recognition that industrial conflict can and will happen and that suppressing it is counterproductive, and the more abstract, occasionally even idealistic belief that conflict need not and ought not to occur. The result is an institutional structure in which the existence of conflict *can* be recognised and accommodated, but only if a sufficient proportion of workers can be persuaded to believe that their employers have the scope to make different choices, and only if employers are willing to accept that workers have a right to try to make them choose differently.

This ambivalence about the employment relationship is built into the most significant international policy model, the common law/ILO model. Apart from specific problems like the lack of any duty to bargain in Ireland and India or the employer's right to dismiss lawfully striking workers that exists in most common law systems, the major lacuna in this institutional model is that it leaves room for tests of the reasonableness of worker objections to management plans and strategies. In principle, the common law abstains from getting into the merits of industrial action in the sense of evaluating the substantive case for worker organization or collective action against an employer in any given situation. However, the associated IR model leaves a great deal of room for those workers who are *not* persuaded that the interests of capital conflict with theirs or who simply do not understand collective representation and are worried about what it implies to prevent their more militant colleagues from taking action. It also leaves a great deal of room for employers to weigh in on the argument by making it understood that demanding or using collective representation is a *risk*; that employees who join unions or go on strike are doing themselves no favours, whether immediately in terms of their relationship with their employer or over the longer run in terms of the performance of the business on which they rely for their employment. This is an especially effective strategy where unionised employment relationships are not well embedded in socio-cultural practice. Unfortunately, the ILO has been unwilling or unable to challenge the framing of the IR policy question as a 'pragmatic' search for the mode of governance of work that can be shown to be the most effective from the perspective of business performance on the basis of positive empirical evidence. Collective bargaining remains guilty until the impossible task of proving it innocent has been achieved.

The result of all of this has been that employers and their political allies have been able to ignore the much more relevant empirical evidence that there are many industrial relations contexts in which independent worker organization and collective bargaining coexist with high business performance. The German economy exists. The Swedish economy exists. Despite these plain facts, employers have maintained a consistent preference for the suppression over the resolution of conflict. Since the political and intellectual opportunity to do so arose in the 1980s, they have exploited the weak institutionalisation of the conflict assumption, leveraging legal requirements for evidence of a 'legitimate' worker desire for collective representation into administrative and organising barriers that, particularly in developing economies, are next to impossible to break down. They have also lobbied for the further weakening of the institutionalisation of the conflict assumption, particularly via more onerous procedural requirements for the establishment of the lawfulness of industrial action. On the international level, employer objections to the conflict assumption have even taken the form of a challenge to the right to strike itself.

All of this means that especially in common law/ILO IR systems but also elsewhere, *what actually happens* in terms of collective worker representation and action depends on the result of an argument, whether tacit or overt, about whether the cooperation or conflict assumptions are better supported by the evidence. This means that the relative plausibility of the conflict and cooperation assumptions is a critical factor in day-to-day IR practice and not just in national and international policy-making. From the perspective of a theory of industrial relations, then, the critical challenge is understanding how the argument between conflict and cooperation might play out. The subject of Chapter 3 is how this argument has been manifest in the academic debate.

Notes

1 This is not to say that there were no formal rules in traditional societies. Rather, "In premodern societies, social labor and political domination are still based on first-order institutions that are merely *overlaid and guaranteed* by law; in modern societies, they are replaced by orders of private property and legal domination that appear directly in forms of positive law" (Habermas, 1987, p. 307). As we will see in Chapter 3, Habermas arguably overstates the degree to which law in modern societies lacks a normative foundation that is accessible to those actors subject to it, but the general point stands.

2 Readers with a background in academic industrial relations will recognise that the two types of IR policy built on the conflict assumption together with the policy arising from the cooperation assumption map closely onto the long-established categories of radicalism, pluralism and unitarism. I have chosen not to use these terms as they tend both to obscure the underlying conceptual continuity between pluralism and radicalism and to gloss over the significant internal variety within unitarism. The importance of these issues will become clear in Chapters 3 and 4.

3 The UK's Trades Union Congress repeatedly offered this argument in its policy statements from the 1960s on. See for example (1977, p. 49).

4 Comparing Fox's account of the UK labour legislation of the 1870s with Barbet's discussion of the background to the French trade union legislation of 1884 shows that the arguments used by legislators on either side of the channel were remarkably similar (Barbet, 1991; Fox, 1986, pp. 156–60).

5 During the same conference at which the Japanese worker delegate complained about feudally-inclined capitalists, there was a bitter argument about whether worker representatives from Mussolini's Italy should be recognised by the ILO. The workers' group, led by Léon Jouhaux, a key figure in reformist trade unionism, argued that as the Confederazione Generale del Lavoro was a mixed organization that included employers it could not be accepted as a properly independent workers' body:

> it cannot be maintained . . . that a mixed organization including both employers and wage-earners can constitute an organization representing the interests of the workers. It was undoubtedly the opinion of the authors of the Treaty [of Versailles] that the interests of the workers and the employers are distinct.
> (International Labour Office, 1924, p. 526)

While a coalition of employers and governments defeated the workers' claim on this and other occasions on which the credentials of the Italian worker delegates were contested (Tosstorff, 2013), the delegation from Nazi Germany in 1933 did not manage to pull off the same diplomatic feat—although according to Tosstorf this was more to do with the offensive racist behaviour of the leader of the Nazi delegation, Robert Ley, than to any change in the balance of the argument.

6 We will have reason to discuss Clark Kerr's famous paper criticising the human relations school in Chapter 3. For the moment, it is enough to note that Kerr's argument with Elton Mayo was not just that his approach was likely to be ineffective, but that it was morally wrong.

7 In his 1977 essay *Labour and Hegemony,* Cox gives a fascinating account of the close relationship between the US Government and the ILO during this period, as well as the role played by the international labour movement as a conduit for covert CIA activity.

8 The common law countries are those whose legal systems are wholly or predominantly derived from English common law. They include the UK, Ireland, the USA, Australia, New Zealand, India, Canada, Nigeria and a number of other former colonies of the UK and dependencies of the USA.

9 "When workmen meet together to discuss their grievances—still more, when they form associations of national extent, raise an independent revenue, elect permanent representative committees, and proceed to bargain and agitate as corporate bodies—they are forming, within the state, a spontaneous democracy of their own . . . the autocrat distrusts the educational influence of even the most subordinate forms of self-government. And when the association is national in extent, composed exclusively of one class, and untrammelled by any compulsory constitution, his faith in its objects or his tolerance for its devices becomes completely submerged beneath his fear of its apparently revolutionary organization" (Webb and Webb, 1902, p. 808).

10 Maupain cites an internal World Bank document that states that "the Bank's treatment of union rights is complicated by (a) the potential political nature of [the ILO's labour standards on freedom of association and collective bargaining] and (b) research showing ambiguous economic outcomes" (Maupain, 2013, p. 78).

11 Up until 2010, the World Bank's 'Doing Business' indicators, a set of statistical indices intended to rank countries in terms of how easy it is to set up and operate a business, included an 'Employing Workers' indicator. Although collective bargaining rights were not in themselves scored negatively as part of the index, the likely outcomes of effective collective bargaining were. Higher scores were awarded to states in which, for example, minimum wages and statutory paid leave entitlements were low, redundancy compensation minimal or non-existent and so forth.

12 In principle, the ILO does have the right to impose sanctions on its member states. However, this has never been done and what those sanctions might be remains a mystery.

13 The representative in question was the late Neil Kearney, General Secretary of the International Textile, Garment and Leather Workers Union. Representatives of the international union federations attend the ILO and are frequently invited to speak but do not have voting rights.

14 Even this rather half-hearted position has frequently been opposed by employers' representatives within the ILO. In 1994, for example, an influential employer delegate who went on to become a senior member of ILO staff made the following appeal: "should the freedom of association also encompass the freedom not to associate? I believe it must. This being the case, we must question why the right to collective bargaining should have any preference or positioning above the right of individuals who choose to bargain individually. The right to representation is fundamental, but again, like all human rights, it is a right available

to an individual. Individuals must be able to decide whether or not they wish to be represented and, if they do, it is their right to decide whether they wish to have their representative work for them alone or to join with others in a group representation" (International Labour Office, 1995, p. 4/37).

15 Collective bargaining in the absence of the right to strike and take other forms of industrial action is frequently described as 'collective begging' (Tucker, 2014, p. 456).

16 "It cannot . . . be deduced from the ILO's Conventions on collective bargaining that there is a formal obligation to negotiate or to achieve a result (an agreement)" (Gernigon et al., 2000, p. 28).

17 Greenhalgh and Russell (2009) argue that 'evidence-based' policymaking in its current form was originally popularised by the three successive Labour governments in the UK that were in power from 1997 until 2010. Du Toit (2012) adds that what he calls the 'evidence-based policy discourse' entered the field of development via the policies and practices of the UK government's Department for International Development.

18 The Bank later lifted its reserve, but as Maupain puts it, "the priority accorded to the economic considerations which underlie [its objections to collective worker rights] still seem to very much inspire the Bank's operational activities and analytical work" (2013, pp. 78–9).

19 The organization best-placed to conduct a large scale global survey on the subject would of course be the ILO, but the question is too politically sensitive to be taken up. Burchell et al. (2014) provide a useful discussion of why this is so.

20 It is not uncommon for collective bargaining in emerging economies to involve little more than a 'rubber stamping' of existing legal minima. For example, many collective bargaining agreements simply state that workers will be paid the minimum wage.

3 Industrial Relations Theory
From Industrial Democracy to the Web of Rules and Back Again

In this chapter I want to start thinking through the main theoretical issues in IR by looking at how the tension between conflict and cooperation has been dealt with in the academic debate.

The Origins of Conflict: Structure vs. Agency at Work

As Alan Fox recognised, the work situation is 'structured' in the sense that it demands that workers play a certain role within a pre-defined system of action:

> the industrial behaviour of individuals and relationships between them are shaped, not only by their being the sort of people they are, but also by the technology with which they work, the structure of authority, communications and status within which they are located, the system of punishments, rewards and other management controls to which they are subjected and various other aspects of 'the structures of the situation'.
>
> (Fox, 1966, para. 60)

The structural demands placed on workers take the form of obligations and constraints backed up by incentives and sanctions. To the extent that workers have choices about what they do, the range of options available and the criteria by which the choice between them is made are limited. Frequently, it will appear to the worker that there is no real choice to be made. The structures of the situation *require* that the worker behave in a certain way if she is to earn desirable benefits or avoid facing undesirable punishments.

That these kinds of structured action situations exist, and not just at work, is indisputable. The interesting question, indeed the critical question from the perspective of social theory in general and IR theory in particular, is the extent to which structural requirements displace other kinds of motivation for action. Does the fact of actors 'being the sort of people they are' continue to affect how they behave in structured action contexts? On the one hand, actors' personalities and their ability to make moral and ethical judgements do not simply disappear in the face of economic and other institutional imperatives. On the other, it seems obvious that social structures have an effect on action independently of their underpinning in ideas and argument. The major task of IR theory is therefore to help us to understand the extent to which workers reactions to the requirements of 'the system' (obligations and constraints) are conditioned by morality, convention, culture and politics, whether in such a way as to promote and improve compliance with rules and incentives (cooperation) or to incite resistance to them (conflict). To put it another way, we need to understand whether the perceived *legitimacy* of the structures of the situation makes any significant difference to how workers behave.

Assumptions about the degree to which structures displace norms feed into the choice of methodological approach. In this sense, the academic industrial relations tradition reflects the unresolved question of the relative importance of structure and agency as causes of workplace behaviour. Industrial and employment relations research in the English-speaking world makes extensive use of theoretical approaches that focus on the structured aspects of the employment relationship in the form of labour markets and job regulation. At the same time, there is a strong current of research and teaching concerned with understanding how workplace behaviour is affected by norms, values and conventions, whether those arising in the workplace itself or those imported from the social world beyond the factory gates.

As a discipline, then, IR has taken both structure and agency seriously. The problem is that these have not been successfully combined in a single approach. No truly satisfactory general conclusions have ever been drawn about the relationship between social behaviour at work on the one hand and, on the other, markets, organizations, conceptualisations of employing organizations and the norms and values of the communities within which workplaces are embedded.

To be fair, it should not be taken as given that this is actually a problem, or rather that it is a problem to which there is a single solution. Sisson, for example, picks up on Hyman's argument that while there is plenty of room for theory *in* IR, a theory *of* IR is not actually possible:

> It is surely not for want of expertise that several generations of scholars have now passed by with little or no movement in the direction of a theory 'of'. It is rather that the context-dependent phenomena that industrial relations deals with do not easily lend themselves to such an approach
> (2007, p. 55)

While it could be the case that relatively little generalisation is possible, I am inclined nevertheless to treat Hyman's claims about what a theory *of* IR implies as something of a straw man. For Hyman, "The premise of the idea of industrial relations theory is that the 'industrial relations system' operates primarily in response to its endogenous laws of motion, its intrinsic principles and logic" (2004, p. 277). This means that unless we have a self-sufficient theory with no need to take into account the insights of economics, law, gender relations and so on then we do not have a theory. Yet, a theory of IR would surely remain a theory *of* IR even if what it achieved was to show how the different aspects of society studied in these other fields fit together and interact in the work situation. We can certainly think of IR theory as a framework for analysis that draws on other disciplines, but this involves more than just suggesting a list of factors that might be relevant to the explanation of action in terms of a contingent balance between the structures of the situation and the sort of people that workers and managers are in any particular workplace.

Industrial Relations Theory

I do not propose to discuss the evolution of IR theory in detail, mainly because the job has already been done better than I could hope to do here. The 2004 collection of papers edited by Bruce Kaufman and published by the International Industrial Relations Association (Kaufman, 2004a) covers the relevant ground splendidly and from a wide range of different intellectual perspectives. Sisson's two papers in the 'Warwick Papers in Industrial Relations' series (2007, 2008), written as part of his 'Employment Relations Matters' project, are masterpieces of synthesis that also offer some immensely pertinent reflections on the relationship between the academic discipline of IR and its objects in the world of work. Hyman's contributions (1978, 1995, 2001b) are indispensable as a counterpoint to those conventional accounts that emphasise the resolution of conflict at the expense of understanding its causes. Finally, the series of papers produced by Kaufman himself over the last fifteen years (2003, 2008, 2010, 2014) has done a great deal to clarify the linkages between the British and US IR traditions and, perhaps more importantly, to show how a reconciliation or synthesis between neoclassical labour economics and IR might ultimately be possible.

Instead of covering this ground again, what I aim to do in this chapter is to offer a reading of the development of IR theory and its preoccupations at any particular moment as reflecting a position in relation to national and international policy debates that roughly mirrors that of neoclassical economics. Bourdieu argues that economics is

> haunted by state thinking: being constantly preoccupied with the normative concerns of an applied science, it is dependent on responding politically to political demands, while at the same time defending itself against any charge of political involvement by the ostentatiously lofty character of its formal, and preferably mathematical, constructions.
>
> (2005, p. 5)

While IR did not start as 'haunted by state thinking' and is certainly no longer so, in its 40-year heyday running from Roosevelt's New Deal to the aftermath of the economic crises of the 1970s, it had many of the characteristics Bourdieu attributes to economics. We see the same emphasis on professionalisation and the formalisation of theoretical propositions, the same concern that research should lead to the development of tools for social change that could be used by 'practitioners'. Instead of mathematical models, the idea of IR systems and typologies of IR context emerged as a step towards the formalisation of the discipline. The emphasis on procedure and rules in abstraction from the substance of those rules and the consequences of their enforcement gave IR something of the 'ostentatiously lofty' air of economics and opened the possibility of its being applied to any situation in which job regulation occurred.

The Webbs, Commons and the First Wave of Institutionalism

Although IR theory has a long pre-history, Beatrice and Sidney Webb's *Industrial Democracy*, first published in 1897, is probably the first recognisable work in the field. The authors' stated intention was to come up with a "scientific analysis" of trade unionism that goes beyond merely noting "the outward form and habit of the creature" and instead allows conclusions to be drawn about its purpose and effects on the basis of the "precise observation of actual facts" (p. v). The timing of *Industrial Democracy* was hardly accidental, arriving as it did roughly 25 years after the legalisation of trade union action in the UK via the Trade Union Act of 1871 and the Employers and Workmen and Conspiracy and Protection of Property Acts of 1875—enough time for the labour movement to shift from being a challenge to the existing socio-economic order to being part of it.

Although their book is ostensibly concerned only with the British trade unions, the Webbs' analysis involves a series of insights of universal and lasting significance for thinking about the organization of work and employment, regardless of its context. Two of these remain particularly relevant for theory building. The Webbs realised that the transformation of trade unionism into a legitimate social force working to reform rather than overturn existing institutional structures had material consequences for how we think about production systems and labour markets. The new collective actors in the economy could and would behave differently from the atomised individuals of marginalist economics. This called for an entirely different way of conceiving the dynamics of employment and wage movement. The second important insight with direct implications for IR theory is that there is no inherent connection between the improvement of the terms and conditions of work and trade unionism. The logic of taking action to mitigate what they called "the evils of unregulated capitalism" via the "deliberate regulation of the conditions of employment" (p. 807) is neither limited to democratic states, nor does it demand the presence of independent worker organization.[1] Collective bargaining is only one possible means of regulating the employment relationship. This in turn suggests that IR should be concerned not with the substance of working conditions or collective bargaining as a specific mode of regulation, but with the governance of work in a much broader sense.

In making these arguments, the Webbs touched on what were to become the two most important themes in IR theory: the *external* argument with classical and neoclassical labour economics and the *internal* argument about the objects and methods of IR. The former deals with why the unregulated capitalism typically envisaged by economists cannot be expected to work in the sense of leading to stable, effective and conflict-free business organization. The latter is concerned with reaching a better understanding of work and employment relationships in the market economic context with a view to designing more realistic public and private policy on IR, given that it is no longer to be expected that workers will simply accept the outcomes of unregulated capitalism and that it is unacceptable to make them do so using the brute force of economic power.

The main theoretical argument in *Industrial Democracy* is focused on the external dispute with economics. This is initially pitched as an argument against 'wage fund' theory, which states that the amount of money available to pay wages is fixed at any given moment and that workers' action to increase it, even if successful in the short term, is inevitably damaging to the workers' own interest. The Webbs started by noting that although wage fund theory had been comprehensively debunked in academic economics, it still needed to be challenged because it persisted in public opinion. They argued that it was a necessary basic principle of any kind of trade union activity that

> the ratio in which the total product of industry is shared between the property-owners, the brain-workers, and the manual labouring class respectively, is a matter of human arrangement, and that it can be altered, effectively and permanently, to the advantage of one class or another, if the appropriate action be taken.
>
> (Webb and Webb, 1902, p. 560)

In a *tour de force* of institutional analysis, the Webbs argued that what they called 'abstract economics' could give no indication of what an appropriate level of wages in the real world ought to be. They even cite one of the original abstract economists, Alfred Marshall, on the subject:

> If the employers in any trade act together and so do the employed, the solution of the problem of wages becomes indeterminate. The trade as a whole may be regarded as receiving a surplus (or quasi-rent) consisting of the excess of the aggregate price which it can get for such wares as it produces, over what it has to pay to other trades for the raw materials, etc., which it buys; and *there is nothing but bargaining to decide*

the exact shares in which this should go to employers and employed.
No lowering of wages will be permanently in the interest of employers
which is unnecessary and drives many skilled workers to other markets,
or even to other industries in which they abandon the special income
derived from their particular skill; and wages must be high enough in
an average year to attract young people to the trade. This sets lower
limits to wages, and upper limits are set by corresponding necessities
as to the supply of capital and business power. *But what point within
these limits should be taken at any time can be decided only by higgling
and bargaining.*
(cited in Webb and Webb, 1902, pp. 648–9; emphasis in original)

The Webbs used Marshall's argument to show that if we start with the
undeniable social fact of the ubiquity of 'combination', even neoclassical
economic theory can be used to show that the institution of 'higgling and
bargaining' is a critical, necessary part of the process of industrial governance. Their analysis showed that, at least within certain broad limits, there
was no division of spoils between capital and labour that could be specified
in advance as 'the best'.[2] Decisions about wages were not ultimately made
by 'the market' because the market did not and could not provide a determi-
nate answer. Any policy approach that pretended it could and did was likely
to be of little use. In short, the Webbs believed that economic theory is inadequate to the explanation of concrete economic behaviour to the extent that
it emphasises monetary exchange at the expense of other, equally important
forms of social interaction. The abstraction of exchange from its social context is the theoretical problem that needs to be corrected.

Industrial Democracy also established the terms of the internal IR debate,
certainly during the first half of the 20th century and arguably beyond.
The basis of the Webbs' analysis was the empirical truth that in late 19th
century England, the collective employment relationship was already the
dominant form: "This practice of Collective Bargaining has, in one form or
another, superseded the old individual contract between master and servant
over a very large proportion of the industrial field" (Webb and Webb, 1902,
p. 177). This meant that IR policy had to be based on an understanding of
the collective rather than the individual logic of the employment relationship. In the particular context of the UK at the end of the 19th century, the
focus of any scientific study of the field had to be trade unions.

The Webbs distilled what they called the 'functions' of trade unionism
into three areas of activity: worker organization and collective bargaining,
the provision of social security (the method of mutual insurance) and con-
ducting political campaigns for the legal regulation of the employment relationship (the method of legal enactment). The combination of these activities
was what provided the deliberate regulation of the conditions of employment and the insulation from financial risk that made capitalism an acceptable form of life. Nevertheless, for the Webbs, trade unionism remained

only one possible manifestation of the collective regulation of employment. Their basic analysis was focused on the nature of industrial society and the problems of governance to which it gave rise, not on trade unionism for its own sake. Reflecting on what they had learned from their study, the Webbs wrote that their abiding impression

> is a sense of the vastness and complexity of democracy itself. Modern civilised states are driven to this complication by the dense massing of their populations, and the course of industrial development. The very desire to secure mobility in the crowd compels the adoption of one regulation after another, which limit the right of every man to use the air, the water, the land, and even the artificially produced instruments of production, in the way that he may think best. The very discovery of improved industrial methods, by leading to specialization, makes manual laborer and brain-worker alike dependent on the rest of the community for the means of subsistence, and subordinates them, even in their own crafts, to the action of others. In the world of civilization and progress, no man can be his own master. But the very fact that, in modern society, the individual thus necessarily loses control over his own life, *makes him desire to regain collectively what has become individually impossible.*
>
> (1902, pp. 849–50; emphasis added)

The Webbs had a direct influence on the US discipline of institutional economics, notably via the work of John R. Commons. At the beginning of the 20th century, academic economics in the US was divided between an institutional school influenced by German social-historical economics and a neoclassical school that based its work on the marginal utility theory originally developed by Menger, Jevons and Walras. Whereas the institutional economists were concerned with understanding the logic of economic behaviour and the problems of industrial order in all their concrete historical specificity, the neoclassical school was focused much more narrowly on "the formulation of uniform or universal laws pertaining to certain 'analytical' factors, 'aspects' or 'elements' in human action, particularly the rational satisfaction of human wants in conditions of 'scarcity'" (Camic, 1991, p. xxxii).

Commons picked up on the Webbs' criticisms of neoclassical economics (Gonce, 2002, p. 757), in particular the argument that there is no balance between capital and labour that will automatically maximise efficiency and that the price of labour has to be settled via the social process of 'higgling and bargaining'. As Gonce puts it, "In Commons's work two opposing resultants of underlying, real economic forces do not impersonally, mechanistically interact and come into static equilibrium. Instead, persons, nonmarket forces, interact and arrive at a contract" (ibid., p. 767). Commons and his colleagues preferred to use political rather than mechanical analogies when talking about the governance of industry (Schiller, 1999), highlighting the conscious will of the parties to come to an agreement in the context not only of a pragmatic recognition that organised social forces exist and cannot be ignored but also of a normative commitment to the principle of mutual respect between different groups pursuing legitimate interests. The relationship between labour and capital is therefore dynamic rather than static (Piore and Safford, 2006, p. 17) and based on deliberate, substantive normative agreement arising from institutional processes analogous to political democracy on the pluralist interest group model.

Among the many contributions of the US institutionalists was the attempt to think through the logic of the collective approach as it applied to the labour process rather than to the labour market. Commons argues that the simple law of contract is an inadequate institutional machinery to deal with the different 'transactions' by which work is organised. He conceived these transactions as the exchange of some kind of property rights, but argued that market exchange is only one of three basic types (Kaufman, 2004b, pp. 104–9). The other two are the rationing transaction (the exchange of property rights commanded by a legal superior: in effect, the issuing of the managerial plans and strategies by which organizations are directed) and the managerial transaction (the exchange of the worker's property rights over her labour power with the employer: the social organization of the labour process). All of these require the presence of a dedicated institutional structure that recognises and provides some means to deal with the highly non-neoclassical phenomena of "bounded rationality, imperfect information, incomplete markets and costly enforcement of contracts" (Kaufman, 2004b, p. 105). It is only by recognizing the reality of these phenomena and integrating them into our theoretical structure that it is possible to conceptualise the economy as what is actually is, i.e. a "mix of markets and organizations, including large hierarchical firms with an employment relationship" (ibid.).

The Second Wave Institutionalists: Rules, Industrialisation and the End of Power

The recognition of the empirical reality of collective worker organization and the consequent inadequacy of neoclassical models of the labour market together with the political realities of the post-Second World War period shifted the emphasis of the industrial relations policy argument from *whether* to accommodate collective worker representation to *how* best to do it. From a concern with the labour market, the focus turned to the labour process, something that institutionalist industrial relations looked well-placed to explain.

Institutionalism's competitors in the argument were the policy manifestations of the cooperation assumption. Taylorism was definitively off the agenda, at least as a tool to persuade workers to throw in their lot with management, and whether the welfare capitalist approach to management might fulfil the political conditions for worker cooperation that the institutionalists had identified had been answered in the negative during the depression years. However, the infamous human relations approach was still in circulation. As Bruce and Nyland put it, human relations "presented conservative business leaders with a set of management ideas and practices that enabled them to deny that workers should become active participants in workplace decision making and in wider society" (2011, p. 384). In this sense it was a direct competitor for the institutional/pluralist approach.

Perhaps the best statement of this distinction as well as of the case against Elton Mayo's work[3] is Kerr's 1949 paper, *Plant Sociology: the Elite and the Aborigines* (Reprinted in Kerr, 1964). Kerr argues that in the analysis of industry, one can adopt either a 'sociological' or an 'economic' perspective. From the sociological—for which read human relations—perspective,

> The test of [managerial] performance is not efficiency, but stability. The industrial plant is not a voluntary association, but a social organism. The view of man is that of the dependent part within the social whole. The task of the manager is to produce coherence, stability and a sense of community.
>
> (Kerr, 1964, p. 44)

Mayo's approach propagated "an image of man and society which stressed supposedly irreducible social elements in collective life" (Rose, 1978, p. 169) that were considerably more important in practice than any kind of rational instrumental calculation. While the Hawthorne research studies that Mayo used to retrospectively justify his arguments are notorious for their methodological errors and bias, they nonetheless highlighted the existence of social processes within the workplace that are independent of the formal system of rules which supposedly define the relationships making up the plant organization. Mayo and his followers, having observed that this informal social fabric could work either to support or undermine the formal organization of the workplace, argued that the manager's role was actively to manage the social system within the plant such that the relationship between workers and managers was harmonious. The basis of authority was to be consent rather than incentives; in this sense, it would have social rather than economic foundations.

From the economic perspective, by contrast, the central task of industrial management is the efficient allocation and organization of productive resources. The continuity with the pre-war institutionalists is evident in the sense that the starting point for Kerr's liberal pluralism is the recognition of the empirical reality of different organised groups with divergent interests. As Hyman (1978) argues, however, Kerr's approach was fuelled as much by politics as theory, one of his principal concerns being to defend post-war US practice against the Soviet model. Certainly he seems to have seen in the tenets of the human relations school something comparable to communism:

The case for the prescription of the plant sociologist is not . . . that the facts compel the prescription but rather that the vision of the plant sociologist is not impossible of achievement if we want it badly enough. The charge against those who do not share the vision cannot be, therefore, that they are blind to facts but rather that they are of the wrong religion and worship false gods.

(1964, p. 81)

Kerr's 'pluralistic industrialism', by contrast, demands that the enterprise have no overarching vision or purpose. It requires absolute neutrality with respect to the specific aims and values of the individuals and groups involved in production. The corollary of this neutrality is the absence of any attempt to organise society along monolithic lines. The possibility of *re*organising in order to pursue more efficient means of production in the face of changed market circumstances must always be kept open. Hence the emphasis on the creation and ongoing revision of the rules that govern the productive enterprise on the basis of negotiation between competing centres of power.

Dunlop and the Systems Turn

As Roche argues (1986), the position taken by Kerr and the other post-war institutionalists lent itself well to a systems analysis in which the conscious coordination of action gives way to coordination based on unintended consequences. It was

a short, if analytically momentous, step to a position in which the purposes of actors and their organizations in industrial relations tended to be regarded as banal, invariant or irrelevant, and in which explanations were elaborated by accounting for apparently unintended consequences of action in terms of the hypothesized goals or 'needs' of social systems.

(ibid., p. 6)

Although it emerged from a basically institutionalist position, this development marked a clear break with the work of Commons and his colleagues in the sense that it instituted the idea of a balance or equilibrium within and between sub-systems that is not actively achieved but arises more or less automatically. Rather than the balance between capital and labour having normative substance in itself as the outcome of compromises consciously made by 'reasonable men', the web of rules is a technical artefact; an outcome of processes operating largely beyond the intentions of those involved.

It is not altogether clear that the sense in which Roche—perfectly correctly—describes the basic assumptions of systems theory is what John T. Dunlop intended with his 1958 work *Industrial Relations Systems*.[4] Reading Dunlop's magnum opus, it is difficult to escape the conclusion that he had only a limited grasp of Parsons's extremely complex social theory.

To be fair, he does say that it is not his intention to 'apply directly' Parsons's 'general analytic scheme' to the industrial relations aspects of industrial society, but on the other hand if this is not what he is doing then he certainly does not make it clear in what sense the work is *not* Parsonian. If we assume that *Industrial Relations Systems* is intended to be at least compatible with Parsons's work, then as Wood and his colleagues (1975), among others, have pointed out (for example, Dimmock and Sethi, 1986; Muller-Jentsch, 2004), Dunlop either makes some very basic mistakes or has some adaptation in mind that he does not spell out.

The most significant problem is the argument that the industrial relations system is analogous to and exists on the same 'analytic plane' as the economic system in the sense that it is a subsystem of society as a whole that deals with certain specialised functions. Yet, Parsons's schema already defines four subsystems of society that cover all of the available territory. The economy is one of these along with the political-administrative system of governance structures, the integrative system of ideas and reasons for action and the cultural system of values and socialisation. Not only is there no room in this scheme for a new subsystem, the governance of economic activity already has a place within the political-administrative system.

Even leaving this important error aside, Dunlop's schema remains inadequate. He argues that just as the economic system takes care of the satisfaction of material needs, the IR system takes care of the regulation of the workplace. The IR and economic systems are the only subsystems to which he makes direct reference, but he suggests that the context of or environment for the IR system (he uses both words) is determined by "the larger society and its other subsystems" (1993, p. 48). Presumably this means that there are more subsystems than just the economic system but for some reason he does not refer to them in discussing the environment for the IR system, specifying simply that it is made up of technology, markets and power. Although Dunlop does not make direct use of biological or physiological analogies, he cites the biologist Julian Huxley in an endnote intended to explain that systems must 'maintain themselves in direct interaction' with their 'environment' (note 14, p. 299). So, the IR system receives *inputs* from its environment in the shape of requirements arising from the technological characteristics of industry, product, labour and capital markets, and the 'locus and distribution of power'. To maintain itself in balance with its environment it then has to produce *outputs* in the shape of rules covering "the full range of rule making that governs the work place" (ibid., p. 46). There is a certain automaticity to this process: "The idea of an industrial relations system implies a unity, an interdependence and an internal balance which *are likely to be restored if the system is displaced*, provided there is no fundamental change in the actors, contexts or ideology" (ibid., pp. 60–1; emphasis added).

It is hard to say exactly what Dunlop believed the mechanisms or causal relationships behind this adaptive capacity to be. He does not discuss the incentives and constraints arising from within the IR system or from other social subsystems that would make actors choose or formulate one type of regulation rather than another. The chapters on the three different aspects of the environment of the IR system do give some idea of the impact that these different factors might have, but these remain at the level of empirical examples. There is no attempt at systematisation. As Blain and Gennard point out in an early review of different approaches to IR theory,[5] the

> 'systems model' does not give an analysis of the processes whereby the rules of the system are made. The focus is on the structure of an industrial relations system and ignores the 'processes' which are the behavioural dynamics of the system. In the model, the actors are viewed in a structural rather than a dynamic sense.
>
> (1970, p. 403)

Dunlop sometimes seems to be working with the first-wave institutionalist assumption that each set of actors in the IR system will take a pragmatic approach to the presence of the others and will make a conscious calculation about the empirical balance of power in deciding how best to pursue their own particular ambitions. Indeed, he has been roundly criticised for failing to make it clear whether his concept of a system is empirical or analytical, a heuristic device to capture an observed social reality or something of wider theoretical significance (Michelson and Wescott, 2001; Wood et al., 1975).

Alongside the system itself, the other components of the theoretical picture are actors and ideology. The actors of the IR system are of course workers, employers and governments. The concept of ideology is what relates these actors to the system: "The Ideology of the industrial relations system is a body of common ideas that defines the role and place of each actor and the ideas that each actor holds towards the place and function of the others in the system" (ibid., p. 53). This at least is slightly Parsonian in the sense that Parsons's overarching intention with his social theory was to relate the internal *action* perspective adopted by individuals and groups to the external *system* perspective of functional interconnection and unintended consequences (Joas and Knöbl, 2009, chapter II). If we are to be justified in taking the methodological step of conceiving the interactions of individuals as a system then we have to have some means of understanding what it is they think they are doing that is logically coherent with the outcomes we observe from a third-party perspective. The worldview of each of the different possible 'industrializing elites' represents a distinct ideology of this kind. However, despite his recognition that incompatible ideologies are likely to lead to conflict rather than to stable IR systems (Dunlop, 1993, p. 53), Dunlop makes no attempt to explain the origin of ideologies or the relationship between the ideology of the industrializing elite and that of other groups like workers.

From a strictly academic perspective, it is difficult to disagree with Roche's conclusion that "Dunlop's [*Industrial Relations Systems*] is of little heuristic, conceptual or theoretical value" and that the evident problems have not been resolved in subsequent work (1986, p. 23). Although I think that there are at least three insights that are salvageable—I will discuss these in a moment—the problems are such that its resonance in the literature is rather mysterious. One possible solution to the puzzle is to adopt a more Bourdieusian perspective and think in terms of the policy needs to which the book and the larger research project of which it was a part responded. It is worth taking a short detour into the wider politics of Dunlop's approach to consider this before returning to our theoretical concerns.

Industrialisation Theory and the End of IR History

"The Inter-University Study of Labour Problems in Economic Development", which had begun in 1954 and which was largely funded by the Ford Foundation, was conceived by Dunlop (Harvard) along with three other labour economists, Clark Kerr (Berkeley), Frederick Harbison (Princeton) and Charles Myers (MIT). According to the authors' introduction to the 1960 work of synthesis, *Industrialism and Industrial Man*,[6] that drew some of the threads of the programme together, they had each come to recognise in the early 1950s that there was a need for the study of labour problems to take on a comparative dimension that up to then it had been missing. In principle, what is presented in the book is a framework for the comparative analysis of industrialisation processes from the perspective of the labour-management relationship. The authors' avowed intention is to break with the established tradition of labour studies, "against Marx, the Webbs, Commons and Perlman, and Mayo, alike. We have redefined the labour problem as the structuring of the managers and the managed under industrialization rather than as the response of unions to capitalism" (Kerr et al., 1973, p. 39). The book maintains and develops some of the most important elements of Dunlop's approach, in particular the idea that institutional coherence and the stability of the structure of social relationships depends on the presence of a "consensus which relates individuals and groups to each other and provides an integrated body of ideas, beliefs and value judgements" (ibid., p. 53). However, beyond the maintenance of the term 'IR system' to refer to the unique structure of institutions and practices in each national setting, there is no reference to the system of IR in the sense of a functional subsystem of society maintaining itself in relation to an environment. Instead, the theoretical thread running through the work is that there is an immanent logic to industrialisation which is separate from politics and culture. Once industrialisation has been accepted as the developmental goal of a society, in the long term there is an almost inevitable convergence around a certain set of values and ideas that the authors believe arise from the inescapable technical logic of the organization of industrial production:

Industrialization transforms an old society or an empty country and creates a new form of society . . . Pre-existing conditions will often obscure the underlying processes at work to some degree. But the logic of industrialization prevails eventually, and such similarities as it decrees will penetrate the outermost points of its universal sphere of influence. Each industrialized society is more like every other industrialized society—however great the differences among them may be—than any industrial society is like any pre-industrial society.

(ibid., p. 56)

As with its companion work on IR systems, the theoretical value of *Industrialism and Industrial Man* is doubtful at best. The basic thesis is simply an extrapolation of empirical trends that has little apparent basis in theory and that arguably contradicts Dunlop's earlier work. In proposing that there is a developmental trajectory common to all industrialising countries, it reduces the idea of variation in IR systems to a question of the variation of routes to a single end-point where any remaining difference in national contexts is largely incidental to the organization of industry. It also skates lightly over the issue of conflict, ignoring the question of the substance of job regulation and the impact of perceptions of (un)fairness and (in)justice.

The political value of the approach, however, was and remains immense. It responded in particular to the needs of the ILO, which according to Cox was the site of a number of conferences and consultations organised by the leaders of the project and which played host to Dunlop during the period of sabbatical leave when *Industrial Relations Systems* was written. The two major outputs of the Inter-University Study fulfilled the ILO's needs perfectly. Indeed, Cox takes the view that they amounted to a "reformulation of the operational ideology" of the ILO (1996, p. 442). An unsympathetic observer might even call it a work of 'policy-based evidence making' on a massive scale.

What is not in doubt is that by the mid-1950s the ILO was in need of intellectual resources. The influx of new member states joining the Organization after decolonisation and the consequently increased importance of direct technical assistance activities as part of the ILO's work gave rise to a need for tools for the comparative analysis of national industrial contexts (Rodgers et al., 2009, p. 31). Another consequence of the expansion of the ILO's membership was a vastly increased gap between the lowest and highest levels of economic development and national income. The (re) accession of the Soviet Union to membership in 1954 also meant that the ILO's conception of industrial relations could not simply assume the backdrop of capitalist forms of industrial organization. Above all, there was a need to come up with some scientific validation for the weakly institutionalised, voluntarist collective industrial relations model that had emerged as the point of political balance between employers, workers and governments within the Organization.

The combined systems-industrialisation approach fitted these requirements almost perfectly. There are three aspects to this. The first is what Hyman called "the elevation of procedural principles above substantive outcomes" (1978, p. 34). As Blain and Gennard have also argued, "The main significance of the 'systems model' for the study of industrial relations as an academic discipline has been its attempt to change the central focus of the subject from industrial conflict and collective bargaining towards rule determination" (1970, p. 395). IR is not about the substance of industrial governance but the maintenance of an agreed order in the production system (Wood et al., 1975, p. 301). It is about the production of rules, not what those rules actually turn out to be in terms of job content, pay, hours, working conditions, workplace discipline and so forth. Roche's point that the systems model in this way removes the *purposes* of the actors from the analytic picture remains true even while, as Hyman (1978) and Fox (1974a) both argue, it also limits the substantive goals and interests that can be pursued. This is the case not just in the sense of the boundaries set by the conventional specification of what is and is not a matter for collective bargaining, but also in the sense that the systems model implies that there are limits to what can be achieved that are determined by the need for job regulation to satisfy the demands of the other subsystems involved, notably the economy. The process is not the conscious normative compromise described by the first wave institutionalists, with the associated implication of responsibility for outcomes, but a norm-free process driven by autonomous economic and social forces. The outcomes of the process will be what they will be and, as Hyman pointed out, "the mere participation in job regulation may of course be wholly compatible with the stagnation or deterioration of material conditions" (1978, p. 34). On this reading, the theory of IR systems is the equivalent of the competitive labour market theory in economics, which assumes that the best approximation of the long-run competitive equilibrium price of labour is the price that is currently paid.

The second aspect of the IR systems-industrialisation model that fits the ILO's policy requirements is the assumption that employers will see collective industrial relations as a rational management choice. As we saw in Chapter 2, the ILO assumes that workers must *choose* to deal with their employer on a collective basis via a spontaneous mobilisation. The Organization is agnostic about 'duty to bargain' provisions and the ability of employers to refuse to recognise unions has never been held to be inconsistent with any convention. The position is defended by reference to the argument that employers and workers who are forced to bargain and do not choose to do so for themselves are unlikely to participate in the process in good faith. For Kerr and his colleagues, as for many others at the time, the absence of any guarantee of collective worker representation in all cases is not problematic because their faith in the logic of industrialisation led them to believe that managers will inevitably come to recognise the greater rationality of collective IR. Employer resistance to collective IR simply makes no sense within their model.

The third aspect is the sequential or developmental trajectory of industrialisation. Kerr et al. make it clear that industrialisation is a process that takes time to achieve. Employers and trade unions cannot just jump into a collective bargaining relationship from one day to the next. Both sides need to serve what can be a long apprenticeship as they learn the skills of organising and representing their members. This means there may be a hiatus of unspecified length between the ratification of ILO conventions on freedom of association and collective bargaining and the eventual appearance of 'mature' industrial relations.[7]

These three aspects of the systems-industrialisation model suit both employers' and workers' organizations because they legitimise their existing institutional roles and privileges while maximising their room for political manoeuvre. Employers, for the most part, simply do not want collective bargaining and will only agree to it if there is no realistic prospect of resisting. Workers' organizations want to maintain a monopoly on worker representation and, in particular, to resist the development of non-union worker representative structures. Both employers and workers' organizations want the maximum freedom to pursue whatever substantive goals seem appropriate and within reach given the existing power constellation.

The focus on procedural rules takes the substance of bargaining claims out of the analysis, reducing the possibility that any such claim—or resistance to it—will be the subject of technical evaluation of its feasibility or desirability. The idea that the substance of the rules is the outcome of systemic pressures that are merely articulated by the participants in bargaining serves to further disconnect outcomes from the conscious—and hence potentially blameworthy—intentions of unions and employers.

The industrialisation thesis provides a means to defuse the potentially critical problems of voluntarism, which in practice may involve, on the one hand, an employer's right to resist or refuse to recognise its workers as a collective actor and, on the other, what in some contexts may be an impossibly strict test for the existence of an authentic workers' shared intention to act collectively. Neither of these problems is critical if it is thought that the choice of collective industrial relations is premised on the demands of rational management. Employers in particular are able to explain away the absence of collective representation by the free choices of workers and managers. Workers' organizations use the principle of voluntarism to maintain their claim to exclusive representation rights and to resist the development of worker representation structures in which all workers have a voice rather than just union members.

The developmental nature of the process of industrialisation adds a further possibility for justifying the absence or inadequacy of bargaining and, within the ILO at least, for ensuring that policy measures to encourage it are not too forceful. The industrialisation thesis conceives 'mature' industrial relations as the end-point of an economic development process of indeterminate length rather than as a condition for its achievement. The absence of collective IR is merely a question of the stage of development that has been reached. Industrialisation is also a process where one stage follows on from another and where different policies and practices are appropriate to different stages. Insisting on too rapid a development of collective industrial relations can therefore be presented as endangering the industrialisation process itself.

The Systems-Industrialisation Model: Is There Anything Worth Salvaging?

Dunlop et al. ultimately fail because their work points to the end of industrial relations history. The systems-industrialisation approach is a grand narrative on the Marxian model that envisages an inevitable end-point to industrial development which, like the proletarian revolution, can be helped along by policy interventions but that is ultimately likely to arrive anyway at some unspecified point in the future. Like Marxism, it demands faith and ideological commitment. Its main function is to justify and mobilise support for an existing model of policy and practice. Ironically, in this sense it falls into precisely the category of social scientific grand narrative that Kerr attacked Mayo for proposing.

Also like Marxism, however, along the way it introduces some useful and important insights—not so many, nor so important, but nevertheless too useful to discard. I want to highlight three of these.

The first and simplest is that workplace order is not exclusively or even principally the result of economic forces. Markets and industrial technology have an impact, but so do constellations of power. The chapters in *Industrial Relations Systems* that deal with each of the contextual influences on the IR system show that Dunlop recognised that the range of variation within each relevant aspect is limited to small number of categories. However, he does not work this insight up into a systematic mapping of possible interactions of the environmental forces. Nevertheless, what we can take away from this is the idea that it is not just economics that has a *systematic* impact on IR systems. This reflects a distinctly Parsonian concern with getting past the exclusive reliance on economics and including other social sciences, notably sociology, as equally important but also equally rigorous elements in the explanation of the employment relationship (Camic, 1991). Dunlop's proposals, while pointing in this general direction, remain inadequate because he conceives power not as a social relation but merely as the set of legal-institutional arrangements that establish the formal competences of unions, managements and government agencies.

The second valuable insight is that the 'systematicity' of rule systems derives from an underlying ideology, i.e. it is ultimately rooted in inter-subjectively shared ideas. It is only where all the different actors involved *understand* their roles in compatible ways—where they have accepted that for actor x in situation y, the appropriate response is action z—that we can expect a stable system of action to emerge. This insight is also very Parsonian in inspiration. As we will see in more detail in Chapter 4, Parsons premised his theory-building on the rejection of what he called 'utilitarianism', challenging both behaviourist accounts of economic action and those proposing that there is something so transcendently rational about the choice of utility-maximising strategies that the historical and socio-cultural context of action is of little or no consequence (Joas and Knöbl, 2009, Chapter II). Like Parsons, Dunlop recognised that the methodological strategy of systems theory only makes sense if the characteristics of systems can be shown to be a consequence of what the actors populating them think and believe. Unfortunately, Dunlop's interesting but underdeveloped ideas about ideology are entirely undermined by his commitment to the industrialisation thesis. The idea of industrialisation implies an ultimate convergence around what he called the 'middle-class' ideology which is driven by the objective requirements of industrial development. As an analytic tool then, Dunlop's concept of ideology is of limited value.

The third of Dunlop's insights that we can hold onto is more an implication of his methodological approach than an explicit theoretical proposition. This is that institutional configurations are not neutral technologies of organization but reflect and embed an underlying ideology. It is not simply the case that the actors in the system have ideologies that are more or less mutually compatible, but that the institutions of the system themselves embed and reflect a particular ideology. We can read Dunlop's observation that the ideology of the IR system will come to bear a close relationship to the ideology of the industrial society of which it is a part (1993, p. 54) as a claim that IR institutions will tend to reflect the ideas of whatever industrialising elite holds the reins of power. This in turn implies, as Dunlop himself points out, that anti-system conflict is different from conflict that remains within the boundaries of the system. Anti-system conflict is a clash of ideologies rather than an institutionalised resolution of differences that, by definition, remain within certain agreed boundaries. Again, however, the value of this insight is rather lost once it is combined with the industrialisation thesis, which relegates analysis in terms of ideology to a secondary role.

There are two notable post-Dunlop contributions to IR theory that share and develop some or all of these insights, although neither of them do so on the basis of a reading of Dunlop. One of these contributions, Alan Fox's 'frames of reference' approach, is extremely well-known. The other, Robert Cox's theory of the 'social relations of production' has been almost entirely ignored in the mainstream IR debate.

Fox and the Frames of Reference

Alan Fox is one of the few scholars of industrial relations or management in the last 50 years who did not start from the assumption that either conflict or cooperation is the 'normal' state of affairs. Although he is usually categorised as part of the British institutionalist school of IR along with his Oxford University colleagues Hugh Clegg and Allan Flanders, Fox based his policy orientation on an analysis of empirical conditions in the context of a series of more fundamental theoretical assumptions, many of which his contemporaries did not share. While Flanders and Clegg were both responsible for empirical research of immense and enduring value, their theoretical contribution was limited. Flanders' argument that IR was 'the study of the institutions of job regulation' added little if anything to Dunlop's basic scheme (Geare, 1977; Hyman, 1978; Kaufman, 2014). If we can characterise it as a school of thought, British institutionalism's most striking characteristic is its firm attachment to the conflict assumption as a basic premise of IR research and policy-making. Although Fox also believed that industrial conflict was to be expected and at least for a time believed that collective industrial relations was the solution, for him this was not a foundational assumption but a conclusion.

Fox argues that actors' responses to the incentives and constraints they face at work cannot be conceived as binary: a 'yes' or 'no' to whatever deal is on the table with nothing in between. Neither is it the case that responses are conditioned primarily either by utility maximisation strategies or individual personality traits. Rather, responses depend on the conceptual models of the employment relationship and its socio-economic context that actors use as a basis for orienting their choices. To put it simply, behaviour at work depends on how employment is *understood* in relation to wider society. Although the specific perspective of different individuals may vary to some degree, the conceptual models that actors use are not idiosyncratic but intersubjective. These 'frames of reference' are forms of shared understanding that are not a deterministic response to circumstances but the result of an ongoing, reflexive and—most importantly—*social* process of interpretation, action and learning.

For Fox, the fault line separating the major types of frame of reference lies exactly where we have located the line between the conflict and cooperation assumptions. He calls the approach to IR that arises from the cooperation assumption 'unitarism' and that arising from the conflict assumption 'pluralism'. What really sets Fox apart from other industrial relations scholars is his recognition that, in the abstract, neither of these conceptualisations of the relationship between employers and employees is more true or accurate than the other. He argues that in any particular historical and organizational context it may be that one perspective is more likely than the other to give rise to effective organizational structures and normative choices widely seen as legitimate. His approach therefore accommodates pluralist forms of analysis without being pre-committed to them, leaving room for other middle-range theoretical orientations should the empirical circumstances warrant it.

This absence of analytical sectarianism is perhaps the main reason why Fox's typology of frames of reference, set out in a series of books and papers produced between 1966 and 1974, still structures much teaching not only in industrial and employment relations but also in human resources management (see, for example, recent HRM and employment relations textbooks: Wilton, 2010; Rose, 2008; Redman and Wilkinson, 2008). Despite this continued pedagogical application, however, Fox's work is no longer influential as a framework for academic research, still less for public policy development and organizational practice. Although it inspired a two-decades long debate about the possibility and range of variation of different 'styles' of managing the employment relationship (a debate conducted largely without the involvement of US scholars; for an account see Legge, 1995, chapter 2), there is little trace today of any significant research into the behavioural implications of different ways of conceptualising or thinking about employment, whether among managers, employees or both at the same time.

Norms, Authority, Compliance and Resistance

Taking his cue from classical organization theory, Fox proposes that the core problematic of industrial relations is how to ensure that the employment relationship is *legitimised* by workers in the sense that the exercise of control by managers is recognised as 'appropriate and proper' (Blau and Scott, 1962, p. 30) or 'just and worthy of support' (Thompson, 1994). In good Weberian fashion, Fox suggests that where subordination is legitimised by workers we can talk of 'authority relations'. Where it is not, and where compliance is the result of a wish to pursue an incentive or avoid a sanction *and nothing more*, we can talk instead of 'power relations'.

Fox argues that regardless of any specific goals or processes, organizations can never operate as effectively as possible on the basis of mere power relations, that is, where workers believe their subordination to management to be morally or ethically ungrounded and comply only from economic necessity. Not only will workers' individual performance be affected (there is an obvious difference in quality of compliance between willing cooperation and 'forced obedience under duress'), but the likelihood of organised collective resistance to management is also increased. In the eyes of the employee, subordination based only on power relations legitimises "whatever action he may be disposed to take to oppose management power with counter-power if he can mobilize it" (Fox, 1971, p. 38).

So, Fox relates conflict and cooperation to legitimacy, but, unlike the classical Weberian organization theorists, he also argues that the establishment of legitimacy is not simply a factual assessment of whether some specific management instruction or a general workplace situation conforms to a pre-existing contractual specification of the employment relationship. Rather, it involves a substantive, multidimensional assessment of the employment relationship as a whole from the perspective of the employee.

In order to capture the demands that the employment relationship makes on the employee, Fox uses the concepts of the 'role' and of 'role behaviour'. Roles, he argues, are largely a consequence of the 'structures of the situation', each a "pattern of required behaviour" which "in some measure . . . exists independently of the person filling it at any one time" (1966, paragraph 62). More specifically,

> Each role includes a technological behaviour system of norms which define the task activities. Secondly, it includes a set of norms designed to focus attention upon the goals defined for the organization by its leaders; specify the kinds of behaviour necessary for achieving those goals; lay down modes of personal conduct; set out the duties and responsibilities of the individual towards the organization; and embody values deemed by its leaders to be required of all the organization's members. Thirdly, some roles include elements which endow them with control over the methods and conduct of work . . . The top management of the organization will allocate the 'right' to issue directives and orders, determine policies . . . define standards . . . Rights and duties relating to such activities are therefore the fourth element of the role system.
>
> (1971, p. 30)

It is evident that Fox recognises that the structures of the situation are principally normative; they are quite literally *made* of values, rules and conventions. However, formal rules are detached from the reasons that justify them. What is more, they may reflect more than one set of underlying reasons for action. Different actors may understand these underlying reasons in different ways and may or may not accept their validity. So, although employees have little influence over the basic pattern of behaviour they are required to adopt—largely dictated by their place within the organization and their need or desire to remain within it—this does not mean that the questions of how they experience and interpret this requirement for conformity, the attitude with which they approach it, and whether and to what extent they may challenge it are either settled or irrelevant:

> bound up with the question of so-called 'structural determinants of behaviour' . . . is the question of how people perceive these structural features, since how they perceive them decides how they behave in response.
>
> (1974b, p. 77)

Workers' perceptions of the structures of the situation are in this sense largely a question of their evaluations of the normative legitimacy of their subordination; of the structural requirement to conform with the work situation—whatever 'conformity' may mean in practice in any given situation. These evaluations arise in turn from their 'frames of reference'. Fox defines a frame of reference as "a distillation of the observer's background, experience, values and purposes" (1974b, p. 77). More specifically, frames of reference arise on the basis of:

- the norms, conventions and values held to be valid in actors' immediate social environments, whether within the workplace or outside it;
- beliefs about the state of power relations in industry and the balance of interests in the economy;
- general socio-cultural attitudes arising from normal socialisation processes; and
- lived experience in the workplace.

Not every possible frame of reference will permit the legitimisation of any given mode of social organization of work. From the perspective of certain frames of reference, subordination may be interpreted as a manifestation of an unjust power structure in wider society. From others, it may appear to be the rational consequence of a technical division of labour. From others still, it might be understood as an institutional structure that exists to help employees to comply with normative obligations they have freely accepted. Each of these different frames of reference implies different expectations about management behaviour and the social structure of the organization. In any given case, these expectations may amount to a more or less accurate depiction of the real situation. The militant trade unionist's default interpretation of any and all management initiatives may be that they are attempts to defraud workers of the fruits of their labour, regardless of how they are intended and of any potential they contain for actually improving the lot of employees. The manager who has worked successfully with union representatives over the length of her career will at first sight see workers' grievances as pointing to serious problems in need of mutually acceptable solutions, perhaps realising only later that they are (to give one unlikely but possible example) actually vexatious complaints prompted by militant union organizers from outside the company.

It is only the actual experience of social and organizational interaction that sheds any light on whether frames of reference are adequate. In the abstract they are neither true nor false. Discussing the concept of 'worldviews', very close to the idea of frames of reference (Cradden, 2004, 2005), Habermas argues that while worldviews themselves may not be susceptible to judgements of truth or falsity, they "make possible utterances that admit of truth" (Habermas, 1984, p. 58). Statements inferred on the basis of worldviews may be more or less coherent with the lived experience of actors, hence more or less 'cognitively adequate'.

The expectations of the militant trade unionist and the union-friendly manager therefore may or not be cognitively adequate, which is to say they may or may not be borne out in practice. If they are not, then those frames of reference themselves are put into question. Frames of reference are not fixed. Fox argues that there is an ongoing feedback process that connects frames of reference and the social organization of work because people will always seek interpretations of their situation that allow them to resolve cognitive dissonance and make sense of their lived experience.

There are two points that Fox is particularly keen to emphasise. The first is that workers' settled frames of reference will reflect the workplace as they experience it rather than as their employers want or imagine it to be. No amount of communication or exhortation will convince workers that managers are behaving reasonably if the day-to-day evidence suggests that management action is exploitative, dishonest or lacking in good faith. If managers want workers to believe the workplace is different, then it has to *be* different.

The second point is about the need for coherence between frames of reference within the workplace and outside it. Even where managers have the best of intentions and where their actions are, to use Flanders' expression, "intelligent and far-sighted" (1975, p. 23), they still cannot expect workers to legitimise their own subordination if the structures of the situation are such that the only values that can support legitimisation are in conflict with socio-culturally dominant beliefs, interpretations and expectations about work. The normative rationalisations of managerial rule that are possible are limited by what is accepted in wider society. This in turn means that management action itself is limited by the values and ideas that characterise the place and time in which an organization is operating. Commenting on the contemporary situation, Fox wrote:

> Of all the values that can legitimize managerial rule, those which appear to be coming to predominate in these [Western] societies are those related to substantive aspirations for a continuously rising material standard of life, and to procedural aspirations for participative decision-making machinery through which substantive gains can be made and protected.
> (Fox, 1971, p. 45)

Fox identifies three ideal-typical frames of reference. Two of these were proposed in his well-known article "Industrial Sociology and Industrial Relations" (1966), written as a background paper for a UK public enquiry into labour-management relations usually known as the Donovan Commission. The third was introduced some years later in his book *Beyond Contract: Work, Power and Trust Relations* (1974a).

Unitarism and Pluralism

The essential difference between the unitarist and pluralist frames of reference is straightforward. The unitarist sees employment as a relationship between members of a single social group, a group with a common purpose or general will. The 'natural' or 'correct' state of the relationship is cooperation, without preconditions, in pursuit of the group's aims. Crucially, these aims exist prior to any plans for action. Membership of the group is pre-mised on the acceptance of these aims and not solely the plans and strategies for action derived from them.

The pluralist, on the other hand, conceives employment as a strategic relationship between strangers which is inherently conflictual. Employee and employer have different and competing interests and hence cannot be said to form a single social group. They have no common purpose, and no general will can be attributed to them. Employment, then, is a relationship characterised by conflict and the resolution of conflict. Any cooperation that arises can only be based on the recognition of the participants' mutual need for the help of the other in attaining his or her separate goals. Common goals in the sense, for example, of an agreed division of labour are subse-quent rather than prior to the decision to cooperate. Membership of the group is premised not on a prior commitment to any particular set of aims, but on a willingness to seek to define plans and strategies which when car-ried out will satisfy the individual or sectional interests of all involved.

Why Pluralism?

Fox's theoretical commitments do not in themselves point to an endorse-ment of any particular means of understanding organizations or, as a con-sequence, to any particular framework of norms for governing them. He repeatedly recognises that no frame of reference has any inherent objective or normative primacy over the others and that even where an organization is run on the basis on wholly unilateral, self-interested management action, workers may nevertheless accept and legitimise this.

> To the extent that employees are totally committed to the same values as management, they may accept that management must be the judge of priorities. In terms of procedural aspirations, they may define for themselves a role of submission to managerial rule and therefore to the substantive norms that management decrees.
>
> (1971, p. 69)

On the other hand, having made this clear, Fox suggests with more than a hint of irony that in practice such legitimisation will be unusual:

> Such value consensus may not, however, exist. Employees may well dis-pute the value placed by managers on minimizing labour costs, upon pleasing consumers or shareholders in preference to themselves, upon seeking new technology to replace old skills, upon developing new products or new markets whatever the threat to the expectations of lower participants. It is for these reasons that the adherence of employ-ees to management's norms must be considered problematical.
>
> (1971, p. 69)

Fox's advocacy of pluralist industrial relations is therefore based on the empirically-grounded belief that cooperation can best be achieved by structural change in industry. The organizational structures of the 1960s, which had been inherited from Britain's industrial past, were based on the assumption of a unity of interest at the level of a stratified class society in which the majority of individuals knew and accepted their place. However, the deference, poverty of aspiration and powerlessness that characterised the working classes in that society had disappeared. The roles that employees were required to take on as a consequence of the existing modes of work organization, work rules and work practices were therefore in conflict with empirical social reality. Work was a denial rather than an affirmation of workers' true social identity—the same, of course, could be said of managers—and hence the organization of industry was preventing cooperation rather than making it possible. In order to improve cooperation and therefore economic performance, industrial structures had to be redesigned. This obviously had to begin with a sober and objective assessment of the nature of contemporary society. Such an assessment clearly suggested that society was experiencing a major clash of values. The dominance of the capital owning classes (and their agents and collaborators in management), as well as their right to claim the fruits of collective labour for themselves was being openly and consciously challenged by organised workers. Fox saw little or no possibility that managers could simply persuade employees to accept their authority without demur. Indeed, as he measured it, the gap between the emergent social reality and the unitarist outlook was so wide that the unitarist perspective represented a kind of cognitive dysfunction. He talks about the high 'emotional yield' that managers got from their ideology, and the 'guilt' they may have experienced if they surrendered what they saw to be their proper decision-making prerogative. Managers could also demonstrate a "genuine incapacity to understand" the conflict generated by pluralistic forces (Fox, 1966, paragraphs 48–49). Perhaps most damningly, he comments that unitarism is "not an analytic tool for social diagnosis and prescription, but . . . an instrument by which managers seek to reassure themselves and public opinion that the cause of failure lies elsewhere" (Fox, 1966, paragraph 51). For Fox in the first part of his career, the pluralist perspective was by far the more accurate reflection of social reality, and it was pluralism that should provide the conceptual basis for the reform of the structures of the enterprise and of industrial relations.

Why Not Pluralism? The Radical Frame of Reference

Later, however, and despite his empirically-based view that unitarist approaches were a dead end, he also rejected pluralist approaches to IR because he did not believe that they provided an effective alternative basis for the establishment of legitimisable forms of industrial organization. As a consequence of an engagement with the arguments of the radical left

(Fox, 2004), he became concerned about the values that were built into pluralist industrial relations and about the political purposes that it might thereby serve. He had concluded that traditional collective bargaining was little more than a panacea that did little to address the true disadvantage of workers within the employment relationship. First, workers are not equal partners in industry: the

> negotiation of order within the enterprise takes place only at the margins. Management and the employee interests do not jointly build up their collaborative structure from the ground floor up. Power and social conditioning cause the employee interests to accept management's shaping of the main structure long before they reach the negotiating table.
>
> (Fox, 1974a, p. 286)

In this sense, pluralist industrial relations actually makes it more difficult to get past 'power and social conditioning' because it ties employees and unions into accepting a conventional interpretation of what it is and is not reasonable for managers to demand. The baseline for discussion is what each side brings to the table, but the inherent or absolute validity of those demands is not part of that discussion. Rather, negotiation is about finding an empirically acceptable balance of claims and counter-claims. While in principle there is no limit to what can be put on the table, in practice pluralism's own ethic of compromise prevents the major underlying issues of inequality of power and status from getting onto the agenda.

Fox's revised diagnosis of the times was that workers were increasingly aware that both unitarism and pluralism were ideological interpretations of the world in the sense that they justified and sustained a particular power structure. As a consequence, rather than interpreting their situation within the structures of the enterprise from the perspective of a pre-given frame of reference, they were basing their frame of reference on an interpretation of their structural situation. This situation was such that neither pluralism nor unitarism were adequate to its explanation. Workers were instead looking at the world through a 'radical' frame of reference from the perspective of which their exploitation was recognised and managerial authority was not and could not be legitimised. Industrial relations, therefore, could in many cases be characterised as the 'continuous challenge' of employers by workers. The radical frame shares the pluralist assumption that there are distinct and competing sets of values and interests at play within the enterprise. However, it also assumes that the capitalist employment relationship, together with the institutional IR structures that support it, cannot correct or compensate for this imbalance in the way that pluralism supposes. Only a fundamental restructuring of economic and social relations can correct the imbalance.

Fox's Legacy

The intellectual development that led to the writing of *Beyond Contract* and the identification of the radical frame of reference left Fox in a dilemma. His analysis of power relations in industry and society was strikingly similar to that of many contemporary Marxists, but he was unwilling to accept that revolutionary change was a viable or acceptable solution. As he put it, his reading simply confirmed "a long-standing belief that the generality of Marxists offered no convincing procedures of defence against abuses of power and no convincing institutions of political accountability" (2004, p. 259). At the same time, his misgivings were sufficiently serious to call into question carrying on with "an active interest in the practical reform of industrial relations" (2004, p. 260). The result of his dilemma was that he withdrew from engagement with the industrial relations policy debate, devoting the rest of his career to teaching and to the writing of his book on the social and cultural roots of the British IR system (Fox, 1986). Nevertheless, his contribution remains vitally important.

The concept of the frames of reference significantly improves on Dunlop's extremely vague formulation of the ideology of IR systems, relating structure to action via intersubjective conceptual structures that are characteristic of particular social groups and that span the boundary between work and society. Frames of reference give meaning to participation in the type of coordinated social action which arises not from shared aims and values but from 'the structures of the situation'. From within their frame of reference, participants are able to understand their structurally-determined behaviour as something other than bare constraint or compulsion. Frames of reference are interpretations of structural role behaviour that explain, rationalise and provide normative support for—or normatively-motivated rejection of—a particular type and range of role requirements and constraints. They enable actors to *grasp* the market and organizational context, endowing it with a normative character and, potentially, the power to motivate action beyond the mere existence of sanctions and incentives. The frames of reference approach allows us to explain the empirical variability of worker responses to what appear to be a uniform set of structural forces.

Also vital is Fox's recognition that there may be a disjuncture between workplace structures and frames of reference. Although he himself does not make this argument directly, his work suggests that dissonance between the frame of reference of groups of actors and the frame of reference embedded in existing institutional structures may explain conflictual industrial behaviour and, in the longer run, pressures for institutional reform. Adopting Fox's approach puts us upstream from any conclusions about conflict and cooperation and shows how they are the outcome of social relations at work rather than an initial premise.

On the other hand, Fox does not manage to improve a great deal on Dunlop's half-recognition of the existence of two aspects to the structures of the situation. In fact, he conflates the market and the internal social organization of work by assuming that managers have little choice when it comes to the division of labour because the market environment effectively determines the internal structure of firms. Fox assumed that managers have very little room for manoeuvre in designing work roles. He believed that the major elements of the social organization of work were determined by the socio-economic structures of industrial society, arguing that low-discretion work roles were a consequence of a society "structurally geared . . . to a complex set of interdependent institutions, expectations, and values shaped predominantly by the principles of low-trust economic exchange" (Fox, 1974a, p. 355). For Fox, managers had little choice but to organise work on the basis of low-discretion roles because trying to establish work and economic relations on a high-discretion, high-trust basis would have had a catastrophic effect on living standards (1974a, p. 354).

For all intents and purposes, then, Fox treats management and the market as a single phenomenon. He assumes that the social structure of rules, roles, incentives and constraints constructed by managers is inseparable from and reflects the economic incentives and constraints of the market. Nevertheless, the alternative view, that markets and management should be thought of as separate, is widely held. Fox's colleague Flanders, for example (1975, p. 88), argues that there are two aspects to the 'structures of the situation': an external market/exchange aspect (market relations) and an internal organizational or institutional aspect (managerial relations). As we will see in Chapter 4, Habermas, following Parsons, distinguishes clearly between the economic and organizational ('bureaucratic-administrative') systems of society and between the money and power media which animate them (Habermas, 1984, 1987).

That Fox does not attempt to draw a line between those elements of the structures of the situation that have their origin outside the firm in the market environment and those that are internal to it is all the more surprising as the conceptual distinction between market and organizational systems is implied at certain points within his own work. As we saw above, the pluralist and radical frames of reference share the belief that there are distinct and competing sets of values and interests at play within the enterprise. However, whereas pluralism supposes that the employment relationship, together with the institutional IR structures that support it, can be such as to compensate for the radically uneven capacity of workers and employers to pursue their own legitimate economic interests, radicalism supposes that only a fundamental restructuring of social relations can correct the imbalance. So there are, in fact, two conceptual dimensions to the adoption of the radical and the pluralist frames of reference. First of all, there is the question of whether the values of capitalism and the market economy are or are not universal; whether or not capitalism involves the pursuit of the aims and interests of the few rather than of the many. This is the dimension on which pluralism and radicalism share a location. Second, there is the question of whether the institutional structures of employment and IR do or do not permit a reasonable balance to be struck between the interests of workers and those of employers/owners. On this dimension, radicalism and pluralism are placed well apart. Arguably, then, frames of reference ought to be characterised not as unified global evaluations of the legitimacy of the structures of the situation, but, to use Flanders' terminology, as reflecting the interaction of views about the legitimacy of market relations and views about the legitimacy of managerial relations.

A second problem with Fox's work is to do with the nature of legitimacy. Whether or not the normative legitimisation of social structures matters for the social scientific explanation of collective behaviour is a question that has preoccupied researchers for well over a century (Joas and Knöbl, 2009). Fox certainly does not seem to have considered the possibility that, as well as accepting or rejecting the normative legitimacy of structurally required role behaviour—and thus being either happy and engaged or angry and demotivated—workers and managers may in some circumstances also see the social organization of work as being effectively non-normative; as representing a kind of economic or organizational necessity comparable to the physical necessity of the need to eat or shelter from bad weather.

Fox's belief that the presence or absence of legitimisation always makes a significant difference to outcomes is in contrast to the arguments of sociologists such as Parsons, Habermas and Luhmann, who believe that social systems—in the case of IR, the structures of the workplace situation—are or can be effectively free of norms. For them there are certain contexts of action in which value judgements are of little or no consequence in the final analysis because of the purely empirical motivation supplied by sanctions and incentives. Habermas, for example, (1984, 1987) argues that behaviour in economic and organizational contexts is ultimately determined by what he calls 'steering imperatives'—the term 'steering' is taken from Parsons' system theory—that reach 'through and beyond' the action orientations of participants in social action, i.e. the things they want to do and the ways of living and behaving they believe to be right. Actors recognise that their choices in these action contexts are constrained by forces external to them, but are either unable to assess the legitimacy of these forces, or are so constrained in their range of possible responses that their normative evaluations cannot change their actions. In the end, they may become so habituated to conformity with structural imperatives that they lose any consciousness that there may be alternatives to that conformity. This possibility has been so frequently canvassed in major streams of social theory that it would seem imperative to give it systematic consideration.

Cox & Harrod: The Social Relations of Production

That Robert Cox's contribution to IR theory should be so little known is perplexing. Cox was not only a close aide to David Morse, the ILO's longest serving and arguably most influential director-general, but for six years was also the director of the International Institute for Labour Studies. He went on to a distinguished academic career at Columbia University in New York and York University in Canada. Although his work has been very influential in the field of international relations, it has remained virtually unknown in industrial relations. In Kaufman's 2004 edited collection on industrial relations theory, for example, Cox is cited only three times in passing and there is no actual discussion of his work.

Despite this, his 1987 book, *Production, Power and World Order* (*PPWO*), is one of the very few works that can compete with Dunlop's *Industrial Relations Systems* in terms of its theoretical ambition. Although the book is pitched as a work of international political economy, something that goes some way to explaining its lack of impact on IR, it could as easily be described as a work of comparative-historical industrial relations—as long as we understand IR in the broad sense of the social relations of production. *PPWO* is a distillation of Cox's fifteen years of post-ILO academic research combined with an analytic approach that had its origins in an International Institute for Labour Studies (IILS) project that was cancelled after his resignation as Director in 1972.

The semi-independent IILS was established by Morse in 1960. It was intended to be something between a think tank and a staff college in which faculty and ILO staff could escape the usual political constraints on policy and action and think more freely. As Cox, who worked closely with Morse on the design of the Institute put it,

> The promotion of constructive change required something beyond a rule book for the enactment of policies. It required an understanding of the processes of change in particular societies. Research might throw light upon the specific nature of change in particular situations and upon dynamics of change in a broader sense. Educational opportunities for a new generation of leaders in different parts of the world could help them cope with the variety of challenges they would face. This is what the Institute was to be about.
>
> (2013, p. 109)

Cox took over as director in 1965 after two other directors who had focused on the educational rather than the research mission of the IILS (Kaufman, 2004b, p. 310). It was only with his tenure in office that the original vision for the Institute started to be realised. The 'Research Project on Future Industrial Relations' was launched in 1970 with "the objective of clarifying thinking about probable developments and alternative futures for industrial relations in the mid-1980s" (Cox and Harrod, 1972, p. iii). Although Cox does not engage directly with Dunlop or Kerr et al. either in the interim report on the project—there was never a final report—or in *PPWO*, he makes it clear in his autobiography that the *Future IR* project was intended to do well what the *Industrialism* project had done badly. He and his principal collaborator, Jeffrey Harrod, wanted to get away from "the bias of functionalist positivism that privileged the integration of all elements of the existing social system towards establishing an equilibrium that would sustain the existing social structure" (Cox, 2013, p. 231). Despite this, the intentions and scope of the two projects were very similar. Both involved a wide international network of collaborators and combined theoretical and empirical work on comparative IR. Both were intended to lead to a framework for the analysis of national or sectoral industrial relations systems that did not assume the presence of a market economy. Both involved the development of a theoretical framework together with a series of empirical studies to inform the development of that framework and subsequently to test its utility. Both stressed the importance of ideology and the connections between ideology, institutions and objective environmental conditions. Both identified a series of ideal types of national industrial relations systems that reflected particular ideologies and stages of socio-economic development. There were three major differences, however. The first is that the *Future IR* approach does not assume that modes of economic organization are necessarily geared towards industrialisation. The second difference is that that Cox and Harrod's approach firmly excluded any notion of a trajectory of industrialisation leading inevitably to a convergence on the bipartite or tripartite collective industrial relations model. The third is that the *Future IR* model equates IR systems with concrete configurations of power.

> For a study considering long-term stability or change, the structure of social relations in production, that is, the relative power of actors (i.e. the individuals and organizations playing a role in these relations) and the formal and informal institutions through which their power may be channelled, is extremely important.
>
> (Cox and Harrod, 1972, p. iii)

We can read Cox and Harrod's work on *Future IR* as a radicalisation of the approach introduced in the *Industrialism* project. As I argued above, the value and interest of Dunlop's work is considerably reduced by its association with the industrialisation thesis and by the inadequacy of its concept of power.[8] The fully developed analytic framework presented in *PPWO* certainly does not suffer from these weaknesses—although it introduces some others as we will see.

The Social Relations of Production

Cox summed up his methodological approach in an article first published in 1980. It is worth citing in full as it provides a much more succinct exposition of the theoretical backdrop to his work than I could hope to produce:

(1) action is not fragmented into a sequence of discrete events but always presupposes a context which gives it meaning (events without such meaning are mere programmed responses to specific stimuli); (2) the first task of analysis is to discern the context or historical structure of social reality within which action takes place, a structure that consists objectively of *power relations* and subjectively of a web of *shared meanings*; (3) ideological analysis, or the attempt to reconstruct *the mental frameworks through which individuals and groups perceive their fields of action*, is the best means of access towards knowledge about the historical structure, knowledge that must be approximated by critically confronting and not just passively accepting the perspective of one group or another; and (4) the further task of political analysis is to know whether actions tend to reinforce or alternatively to transform a historical structure, and this can only be understood in terms of the consequences of actions rather than the motivations behind them.

(Cox, 1996, pp. 474–5; emphasis added)

The 'historical structure of social reality' in the industrial relations context is what Cox calls the 'social relations of production'. In the earliest versions of his analytic framework, Cox proposes that the term 'industrial relations' should be "defined functionally rather than institutionally. It is used to mean social relations in production" (1971, p. 3). In *PPWO* he drops 'industrial relations' altogether and refers only to social relations. Rather than 'industrial relations systems', used in the *Future IR* project, he prefers in his later work to talk about 'modes' of the social relations of production (SRP). These different modes, 12 in all, are made up of three sets of factors: objective factors (or relationships of forces), subjective factors (or forms of consciousness) and institutional forms. Four of the modes are pre-capitalist ('simple reproduction'), six are capitalist and two are what he calls redistributive, amounting to the earlier communal and later command economy phases of the communist bloc economies.

The objective factors concern power and control in the workplace and in wider society. Cox assumes that each mode of SRP has a dominant and subordinate group. The position of the dominant group reflects the accumulation of resources which, although derived from production, have over time been invested in social influence. The dominant class is able to draw on resources (wealth, status, prestige) that are not *immediately* derived from the production process. This in turn gives it a capacity to control both *what* is produced and *how* it is produced that the subordinate group does not have. We should note that Cox does not include markets among the objective forces that influence the mode of social relations of production. Although he does not make this argument explicitly, he appears to relegate markets to the status of decision criteria used by the dominant class in the six modes of the social relations of production that he counts as capitalist. As he puts it, "capitalist development is driven by opportunities for realizing profits in the market, and *perceptions of these opportunities* determine what is produced" (Cox, 1987, p. 399; emphasis added). For Cox, markets should not be thought of as independent forces but merely as a manifestation of the power of the dominant class specific to those modes of production in which the division of labour and the distribution of rewards can be determined via nominally free contractual transactions.

The production process itself is a further objective factor. There is a complementarity of roles within the enterprise based on a particular division of labour bound together by a structure of authority. This structure runs the gamut from direct coercion to custom and tradition to administrative fiat to market transaction. Technology also has in impact in the sense that it further structures the relationship between those who command and those who obey. Cox gives the examples of a workshop in which a group of craft workers work together cooperatively, an assembly line in which fragmented tasks are continuously coordinated and an automated factory (1987, p. 20). However, technology is not an independent variable as the choices about technology are made by the dominant class. These choices are often driven by the wish or need to maintain or increase control over the production process rather than by the working through of any inherent logic of technological development. The final objective element of modes of SRP is the distribution of the rewards of economic activity. The range of possibilities here is the same as with the division of labour in the production process: coercion, custom, administrative fiat and market transaction, although Cox is careful to point out that none exist in a pure form. For example, even where the distribution of rewards is based on a market transaction, custom has a heavy influence on expectations about the relative returns thought proper for the dominant and subordinate groups and for different types of work.

With respect to the subjective aspects of modes of SRP, Cox argues that "Participants in a mode of social relations of production share a mental picture of the mode in ideas of what is normal, expected behaviour and in how people arrange their lives with regard to work and income" (1987, p. 22). He divides these intersubjective factors into two types, ethics of production and rationalities of production. "Ethics of production characterize the quality and intensity of producers' participation in the production process" (ibid., p. 24). They derive from differences in the sense of obligation and motivation that arise depending on the nature of the social bond existing in any situation. Family, kinship and tradition give rise to very different attitudes to obligation than does a relationship based on contract. Likewise, behaviour directed by external sanctions and that governed by internalised norms of conduct will give rise to very different qualities of compliance. Cox identifies five different ethics of production (1987, pp. 23–4):

- *Custom*, in which work is thought of as an activity flowing naturally from social bonds transcending work;
- *Coercion*, in which work is something that has to be extracted from others against their will;
- *Clientelism*, in which work is based on an exchange of protection and loyalty between master and servant or, in the contemporary world, on bureaucratised relationships within large corporations;
- *Contract*, in which work is a partial and limited exchange negotiated either individually or collectively and in which the contract is intended to regulate an inherent conflict of interest;
- *Inspirational*, in which work is a claim made by the community over the individual in the context of the construction of that community.

While ethics of production condition the attitude of individuals to their work, rationalities of production are "the interpretive structures of thought and mental rules for making decisions that are characteristic of specific social groups" (ibid., p. 25). The mental processes typical of bureaucrats, for example, differ from those of entrepreneurs, as do those of the leaders of business unions and revolutionary syndicalists. "Members of these different groups tend to look for different kinds of facts, to process them according to different decision rules, and to devise different strategies of action based on the same facts" (ibid). This does not mean, however, that each different rationality is not coherent and rational on its own terms.

Cox makes the rather odd claim that the intersubjective aspects of each mode of SRP all incorporate a bias favouring the dominant over the subordinate group, despite an appearance of reciprocity. The obligations of the peasant to the lord, for example, are significantly more onerous than those of the lord to the peasant, but feudal modes of thought justify the suppression of rebellion in the name of the preservation of the divine order.

The third part of the picture involves institutions. These typically correspond to the subjective and objective factors that characterise each mode of SRP, but according to Cox should not be taken as determining the mode. The social and objective factors are the determinants of the mode of SRP and the institutional structure will not necessarily reflect this real or essential structure of relationships. As Cox puts it, there may be a 'hiatus' between real structure and formal institutions. He identifies four possible institutional structures: direct domination, which in fact is the *absence* of institutional structure; corporatism, in which production relations are bureaucratised and opposition is eliminated, coopted or controlled; delegated bargaining, in which opposition is accepted but institutionalised through an external bureaucratisation like collective bargaining; and self-management, in which both external and internal bureaucratisation are rejected.

The three sets of factors making up a mode of SRP are related as shown in the diagram below (reproduced from (Cox, 1987, p. 29) Cox goes on to explain the character of each of the 12 different modes of SRP in relation to

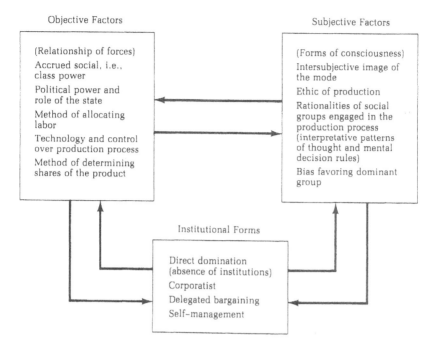

Figure 3.1 Cox's 'Dimensions of a Mode of Social Relations of Production'
Reproduced from Cox (1987), p. 29

these dimensions. Table 3.1 below briefly sets out the different modes. Cox does not argue that entire national economic systems can be characterised by just one mode of production relations. Rather, in any given society at any particular historical moment there is likely to be a dominant and one or more subordinate modes of production relations. Just about any mode of production relations can co-exist with self-employment, for example, and all necessarily co-exist with household production.

The End of IR History (Version 2.0)

There is little to be gained here by describing each of the modes in more detail, not least because only four, or perhaps five, are any longer of real significance. Cox's approach to the development of the categorization was largely empirical (Cox, 1987, p. 32) and it is not intended to be conceptually exhaustive. For example, it excludes modes of production relations like self-managed autonomous worker collectives that are envisagable but that remain very rare in practice.

What is of more enduring value in Cox's scheme are the theoretical proposals he makes about the objective, subjective and institutional components

Table 3.1 Cox's Modes of the Social Relations of Production

Simple reproduction		Subsistence	Hunting, gathering & cultivation ordered principally by kinship relations
		Peasant-lord	Agricultural production in which producers are dominated in a feudal relationship with land-owning nobility
		Primitive labour market	Industrial or agricultural production in which precarious and generally unskilled workers are completely detached from any social or legal protection
		Household	Household production including childbearing and child care, cleaning, food preparation etc
Capitalist development	*Competitive*	Self-employment	Production in which contracts set a price for a finished product or service rather than an amount of labour power
		Enterprise labour market	Industrial production by 'peripheral' workers in a core/periphery model; 'nonestablished' workers share a labour market with established employees but have lower rights
		Bipartism	Unionised industrial/service production
	Monopoly	Enterprise corporatism	Industrial/service production in corporation that denies the legitimacy of conflict: welfare capitalist, human relations or most cooperative extreme of unionised relationship ('symbiosis') between union and management).
		Tripartism	Industrial/service production in which government is a party to bargaining
		State corporatism	Industrial/service production in which the power of the state dominates over both unions and managements, e.g. fascist Italy
Redistributive development		Communal	Collective agricultural production typical of (although not exclusive to) the early stages of a communist economy
		Central planning	Production in centrally planned command economy

Derived from Cox (1987), chapter 1.

of each mode, about the relationships between them and about stability and change. A stable mode of production relations involves a kind of congruence or continuity between the three dimensions: the objective factors or relationships of forces are 'matched' by the intersubjective content, and specific institutions 'embody and stabilize' this match. By contrast, social transformation is driven by the actual or potential disjunctions among the three aspects, that is, situations in which there is some kind of mismatch between different dimensions of the mode.

Although these are extremely valuable insights, Cox says frustratingly little about the possibilities for change arising from the absence of congruence between the different dimensions. He gives no indication of how the subjective and objective dimensions might come to be out of line with each other and what might happen if they are. His argument that the intersubjective aspects of each mode of production relations always contain a bias towards the dominant class suggests that he sees a connection, but he does not elaborate on this. Neither does he discuss what is likely to occur in circumstances in which the dominant and subordinate classes do not share a form of consciousness. This leaves us wondering to what extent there is any scope at all for ethics and rationalities of production to encompass a logic of opposition to the dominant class.

This brings us to Cox's thinking on the objective relationships of forces that form the backbone of each mode of SRP. Although, as we saw above, Cox recognises that markets have an impact on business decision-making (in those modes of production relations in which prices are set by markets), like Fox he does not see them as a force that is even potentially independent of the interests of the capitalist class. Strategic decision-making, the division of labour, the distribution of rewards between labour and capital, and the structure of authority within businesses all arise from the logic of class interests. Even technological development is driven by the interest of the dominant class in maintaining and enhancing its control over production. In Cox's scheme, there is no way to include any neutral or positive conception of the market that might be shared by workers, nor any means of management in capitalist contexts that workers might recognise as legitimate. None of the ethics of production that he proposes involve spontaneous and willing cooperation with authority.

Cox's scheme is on this reading much more firmly grounded in the conflict assumption than that even of the pre- or post-war institutionalists. Some kind of class domination is assumed to characterise every existing mode of production relations and it is very difficult to see how a mode of production relations that is *not* based on domination could arise. Although he envisages at least one type of rationality of production (syndicalist trade unionism) that would seem to be wholly incompatible with class domination, he does not attempt to project what types of relationship of forces would 'match' that subjective conception of the employment relationship. Similarly, although he includes 'self-management' as an institutional form, this appears to be incompatible with all of the modes of SRP that he proposes. Cox ultimately gives us little reason to believe that a consensual form of capitalism will ever be possible.

The Return of Institutionalism

Before drawing the threads of this long chapter together, I want to briefly discuss one of the more recent developments in IR theory: the return of institutionalism.

Neither Cox nor Fox had any significant impact on the development of industrial relations research, the result being that, as Piore and Safford (2006) argue, the standard IR model remains heavily influenced by Dunlop. The model involves a fixed set of institutional participants (workers, employers and governments) interacting in a systematic way on the basis of predictable motivations in the context of technological, economic and political constraints which, while relatively stable, may be subject to change over time. Variations in job regulation regimes can be traced to variations in these constraints across industrial and national contexts, and the evolution of regimes to autonomous changes in these different aspects of the system environment. Godard argues that there has been at least some movement since Dunlop. What he calls 'the new industrial relations' has left behind the convergence assumption of Kerr et al's *Industrialism* project, leaving more room for diversity in industrial relations systems as a result of strategic choice, ideologies and institutions (2004). Nevertheless, it is still largely assumed that change is

> ultimately driven by economic and technological forces and that these forces tend to be immutable and largely invariant across nations. Actors may respond to these forces in somewhat different ways depending on their ideologies, and established institutions may filter the pressures associated with them. But while the nature and valence of change may vary, those changes that do occur tend to be broadly similar across all developed nations
>
> (Godard, 2004, p. 232)

Godard goes on to argue that while the new IR is a useful contribution, it can do little to explain the major empirical phenomenon of the past 30 years, which is the increasing level of variation and diversity in industrial relations systems. He explains this failure by reference to the inability of the standard model to accommodate the impact of the wider institutional environment on "the interests and orientations of the parties, the power resources that they are able to draw upon, and the various pressures and constraints to which they are subject" (ibid., p. 234).

Coming from a different angle, Piore and Safford (2006) argue that the traditional framing of IR questions has been overtaken by the blurring of the boundaries between work and wider society and between workplace identities and other forms of self-identification. The effect of this blurring has been to significantly increase the effect on behaviour of normative factors like social recognition, symbolic value, ethics and morality, eroding the instrumentally rational types of behaviour upon which the accuracy of the systems model depends. Ackers too suggests that while traditional IR "abstracts both substantive and procedural workplace 'rule-making' from the wider economic and social dynamics of society" (2002, p. 5), the frontier between the systemic domain of work and industry and the more normatively-structured domain of family and community is crumbling, rendering the analyses of traditional IR increasingly irrelevant and its policy prescriptions increasingly ineffective.

IR by its continuing economistic emphasis on internal workplace relations and its exclusion of explicit ethical considerations, has become stranded by the shifting tide of social change and cut off from the major public policy debates about the future of Western society.

(Ackers, 2002, p. 3)

All of these arguments point clearly to the need to introduce a renewed emphasis on the normative aspects of IR. State traditions, the immediate socio-cultural context of work and the social and institutional aspects of workplace relations seem to be at least as important in explaining behaviour in organizations as individual, instrumentally-oriented responses to systems of incentives and constraints like the market economy. This has led authors like Godard (2004) and Sisson (2007) to argue that industrial relations needs to take a new institutional turn. This would not involve any renunciation of the existing basic analytic framework of industrial relations, but it would recognise that the goals and orientations of the actors in that framework are not fixed but shaped by rules, norms and institutional arrangements that do not simply represent empirical incentives and constraints but provide actors with "cognitive and normative templates for interpretation" (Godard, 2004, p. 247).

All this is, of course, perfectly reasonable and must count as an advance in the sense that it instills an entirely appropriate initial agnosticism about the degree to which policy measures and management actions will prompt conflictual or cooperative responses from workers. The problem is that it does not address the perennial problem of institutionalism, which is precisely the conflation of regulative, normative and cognitive elements within a single concept that covers an extremely wide range of formal and informal social structures and systems.

Cited by Sisson (2007), the Penguin Dictionary of Sociology defines 'institution' as "a term widely used to describe social practices that are regularly and continuously repeated, that are sanctioned and maintained by social norms, and that have a major significance in the social structure." Kaufman defines 'institution' as

> a collective entity that 'expands, liberates, and controls' the behavior of individuals (Commons, 1934). An institution is synonymous with a 'governance structure': a set of explicit or implicit rules that delimit the rights, responsibilities, and duties of all parties, as well as penalties for violations of these rules (Williamson, 1985). Examples include formal organizations, such as governments, corporations, political parties, families, and churches, and informal collective entities, such as national or ethnic cultures, social norms and customs, and ethical belief systems. A market is also an 'institution'.

(Kaufman, 2004c, p. 56)

Just to give one more definition, Neale proposes that 'institution' is a term used to describe the regular, patterned behaviour of people in a society and . . . the ideas and values associated with these regularities. Various phrasings have been used to define institutions or an institution: a usage that has become axiomatic by habitation; collective action in control of individual action; widely prevalent, highly standardized social habits; a way of thought or action embedded in the habits of a group or the customs of a people; prescribed patterns of correlated behaviour.

(Neale, cited in Bray and Wailes, 1997, p. 56)

These very broad definitions suggest that institutionalism is simply trying to cover too much ground at once. It fails to draw a line between *formal* institutions in which regulation is both written and backed up by sanctions, and *informal* institutions in which customs, conventions and practices are maintained solely by the force of habit or the potential for social disapproval. Nor does institutionalism distinguish between practices like markets, in which norms and conventions limit the choices available to individuals but do not supply the primary motivation to participate, and practices in which collectively prescribed patterns of behaviour are in themselves the cause of action. The most problematic outcome of these inadequacies is that the very specific role of the firm as a structure of formal rules dedicated to coordinating and controlling workplace behaviour is lost to view amid the array of other institutional influences on action.

What is more, the failure to distinguish between formal and informal institutions means that although institutional factors have been offered as an explanation for the observed variation in the reaction of the same kind of actors to what appear to be the same external pressures, institutionalism has nothing to say about the potential for actors' responses to the demands of formal institutions to vary. Institutionalism simply identifies a series of complexes of social action in which structure *and* agency may both be at work without making any attempt to separate one from the other.

So, although the institutionalist intuition is wholly defensible in the sense that action in response to what Cox would call relationships of forces is obviously conditioned by normative factors, "the emphasis on historical and social specificity inherent in this approach works against the identification of universal causal mechanisms that hold across time and space and therefore limits the level of theory development" (Bray and Wailes, 1997, p. 61). We find ourselves back at a concept introduced at the beginning of this chapter, which is whether anything more than theory *in* IR—the lightly structured empiricism that the institutional approach implies—is possible.

Conclusions: Cox, Fox and Post-Institutionalist IR

A theory of IR needs somehow to strike a balance between Dunlop-style systems approaches, in which individual and collective goals and orientations entirely disappear from view along with the conflict and cooperation their pursuit may engender, and institutionalism, whether new or old, in which the task of the researcher is reduced to mapping the many possible ways in which values, culture, history and state traditions either impede or promote the workplace behaviour that neoclassical economics predicts. Caricaturing the two ends of the spectrum like this is unfair to the researchers in both broad traditions who have done a great deal of valuable work over the years, but it helps to illustrate the nature of the synthesis that is needed.

Fox and Cox's work is invaluable in this regard. Cox's analytic model is based on the interaction between objective and subjective factors in the context of a fixed institutional framework that may or may not be coherent with this 'real structure' of social relations. Fox's concept of the frames of reference adds depth and precision to Cox's rather sketchy picture of the relationship between the subjective and objective aspects of the mode of production relations. Although Fox's approach lacks clarity about the origins of 'the structures of the situation' in reaction to which conflict or cooperation may arise, it offers the absolutely critical possibility of not taking a position on the outcome of social relations at work before we have even begun our analysis.

Although, as far as I am aware, neither references the work of the other, there are striking similarities in Fox and Cox's analytic frameworks and methodological approaches. What is more, each can—to some extent—compensate for the weaknesses of the other. As an historian and political scientist, Cox had a better grasp of the overall structural features of capitalism: the state and class power. As a sociologist, Fox's explanations of workplace behaviour are more precise and better-grounded in normativist theories of action that recognise the importance of conventions, values and ethics at well as structural motivations. At the same time, to the degree that each strays onto the preferred territory of the other, their approaches are largely compatible.

The most striking point of contact is around the subjectivity of actors in the system. If we combine Cox's ethics and rationalities of production into a single conceptual structure it would be difficult to say how this differs from a frame of reference as defined by Fox. Fox and Cox also agree that IR research should start with what Cox calls 'ideological analysis' or the reconstruction of mental frameworks. Both authors propose that subjectivity is in a dynamic relationship with a series of objective factors in the workplace environment and wider society. They agree that stable industrial relations depends on the existence of a certain congruence between subjective and objective factors. Conflict arises when the narratives of work and employment that are possible cannot make sense of the conditions and relationships that make up the structures of the workplace situation as these are experienced by workers in relation to the wider social context. Dissonance between these different aspects is the driver of change. However, Fox has the better of the argument with respect to the role played by actors' mental frameworks. As we noted above, Cox's account of the ethics and rationalities of production is rather ambiguous on the issue of whether and when subjectivity can act as a vector for the mobilisation of counter-power rather than serving to support and stabilise relationships of forces. At certain points he seems to imply that it is always the former. By contrast, Fox makes it clear that while frames of reference exist *in relation to* the structures of the situation, they may either validate or put in question the legitimacy of those structures, giving rise to either cooperative or conflictual attitudes. Fox thus connects conflict and cooperation to legitimacy, legitimacy to the mental frameworks of actors and these frameworks to a combination of socialisation, culture, history and experience.

On the structural or objective side of the equation, Cox draws two useful distinctions that Fox does not. First he distinguishes between what he calls 'relationships of forces' and the formal institutional structures of workplace governance. Second, within his category of relationships of forces, he distinguishes between class power and the state, which exist beyond the enterprise, and the internal structures of work organization, management control and the distribution of rewards.

There are two areas in which neither scholar can help us, however. Unlike Commons, Dunlop, Flanders and many others, neither Fox nor Cox seem to believe that a useful distinction can be drawn between market forces and the interpretation and expression of those forces via the structures of authority of the enterprise. Cox conceives the project of management simply as an expression of class interests. Fox's view is closer to a kind of sociotechnical determinism. He believes that managers' room for manoeuvre is limited by interlocking and interdependent institutional and conceptual structures that embed an historically specific understanding of the rational organization of production. In neither case is a clear distinction drawn between the external force of the market and the internal structure of authority in the organization. As with the new institutionalism, the market is not conceived as an analytically distinct force, while the firm is obscured behind justifications for authority drawn in terms of the need to react adequately to external pressures. As we will see in Chapter 4, there are good reasons to ensure that we maintain a sharp distinction between markets and the bureaucratic-administrative systems of the firm.

The second gap is with respect to normative evaluations of structural forces, which is to say with conflict and cooperation. The value of Cox's approach is undermined by his inability to take seriously the possibility of cooperation. All of Cox's modes of production relations are characterised by the domination of one class by another, the 'forms of consciousness' he proposes include a bias in favour of the dominant group, and although he suggests that self-management is a possible institutional structure, he cannot give any account of how it could reflect an egalitarian social reality. While Fox accepts that unitarist or cooperative forms of work relation are at least a theoretical possibility, he offers no means of conceptualising a situation in which frames of reference are characterised by passivity—neither conflict nor cooperation.

Because of these problems we cannot simply combine Fox and Cox's insights into a new theory. Neither can provide a truly adequate theory of action in economic and organizational contexts. Such a theory would need not only to explain both individual and collective action, but to explain it in a way that is coherent with the existence of economic and organizational order where this exists, and with economic and organizational conflict where it does not. For this, we need to go beyond the IR research tradition and venture into the territory of social theory.

Notes

1 "The wise autocrat of to-day, conversant with the latest results of economic science, and interested in the progressive improvement of his state, might, therefore, be as eager to prevent the growth of industrial parasitism as the most democratic politician. Hence, we can easily imagine such an autocrat enforcing a National Minimum, which should rule out of the industrial system all forms of competition degrading the health, intelligence, or character of his people. The rapid extension of factory legislation in semi-autocratic countries during recent years indicates that some inkling of this truth is reaching the minds of European bureaucracies." (Webb and Webb, 1902, p. 807)

2 "Whether the general level of wages in the trade should be raised or lowered by 10 per cent; whether the number of boys to be engaged by any one employer should be restricted, and if so, by what scale; whether the hours of labor should be reduced, and overtime regulated or prohibited, are not problems which could be solved by even the most perfect calculating-machine." (Webb and Webb, 1902, p. 184)

3 As Michael Rose points out, the identification of the human relations approach with Mayo alone is arguably unfair, but to do justice to the diversity of the school is impossible here. It nonetheless remains the case that the principal outlines of the approach were established by Mayo. See Rose (1978, part III).

4 References in what follows are to the revised edition of 1993.

5 Although I have to admit to not having conducted a truly thorough bibliographical search, there seems to have been quite a long delay between the publication of *Industrial Relations Systems* and any serious critical engagement with its arguments.

6 References are to the UK 2nd edition (Kerr et al., 1973).

7 This is one of the aspects of industrialisation theory that has become a permanent part of ILO internal arguments. In the 1994 debate on the 'social clause' for example, one employer delegate argued that "We need to understand carefully the unintended consequences of an improper sequencing of social and economic development. Social development is necessary. But it cannot take place without economic development. Any impediment to the economic development of developing countries would have the intended or unintentional additional consequence of impeding social development" (International Labour Office, 1995, p. 4/33).

8 According to Harrod (2008), to the extent that the *Future IR* analytical framework addressed these problems, the result did not go down well in the ILO. The idea that the ILO should recognise the existence of a number of different, stable types of industrial relations system and tailor its work accordingly rather than gearing everything towards supporting the development of bi- and tripartite collective IR put the legitimacy of the ILO's existing constituents into question. In a remarkable piece of empirical analysis, the interim report of the *Future IR* project exposed the highly embarrassing fact that the ILO-supported systems covered

less than 10% of the world's workforce. The idea that collective IR is the reflection of a particular power structure rather than a rational technical response to industrialisation also strongly suggested that the ILO's constituents had a vested interest in the bi-tripartite [bi- or tripartite?] model; that, to use a contemporary turn of phrase, collective IR was not the policy choice because it is *what works* but because it suits those who occupy positions of influence for their own particular reasons. That the interim report of the *Future IR* project was published at all is a testament to Cox's influence and support within the ILO and its constituents—by his own account he had been a serious candidate to replace Morse as Director General on his resignation in 1970 (Cox, 2013). However, once he had resigned over a serious difference of opinion with new Director General Wilfred Jenks about the potential political review of publications by IILS staff, there was no one left with sufficient weight to carry the programme. It was closed down and its staff dispersed. Harrod too resigned rather than take the only alternative on offer, a post within the ILO itself.

4 System, Lifeworld and Points in Between

In Chapter 3, I argued that in its attempts to explain industrial behaviour, IR theory has consistently highlighted the importance not only of objective structural influences but also of a range of different kinds of subjective and intersubjective influences, whether these are called frames of reference, ideologies, forms of consciousness, ethics and rationalities of production, or informal institutions. Power and control at work are manifest principally as structural forces (sanctions and incentives) and it is the requirements arising from these forces that are the object of conflict or cooperation. Intersubjective factors can either support or undermine the efficacy of the exercise of power by legitimising cooperation or conflict. There are two questions on which there is no consensus: first, whether structural forces will necessarily give rise to requirements that are *not* in the interests of workers; and second, the degree to which intersubjective factors are autonomous with respect to structural forces rather than tending merely to reflect and stabilise some particular power configuration. I also identified two further requirements arising from problems with Fox and Cox's theoretical schemes: first, the need to accommodate the possibility that actors may not recognise the structures of the workplace situation as an appropriate subject of normative evaluation; and second, the need to draw a clear distinction between market forces (exchange) and the structure of authority within the organization (power).

In this chapter and the next, I want to go back to first principles to start to construct an approach that deals with these problems and lacunae by weaving some of the threads of the existing IR tradition together with one of the major contemporary approaches to critical theory, Jürgen Habermas's *Theory of Communicative Action*. My aim is to relate structure, subjectivity and institutions in a way that allows us to identify how each aspect influences and is influenced by the others.

Structure and Agency (Again): Systems Thinking and Positivism

The problem of collective autonomy in the face of social structures and systems is not one that is confined to industrial relations theory. In fact, whether we are at the mercy of forces that are beyond our control or whether we are, or could be, the mistresses and masters of our own destiny has been perhaps the most important theme in social theory for the last 150 years. Leaving aside despotism, discrimination and other forms of purely political oppression, the biggest obstacle to our collective agency as human beings is the idea that some parts of society are made up of structures or *systems* in which the actions of each individual are linked in a consistent, predictable way with the actions of a large number of other individuals. We can call this the 'systems intuition'. Thinking of action in this way involves the belief that in certain circumstances, decisions about social action are not made by the free collective choice of those involved but arise from the quasi-automatic reaction of individuals to an action situation that, from their perspective, is unalterable. Commenting on Herbert Spencer's work, Durkheim describes this approach as the belief that "social life . . . can naturally organize itself only by an unconscious, spontaneous adaptation under the immediate pressure of needs, and not according to a rational plan of reflective intelligence" (Cited in Habermas, 1987, p. 115). Adaptive systems of this kind are usually thought to operate more or less autonomously, independently of the historical and socio-cultural context. However, this does not mean that they operate randomly. Rather, like other living systems, they follow laws of action that can in principle be known and that allow the prediction of the output that will arise from different inputs in different systemic contexts.

Many have argued that these kinds of system—the original model being, of course, the economy—achieve a level of coordination between human actors that would not otherwise be possible. In particular, they allow the fulfilment of certain functions critical to material reproduction that could not be achieved via conscious action. The partisans of this perspective argue that the systemic parts of society cannot be placed fully within the scope of democratic decision-making, or as the Webbs put it, 'of human arrangement', either because they are simply inaccessible to human intervention and cannot be controlled or because the attempt to intervene is ultimately bound to disrupt the valuable function they perform. All that can be done is to adopt a methodological perspective on social action that abstracts from the particular motivations of individuals and instead focuses on structures and systems themselves, not as the *result* of social behaviour and integration but as objective phenomena that represent the scientific facts of social life. From this perspective, social science is the quest to understand the functional characteristics of systems sufficiently well to be able to say that input x in social context y will consistently lead to output z. Once the causal laws of systems are known, policy can be designed on the basis of a neutral scientific assessment of the inputs that will lead to the desired outputs. Politics is simply a matter of defining the *ends* of policy. The *means* are a matter of finding the appropriate technique.

This introduces the idea of *necessity* into policymaking. The range of effective means to any given end is limited by the laws of the system— its functional characteristics. This in turn implies that goals can only be achieved if the choice of means respects certain scientifically established, necessary technical limits. The logic of the policy design model is that of the hard sciences. For example, if the goal is to cut production costs, then producing aircraft with only one wing instead of two will certainly achieve this, but the laws of aerodynamics mean that the aircraft will not fly. A logically equivalent social scientific statement would be that if the goal is to increase the incomes of the working poor, then introducing a minimum wage will certainly achieve this, but the laws of the labour market mean that a significant proportion of those workers will end up unemployed. The assumption is that the technical parameters of labour market policy, like those of aircraft design, are what they are, no matter how much we might wish them to be otherwise. When economists say that a minimum wage is not a good means of improving incomes they appear to be stating a fact with the same logical status as the facts stated by the aeronautical engineers who say that reducing the number of wings from two to one is not an acceptable cost-cutting policy. Even though the process of coming to those conclusions is not and cannot be democratic, and even though the conclusions have a significant effect on policy, in neither case is there any unwarranted intrusion into the decision-making process from those without a mandate to take policy decisions. Rather, they are simply stating necessary truths that are relevant to policy design.

The conception of social science that underpins this policymaking model is usually known as 'positivism'. As Bohman puts it, "This conception of practical knowledge would model the role of the social scientist in politics on the engineer, who masterfully chooses the optimal solution to a problem of design" (2016, p. 18). This is the approach favoured by those who argue that there is a need to make an *empirical* case for collective bargaining. However, as we saw in Chapter 2, even if we accept the positivist framing of the 'business case' argument, it looks as if positivism raises more questions than it answers, at least in those cases like collective bargaining where the motives of actors are unlikely to be economic in any simple or straightforward sense. On the other hand, it would be difficult to say that there is a cut and dried answer to whether and to what extent it is a useful approach. Nevertheless, settling on some satisfactory conclusions is essential because the extent to which positivism is defensible tells us the extent to which human actors are *not* potentially in complete control of their own destiny. To get a grip on the question, we need to think about what positivism implies about human behaviour and how the issue has been dealt with in sociology and social theory.

Talcott Parsons and the Systems Intuition

As a methodological strategy, positivism can only work if the systems intuition is broadly true. If it *is* true, it must be because there are underlying mechanisms that can explain the consistency of action ('order') that gives rise to the system. In the 19th and early part of the twentieth centuries, behaviourist explanations for social order were very common. Parsons called these types of explanation 'radical anti-intellectualist positivism', arguing that they explained order by reference to "the conditions of the situation of action objectively rather than subjectively considered, which for most practical purposes may be taken to mean in the factors of heredity and environment in the analytical sense of biological theory" (Parsons, 1949, p. 67). From this perspective, there is nothing rational about systemic social action; it is merely the reflection of some psychobiological process beyond the control or even the consciousness of individual actors. Behaviourism is to be contrasted with what Parsons describes as "the interpretation of subjective states of mind" (Camic, 1991, p. xxxix), which is to say the method of interpretive understanding pioneered by Max Weber. Weber argued that "Statistical uniformities constitute understandable types of action, and thus constitute sociological generalisations, only when they can be regarded as manifestations of the understandable subjective meaning of a course of social action" (Weber, 1978, p. 12). Social order has to be explained based on an understanding of what it is that actors think and believe they are doing when they engage in the action that, from an external third-party perspective, can be seen as a system. I will not waste time arguing the case against behaviourism, not least because it is entirely contrary to my avowed goal of working towards a *consensual* capitalism. For the moment, then, we can stick to explanations of the existence of systems that start with 'subjective states of mind'.

Perhaps the most historically influential proposal about the subjective state of mind of individual actors is utilitarianism. This is the belief that individuals decide how to act on the basis of a conscious, rational calculation of what course of action will maximise pleasure and minimise pain according to their own unique conception of the good. If this is the case, then the connection between actors takes the form of contracts of exchange that actors draw up and enter into according to whatever egocentric calculation best suits them. By providing information about the egocentric calculations of *other* actors (supply and demand at particular price levels) and thus the potential exchanges that are available, the market links every contract with every other contract, thus creating a system. But as Durkheim argued in criticising Spencer, contracts of exchange simply do not create enough of a connection between individuals to be a plausible explanation for order in the context of utilitarian assumptions about action:

> if interest relates men, it is never for more than a few moments. It can create only an external link between them. In the fact of exchange, the various agents remain outside of each other, and when the business has been completed, each one retires and is left entirely on his own. Consciousnesses are only superficially in contact; they neither penetrate each other, nor do they adhere. If we look further into the matter, we

shall see that this total harmony of interests conceals a latent or deferred conflict. For where interest is the only ruling force each individual finds himself in a state of war with every other since nothing comes to mollify the egos, and any truce in this eternal antagonism would not be of long duration.

(Durkheim, cited in Habermas, 1987, p. 116)

Parsons picks up on the idea of 'eternal antagonism', asking how there can be any guarantee that the freely chosen ends of a large number of actors will be sufficiently compatible to give rise to social order. He takes the view that if we want to explain order

we cannot assume straightforward 'randomness of ends' . . . among the members of a society; it is wrong to assume that people have only very specific, individual goals and conceptions of utility, not all of which or which only randomly tally with those of others, if indeed there is any overlap at all.

(Joas and Knöbl, 2009, p. 32)

But since order—for example the economic system—does exist as an empirical fact, the question that needs to be answered is "Where do the goals of action, actors' notions of utility, their 'ends', in fact come from?" (ibid. p33). Durkheim's answer was 'moral and legal rules', and Parsons expands on this to offer a *normative* theory of action that attempts to show how even the most apparently egocentric, self-interested actions demand a backdrop of widely accepted norms of action.[1]

Parsons's strategy is to introduce the idea of 'generalized values', which are values that can be presumed to motivate or bind all actors in the same way at all times and places. The pursuit of individual utility is one such value. Each value corresponds to a 'steering medium' which is a highly specialised means of communication that directs or 'steers' the choices of actors. Money is the medium that corresponds to utility. The pursuit of these generalised values is what drives individual choices, but, as norms must be, they are social in origin. The assumption that actors are driven by interest maximisation is therefore neither self-evident nor universally applicable. Rather, it is the outcome of a specific set of historical circumstances and cannot simply be assumed to be the case. As Henri Bergson said, "It takes centuries of culture to produce a utilitarian such as John Stuart Mill".[2] Parsons argues that although what individuals perceive or experience as utility maximisation clearly does exist, it could not exist as part of a stable system of action without the support of rules, values, shared ideas and socialisation processes that go a long way to harmonising how individuals define their own interests and the acceptable means by which they can be pursued. All this of course is highly reminiscent of Fox, Cox and Hyman's arguments about the essential ideological backdrop to collective bargaining.

The way Parsons goes about working this idea up into a complete theory is especially interesting from the point of view of industrial relations theory as it reflects Parsons's attempt to reconcile his initial academic training in institutional economics with the orthodox neoclassical approach he learnt after finishing his doctorate. While he very much admired the precision and theoretical power of abstract economics, he recognised that if not combined with a sociological analysis of norms and values it was incomplete and might even be dangerous. For example, Camic refers to a paper in which Parsons discusses

> the close ties between dogmatic orthodoxy in economic theory and 'capitalist apologetics', or the political conviction that practical affairs *should* correspond to neoclassical premises and that 'to modify the social order away from this pattern [is] not only foolish but vicious as well'
>
> (1991, p. lxii)

However, he did not want to fall back on institutional economics because of its strongly empiricist leanings and lack of any coherent analytical structure. Rather, he believed that the answer was to try to develop a sociology of action that would have the same relationship to values as economics does to individual interests (Camic, 1991). The generalised values that made economic action possible could not be explained from *within* economics and had to be grounded in a different type of social process that was able to explain the emergence and persistence of normative phenomena.

The eventual result was a dauntingly complex theory of social systems in which the economy is merely one of four principal subsystems of society along with the political-administrative system of governance structures, the integrative system of ideas and reasons for action and the cultural system of values and socialisation. Each of these systems has its own steering medium, which, from the perspective of the rationality criteria also proper to each system, indicates how the corresponding generalised value can best be pursued. In the economic system, for example, applying the rationality criterion of *profitability* to social interactions steered by the *money* medium (exchanges) indicates to the actor what course of action will maximise her *utility*. In the political-administrative system, applying the rationality criterion of *sovereignty* (legally correct direction from a superior) to interactions steered by the *power* medium (directives) indicates to the actor what course of action will lead to the most *effective* realisation of collective goals (Habermas, 1987, p. 274).

There is little point in getting further into the intricacies of the overall scheme here. Suffice it to say that in his quest for analytical rigour, Parsons ends up by reducing the scope for human agency almost to nothing. His scheme is so complete that it is almost impossible to grasp the point at which any genuine collective choices are made. He conceives the influence of norms on economic action almost entirely as the interaction of subsystems, each of which forms part of the environment for the others. Actors are locked into a logic of action arising from unintended interactions not just in markets and bureaucracies but also in the realm of culture and values. In this sense, the theory of action ends up being almost entirely sidelined by systems theory (Joas and Knöbl, 2009, p. 84).

Of course, it could be argued that human agency *has* effectively disappeared; that the possibility of genuine collective or individual choice is excluded by the dominance of system imperatives. This is the position argued by Niklas Luhmann. Luhmann accepts the ultimate implication of systems thinking, which is that the idea that we choose our goals no longer makes any sense. He rejects the action frame of reference altogether, arguing that social action has no aim and is merely the playing out of the logic of the system (Joas and Knöbl, 2009, chapter XI). What appear to us to be the least structured, most freely made choices are in fact determined by forces beyond our control or even consciousness.

Luhmann's argument is extreme, but only because his systems theory is comprehensive. More limited systemic assumptions are almost banal, particular when it comes to the economic domain. As Andrew Sayer (2004) points out, the tendency for market forces to gain a degree of autonomy from actors' intentions and actions and hence to "displace moral and traditional norms in structuring society" (p. 2) has been identified by, among others, Karl Marx, Max Weber and Karl Polanyi, not to mention the massed ranks of neoclassical economists for whom it is their most critical article of faith. As Bourdieu puts it, orthodox economics "is based on an initial act of abstraction that consists in dissociating a particular category of practices, or a particular dimension of all practice, from the social order in which all human practice is immersed" (2005, p. 1). Economists believe that an adequate analysis of economic action is possible "outside of any reference to the work of historians or social anthropologists, of social realities as complex as the family, intergenerational exchanges, corruption or marriage" (ibid., p. 3).

Bureaucratic contexts have also frequently been treated from a systems perspective. Classical organization theory, for example, plays down the significance of individual perspectives and motives in favour of a focus on the establishment of managers' formal or legal right to obedience. In Herbert Simon's frequently cited formulation, subordinate members of the organization "hold in abeyance [their] own critical faculties for choosing between alternatives and use the formal criterion of the receipt of a command or signal as [their] basis for choice" (2013, p. 179). Similarly, Habermas has proposed that the payment of a wage gives rise to a 'generalized willingness' on the part of the worker to follow (legal) orders. In becoming a member of an organization, a person takes on the role of 'employee'. This, he argues, has the effect of excluding personal motivations from the interior of organizations, rendering them "independent from concrete dispositions and goals, in general from the particular contexts of life that might otherwise flow into them from the socializatory background of personality traits" (Habermas, 1987, p. 308).

System, Lifeworld or Somewhere in Between?

Despite its ubiquity, systems thinking as a theoretical and methodological approach has been subject to a great deal of criticism. Readers of this book are likely to be familiar with the extensive empirical evidence that contradicts the assumptions of neoclassical economics so there is little need to go into it here.[3] We can be content with Bourdieu's trenchant summary:

> in many situations, economic agents make choices systematically different from those predicted in the economic model: either they do not play the game in accordance with the predictions of game theory, or they resort to 'practical' strategies, or they evince a concern to act in conformity with their sense of fairness or justice and to be treated in the same way themselves.
>
> (2005, p. 8)

Similarly, the idea that organizations will simply work according to some predetermined functional pattern so long as what employees are required to do remains within certain pre-specified contractual limits is difficult to sustain. What has been repeatedly recognised is that even incontrovertibly legal employment relationships prompt a very wide range of responses from employees. These responses run from enthusiastic commitment through resigned acceptance all the way to determined resistance and conflict (Thompson and Newsome, 2004, p. 145). Yet, if employees were in fact 'holding in abeyance their own critical faculties' or had adopted an authentic 'generalized willingness' to follow orders, then it is difficult to understand how such a wide range of responses to legal instructions could come about. Theories that premise the functional characteristics of organizations on the purely formal aspects of the employment relationship are clearly not giving us the full picture. As Granovetter argues, "norms and identities result from and structure interaction in cognitive and emotional ways that escape reduction to self-interest, and indeed are key in actors' definitions of what their interests are" (2002). To put it another way, we cannot say a priori that structure is more important than agency; that social institutions are effectively independent of the values and beliefs of the actors that constitute them.

On the other hand, it seems at least as implausible to argue that the structuring effect of rules on behaviour in any social institution, but particularly in employing organizations, depends on a principally local negotiation of order. Authors like Anselm Strauss—one of the originators of grounded theory—have argued that social order is not fixed but is time-bound and unstable, arising from interactional processes in specific localised situations rather than being imposed from 'above'. Strauss argues that the rules and regulations that define social structures are "not necessarily prescriptive nor peremptorily constraining" (Strauss, 2008, p. 255). Yet, organizations are capable of consistently producing extraordinarily complex products like cars or smartphones over very long periods. Although it remains perfectly plausible to argue that the local negotiation of order is of material significance, it would surely be unwise to assume from the outset that local interactions based on the entirely contingent 'concrete dispositions and goals' of organization members are the primary causal antecedents of organization behaviour.

It appears, then, that we are not dealing with a simple opposition between structure and agency. The question is rather *how far* action in systems contexts is influenced by culture and values rather than incentives and sanctions or alternatively *where to draw the line* between those contexts of life in which systemic motivations are dominant and those in which genuine choice remains possible. Habermas's argument is that while Parsons is entirely right to argue that in certain action contexts, systemic motivations "reach through and beyond action orientations" (Habermas, 1987, p. 116), he extends the reach of these motivations too far into the territory of culture, convention, morality and aesthetics. For reasons we do not need to go into here, Habermas argues that only two of the four subsystems that Parsons proposed can be counted as genuinely systemic. He thereby divides the terrain of human action into the economy and the political-administrative system on one hand—he usually refers to this simply as 'system'—and what he calls 'the lifeworld' on the other. The lifeworld is the normative sphere in which human agency remains effective. Although the behaviour characteristic of economic and political systems is ultimately grounded in the lifeworld via the generalised values that Parsons identified, the two spheres have become 'uncoupled', with the systemic spheres breaking away and congealing into 'blocks of norm-free sociality'. For Habermas, the distinction between these spheres is not merely a question of methodological approach but of a real difference in the means of coordination of social action that requires the development of two different theories of action. In the rest of this chapter, I want to explain and discuss Habermas's approach before proposing some modifications to it that will make it more useful as a basis for finally developing our theory of industrial relations.

Communicatively Structured Interactions and Legitimate Law

In principle, the dissolution of the traditional practices, religious ethics and morality that justified all forms of social domination in premodern societies leaves room for the emergence of what Habermas calls 'post-traditional' morality and legality. It is impossible to do justice to the depth and complexity of his account here, drawing as it does on a synthesis of the major social theorists, sociologists and philosophers of the 19th and 20th centuries including Marx, Weber, Durkheim, Mead and Austin. However, the very short version is that under ideal circumstances, what modernity permits is the development of genuinely consensual norms whose legitimacy is not externally validated via some religious or other traditional cultural authority but actively established in 'communicatively structured' interactions. These are interactions in which the participants conduct a substantive discussion aiming to arrive at a consensus about how to coordinate their actions. This discussion has no a priori limits on what is and is not relevant to coming to an agreement and no means of persuasion can be mobilised except argument. In modern human societies, the most fundamental source of motivation is the 'peculiarly constraint-free force of the better argument' (Habermas, 1984, p. 24).

This approach represents an important break with the individualistic theories of action that dominate contemporary social science. For Habermas, the key to understanding social action is not to be found in some kind of individual calculation or inference leading from circumstances to action, but rather lies in understanding what those circumstances are thought to be and how they come to be defined. He defines 'communicative action' as social action in which there is either a direct attempt to establish a definition of the situation, or in which an actor, in attempting to pursue some more immediate goal, relies on a partner's agreement that the assumptions made about their common situation are valid, while remaining open to the possibility that these assumptions may be rejected or subject to modification.

Drawing on the language philosophy of J L Austin and John Searle, Habermas proposes a theory of action that he calls 'formal pragmatics'. He argues that in speaking, actors 'raise claims to validity' of three kinds:

the truth of propositions about objective states of affairs;

the rightness or legitimacy of proposed norms and values;

their own truthfulness or sincerity in the sense of their intention to say what they say and nothing more, rather than to deceive or manipulate their audience.

The meaning of a statement depends both on its propositional content (its meaning in the abstract or formal sense) *and* on whether a hearer accepts or rejects the underlying validity claims raised by a speaker in uttering it. Successful communication is communication in which a hearer unreservedly accepts the claims a speaker raises.

Habermas gives the example of a professor in an academic seminar asking a student in the audience to get her a glass of water (1984, p. 306). The student can either accept the request and fetch a glass of water, or he can reject it on the grounds that one or more of the claims to validity raised by the speaker cannot be sustained:

The nearest water tap is so far away he could not get there and back before the end of the seminar (rejecting the *objective* physical possibility of complying with the request).

It is unreasonable to ask a student to take on this kind of service role (rejecting the *normative* rightness of his complying with the request).

The professor does not need water. Her real motive is to humiliate the student (rejecting the *subjective* truthfulness of the speaker in making the request).

Quite simply, a hearer will accept a speaker's claims only where there are good reasons for them. What is important is not that these reasons *are* actively and openly considered, but that in principle they could be. As Habermas puts it, a communicative actor will raise with her statement only *criticisable* claims to validity. In this sense, suggests Cooke, "everyday communicative action involves a rudimentary process of 'argumentation'" (Habermas, 1998, p. 4). This is not to say that every interaction involves some explicit process of argument in which individual actors can take part or even that they can passively follow a discursive struggle as it unfolds. Rather, we are surrounded by ideas and argument, whether built into culture and institutions, assumed in political debate, taught in schools and universities, or transmitted or embodied in any of an almost unlimited range of other ways. When we go about our everyday lives in the company of other individuals, we rely on the conceptual anchoring that these ideas provide. Rather than having to establish shared meanings from scratch every time we encounter and interact with other people, we assume that a vast array of things are already understood. Habermas—among others— refers to this shared background knowledge as the 'lifeworld', defined as a "culturally transmitted and linguistically organized stock of interpretive patterns" (Habermas, 1987, p. 122). When we look at the social world around us, our first assumption is that what we see is more or less what everyone else sees. If there is some question about what we should (collectively) do then we do not have to start from first principles to answer it. As Thomas McCarthy puts it, "In the form of 'language' and 'culture' this reservoir of implicit knowledge [the lifeworld] supplies actors with unproblematic background convictions upon which they draw in the negotiation of common definitions of situations" (in Habermas, 1984, p. xxiv). Nevertheless, for all that, these background convictions anchor meaning and communication, they can in principle always be brought into the foreground to be discussed, criticised and potentially revised on the basis of good reasons. They are not insulated from criticism like the religious and metaphysical foundations of traditional worldviews.

The Legitimacy of Positive Law

In many circumstances, however, we are not free to resolve social interactions on the basis of whatever arguments appear to us to be valid. Rather, interactions are structured by formal rules. For example, whether or not a person can legally reside in a country is not a question that is up for discussion between a migrant and an immigration official. The migrant does not make a free-form argument about why she should be permitted to enter and remain that the official accepts or rejects having weighed up its inherent merits. Rather, the migrant is required to provide evidence that establishes a certain pre-determined set of facts—country of origin, level of education, language competences, family situation, employment history, criminal record and so forth—and the official must verify these facts according to certain pre-determined standards of proof. If the migrant verifiably meets the required criteria, then the official is obliged to issue the appropriate permit. Similarly, a medical student who has completed her studies does not go before a medical registration board and make a substantive case that she has the expertise and clinical competence to practice medicine. Rather, she provides the various certifications she has amassed over the course of her studies to the board, which verifies their authenticity and issues a licence to practice. If the student has the correct set of qualifications, then under normal circumstances the board has no right to refuse her a licence.

Formal rules are formulae that pre-establish the outcome of an interaction between particular types of actors in a given set of circumstances. They take the substantive decision about action out of the hands of the immediate participants, leaving them instead simply to follow a series of cognitive steps that point to a particular outcome. Certain aspects of the situation in which the participants find themselves are deemed in advance to be pertinent to the determining the outcome while others are not. Habermas describes action situations that are rule-bound in this way as 'formally organized'. This is contrast to the informal, open-ended interactions that he describes as 'communicatively structured'.

Formal rules are an alternative to communicative action against the backdrop of the lifeworld. Rules help us to solve a problem with modernity, which is the enormously increased burden placed on communicative processes once no form of life or structure of social relationships can be taken as given. If nothing is insulated by tradition and the religious worldviews and notions of natural law that support it, we are thrown back on our own interpretive accomplishments which very quickly become overburdened. Habermas (1987) argues that formal rules arising from positive law relieve that burden. Positive law, in contrast to natural law, is any law that is made deliberately, by the conscious and free choice of the lawmakers, rather than referring beyond that choice to principles that in some sense already exist. This is what distinguishes modern from premodern law, in which domination is based on traditional institutions "that are *merely overlaid and guaranteed by law*" (Habermas, 1987, p. 309; emphasis in original). There are two means by which positive law can relieve the burden that modernity places on communicatively structured interactions. The first is that rules save actors from having to negotiate each aspect of an interaction every time an interaction of that kind occurs. They "reduce the expenditure of interpretive energy" (p. 262). The second reason is that they help us to negotiate complexity in the sense that they "overcome the risk of action sequences falling apart", sparing societies from having to bear the "costs of dissensus" (p. 263).

Of course, this stabilising effect could hardly be very effective if there were not some means of *enforcing* rules. Formal rules ultimately depend on the power of the state to *require* compliance via the imposition of sanctions. At the same time, and excluding the case of absolutist regimes, rules limit the use of power to those situations in which the enforcement of a rule can be shown to be an effective means of pursuing a collective or general interest. This is usually referred to as 'legitimacy'. Although, as Weber argued, legitimacy can be secured by reference to tradition, it is characteristic of modernity that it refers most frequently to rationality. In the absence of

> religious or metaphysical support, the coercive law . . . can preserve its socially integrating force only insofar as the addressees of legal norms may at the same time understand themselves, taken as a whole, as the rational *authors* of those norms.
>
> (Habermas, 1996, p. 33; emphasis in original)

We can parse the legitimacy of a rule into the same three components that Habermas argues underpin communicative acts. If a rule is to be one that we can freely accept,

> it must be objectively effective in the sense that compliance with it will have the desired effect;
>
> it must be normatively right in the sense that the goal it is designed to realise is a valid one and that the means of realization does not require actors to engage in actions that would be wrong in themselves; and
>
> the subjective intent of lawmakers must be that the law should have only its stated impact and not a hidden collateral effect.

In the simplest cases, the legitimacy of a rule can be self-evident. Rules about dangerous driving, for example, or ticket-based queuing systems that ensure that clients are served in the order they arrive are visibly rational. In more complex situations, though, it may be that no-one directly involved in a rule-governed interaction is in a position to make a substantive case for the accuracy of any technical knowledge that underpins the rules or perhaps even for the validity of their normative goals. Most of us, for example, are in no position to judge whether the rules governing medical licencing are sufficient to ensure that all licenced doctors are in fact competent to practice. The knowledge required to make such a judgement is 'beyond the horizon' of our lifeworlds.

Procedural Legitimacy and Warranted Belief

In these cases, rules may still be recognised and experienced by actors as legitimate because of a belief in the procedure by which the rule was formulated:

> the permission for legal coercion must be traced back to the expectation of legitimacy connected with the decisions of the legislature. The positivity of law is bound up with the promise that *democratic processes of law-making* justify the presumption that enacted norms are rationally acceptable.
>
> (Habermas, 1996, p. 33; emphasis added)

We can accept and comply with rules because we understand that they are the result of decision-making procedures of which we do not have first-hand knowledge but which we believe to have been appropriately rational: technically and scientifically grounded in the case of medical registration, for example, or democratically grounded in the case of immigration regulation. We believe that the rules represent an accurate model of objective and social reality. Where this is the case, there will be no difference between how we behave in the face of the 'rule-guaranteed' situation and how we would behave were we able to make a direct technical assessment of a doctor's skills or certain kinds of treatment, or to come to a substantive understanding of the motivation and likely contribution of the applicant for residency. In practice, the presence of any enforcement procedures is of little consequence as we would follow the rule in any case. For example, the parents of a seriously ill child do not have that child treated by qualified and licenced medical practitioners because and only because they risk the intervention of social services if they limit the child's care to faith healers.

There is, then, a category of rules that can be willingly complied with not because their substantive legitimacy is immediately evident to those subject to them but because they emerge from procedures that give rise to a *warranted belief* in their legitimacy. This category includes ad hoc directives issued by experts and office-holders. The rule in this case is that we accept direction given by those who are legally entitled to issue binding commands and who are acting within the scope of their formal authority. The substance of these commands are not the subject of specific law-making processes but are nevertheless backed by a different kind of procedural warrant. A senior police officer ordering the evacuation of an area of a city because of a bomb scare is not applying a substantive rule that already exists but exercising their judgment as a trained and experienced professional in the interests of public safety. Nevertheless, their evacuation order has the force of law and is likely to be complied with in so far as that training and experience is recognised as a procedurally valid basis for decision-making.

Judicial vs Ontological Truth

In a paper on Weber's sociology of law, Andrini (2004, pp. 146–7) makes a critical observation about procedurally-validated rules of this kind. This is that *judicial* truth has to be distinguished from the actual *ontological* truth. Ontological truth is what *is* true; it refers to the actual characteristics of the situation and to any action that is right and effective within it. By contrast, judicial truth has a hypothetical character. The point of medical registration laws, for example, is to ensure that only those who are competent to practice medicine safely are allowed to do so. However, what the law *states* is that only those who have a medical licence will be allowed to practice medicine. But the statement 'Ms. X has the necessary qualifications to be licenced as a medical practitioner' is not in itself the same as the statement 'Ms. X has the necessary competence to practice medicine safely'. These statements can be taken as functional equivalents only if a long series of other statements about the technical effectiveness of the medical education and certification system are also believed to be true. The competence of the medical student is not guaranteed by the procedure of applying the rule but only deemed to be likely. Although procedures for the certification of medical competence are very reliable, there are always cases of formally qualified medical practitioners who in practice are incompetent. There are also cases of individuals who would be perfectly competent practitioners but who, for whatever reason, are unable to meet the certification requirements—perhaps because they possess only unrecognised foreign qualifications—and are thus refused a licence to practice. Similarly, the senior police officer's evacuation order is not logically equivalent to a statement that it is dangerous to remain in the area of the city in question. It may be that in reality there is no danger, but the experience and training of the officer give us good reason to believe that danger is likely.

When we use judicial truth in place of ontological truth, we are assuming the validity of the objective, normative and subjective claims which logically have to be valid if complying with the rule in question is to be the right thing to do. Rules and authoritative directives refer beyond their formal specification to norms and technical knowledge that are not immediately available to the actors involved in whatever social interaction is taking place. Rules are applied regardless of whether the actors subject to them have what we could call 'first-order' reasons to believe they are right and effective. However, this will not be experienced as compulsion if actors accept that good reasons for the rule could be provided if necessary.

Truth, Legitimacy and Knowledge

Nevertheless, the possibility of compulsion is anything but irrelevant. Once a rule is in place it will be applied regardless of whether these good reasons actually exist; regardless, that is, of the ontological truth of the matter. The argument about the ontological truth is closed and inaccessible to actors directly involved in rule-governed interactions. For example, there are certain jurisdictions in which the use of cannabis as a medical treatment is illegal, despite evidence showing that it can be a safe and effective drug. In this sense, judicial truth (cannabis is sufficiently harmful that it must be banned even for medical use) takes priority over ontological truth even though there may be a perceptible 'gap' between the two. Rules that are *procedurally* legitimate may nevertheless not be *substantively* legitimate. In this case, it is only the sanction or fear of it that results in compliance.

This means that behaviour oriented towards rules implies the adoption of an attitude towards judicial truth in relation to ontological truth. We can adopt Weber's threefold distinction of legitimacy, habit and expediency (Weber, 1978, p. 31) to capture the range of possible attitudes. Actors may abide by the rules out of a sense of conviction because they recognise them as legitimate. This implies that they recognise no substantive difference between the judicial and ontological truth. However, they may also abide by the rules simply because they *are* the rules, from a purely habitual or customary conformism. This implies no attitude whatsoever to the truth of the matter. Finally, actors may reject the rules entirely, complying only to the extent that they are forced to do so through fear of suffering whatever sanction is attached to non-compliance. To the extent that they comply, it is from a sense of constraint, of the absence of free choice. This attitude of expediency implies a rejection of judicial truth.

We can characterise cooperation and conflict, then, by reference to how the constraints and sanctions that rules create are understood and experienced by actors. Conflict will arise when actors are constrained to follow a rule despite perceiving a significant gap between ontological and judicial truth, between the action situation as actors know or believe it to be and the situation as the rule implies that it is. For example, actors may believe that it is possible for medical students to 'buy' their qualifications by bribing examiners. Cooperation will follow when no such gap is perceived. The rule would be willingly followed even in the absence of sanctions. The situation in which actors have no attitude to the truth of the matter beyond the simple recognition of the existence of rules that need to be followed is a more difficult to categorise, but this is a subject to which we will return in a moment.

Whether actors cooperate willingly with the implementation of rules or comply simply because they have no choice is intimately connected with knowledge. It depends on the confrontation of the actors' beliefs about the social and objective worlds and that which would have to be true if judicial truth and ontological truth were to be effectively the same thing. Just like the communicative statements made in everyday interaction, the meaning of rules depends not just on their bare content but on the validity claims raised when compliance is demanded. Formal rules and authoritative directives imply a judicial truth: a 'way things are' that makes it possible for actors bound by the law to understand themselves as its rational authors and hence for the potential for coercion to have no impact on their freedom. If the use of power to enforce rules is to be permissible, then it has to be possible to show that judicial truth is an accurate reflection of the ontological truth. The perception of a gap, of claims to validity that do not appear to be sustainable but are nevertheless embedded in the law, demands that corrective action be taken. If it is not, the power to require compliance is not legitimate authority but mere empirical compulsion.

Closing Truth Gaps: Revision and Contestation

Rules and directives that refer principally to objective facts susceptible to scientific verification often have routinised revision processes intended to preserve the congruence of judicial and ontological truth. Medical systems, for example, include formal processes for reviewing research and deciding when new knowledge is sufficiently different from any previous consensus as to require a change in the relevant rules (treatment protocols, prescription guidelines, medical school curricula and so on). This is not to say that these routinised processes always proceed in such a way as to avoid controversy, however. Citizen-led movements to change medical practice on the grounds that current regulation does not reflect the latest available evidence are a regular occurrence. Arguments made by these movements focus on the technical arguments for adopting new treatments or practices.

Changes in the law can also be based on the recognition of non-technical learning and social change. In jurisdictions where marriage is restricted to straight couples, the judicial truth is that gay relationships are different in some way that means that it is inappropriate to give them the social and legal recognition that marriage affords. This distinction arises from traditional conceptions of marriage defined exclusively in terms of reproduction and the family. A rather more common and widely accepted contemporary definition of marriage, however, would be that it is a commitment made by two individuals to share their lives based on love, sexual attraction and a healthy dose of pragmatism. There is nothing in this definition that distinguishes gay from straight relationships. Once this contemporary conception of marriage has been recognised as a social reality the traditional restriction of marriage to straight couples becomes impossible to defend. Campaigns for change in these types of law are usually focused on establishing that social reality is not—or is no longer—as it is assumed to be in the law.

Change in rule systems can also be demanded for strictly normative reasons. The validity of pursuing the goal of the preservation of life in all circumstances, for example, has been questioned in the face of medical progress that has increased our capacity to keep people alive but with a questionable quality of life. As a result, the goal of preserving life comes into conflict with the equally important goal of minimising suffering. This has led in some jurisdictions to changes in the law that mean doctors do not risk prosecution if they accept a patient's request to end their life rather than preserve it.

While all these types of challenge can be made without contesting the sincerity of lawmakers or office-holders or the fundamental legitimacy of law- and decision-making processes, rules and directives can also be contested on the grounds that they do not represent sincere attempts to pursue the public interest. Challenges to existing rules may be made on the grounds that their stated goal is not what lawmakers subjectively intend to achieve and that the real reason for the law is invalid. Those who want to question the subjective intent of lawmakers may do so on the basis of direct evidence about lawmakers' intentions. Although President Trump's executive order denying entry to the USA to travellers from certain countries makes no mention of religion, the order has been ruled unconstitutional on the basis that Trump has publicly stated on a number of occasions that he wants to see a 'Muslim ban'. Challenges to lawmaker intent may also be indirect. Campaigners against certain voter identification laws in the USA have argued that there is at least a political motive and possibly also a racial motive behind these laws which—their authors claim—are intended only to ensure that elections are properly democratic. It can be established that citizens with lower incomes are less likely to have or to be able to obtain a photo ID document. These citizens are disproportionately Democrat voters and also disproportionately from minority ethnic backgrounds. This might count as an unfortunate but acceptable side-effect of the law if there was a real problem with voter fraud, but campaigners against voter ID laws have shown that election fraud is vanishingly rare. The problem the law is intended to correct essentially does not exist. Thus, it makes sense to believe that the law is intended to achieve a goal other than the stated goal. Campaigners for the legalisation of medical marijuana frequently make arguments that follow a similar logical structure. Typically, these movements will not argue that the lawmakers have simply made a mistake in their scientific assessment, but rather that the ontological truth is so evidently out of line with what is assumed in the law that an honestly mistaken assessment of the evidence is very unlikely. There must logically be some other, invalid reason for the rule like private gain or the pursuit of conservative religious goals that are not widely accepted. The subjective intent of lawmakers is contested via a deduction from other types of evidence.

Winning the Argument

We can see now that there are two senses in which power demands justification grounded in ideas. First, the legal use of the empirical power to require compliance with rules and directives demands that an appropriate law- or decision-making procedure has been followed. This in turn demands at least the semblance of a rational argument for why compliance with the law is an effective means to the end of realising valid collective goals and values. Second, compliance with rules and directives is not simply a question of the fear of sanctions. If this were the case, citizens would simply ignore the law in situations where there was some advantage to them in breaking it and the chances of them being caught and punished were low. The 'stability of an order', as Weber put it, depends on actors' willing cooperation in the implementation of rules, which depends on the degree to which the law is recognised as legitimate. This in turn depends on actors' perceptions of whether the judicial truth and the ontological truth are adequately congruent and hence on what it is that actors think and believe about the world. If there is a persistent truth gap that does not seem to be being closed in the face of objective and normative arguments for change that appear to actors to be valid, this puts into question the efficacy of law-making processes but also the sincerity of law-makers' intentions.

The absence of substantive legitimacy cannot be compensated by the mere legal capacity to coerce. We do not have to deny the empirical reality of coercion to recognise that power is not self-justifying and cannot force the recognition of the well-foundedness of an idea. Rather, power in the sense of legitimate authority ultimately turns on *winning the argument*; on actors being persuaded that compliance with the law is the right thing to do.

It is frustratingly difficult to say when and if one argument will win against another. Recent political events confirm that that there is no guarantee that what would conventionally be counted a strong argument will win out against a weak one.[4] At the same time, whether an argument in support of a rule is convincing is not purely contingent or historically specific. We all have an idea of what a rational decision-making process involves and what its outcomes should be. We have an intuitive understanding of what communicatively structured action involves and of its inherent connection to validity. Where we recognise advances in knowledge, we assume that there is a connection between the winning argument and the truth. To take up the medical example once again, whatever decision-making process doctors and medical researchers use in going about their work, it has undeniably led to an ongoing increase in the effectiveness of medical treatment. Despite being unable to understand the arguments being made in research labs and clinical practice review boards, we can be sure that the winning arguments are those based on the more accurate understanding of human physiology, pharmacology and so on. Similarly, even without participating in the debate, we can be confident about the validity of the non-heteronormative concept of marriage in Ireland from the large majority of the Irish population that voted to extend the right to marry to gay couples in the 2015 referendum, not to mention the high turnout and the moving spectacle of thousands of expatriate Irish citizens travelling home specifically to vote in favour of marriage equality.

Contractual-Administrative Rules and the Limits of Ontological Truth

So far, the only examples I have discussed involve *recognising* some kind of independent objective or normative reality like effective medical treatment, the danger posed by an explosive device, conceptions of marriage or the point at which a person's suffering is such that it is reasonable for them to choose death over life. The nature of these different phenomena can in principle be defined independently of any existing rules. In situations in which the validity of the rules and directives is not immediately evident, for example where actors do not have the technical knowledge required to understand why the rules are as they are, those bound by the rules nevertheless trust that their substantive rationality—rightness and efficacy—could be explained if necessary; in principle, given enough time, the issue could be settled via a communicatively achieved consensus before any action is taken. Actors see the rules from the perspective of a warranted belief that the ontological truth is more or less as the rules assume and imply that it is. None of this means that finding a rational consensus will be easy, but it is at least possible in principle.

In these purely technical or purely moral-political contexts, the predictable consequences of rule following are the justification for following the rule, but only because this rule or directive recognises a causal relationship that already exists in nature or consensual morality. If all parents comply with the obligation to vaccinate their children, the chances of an outbreak of viral disease are significantly reduced. This is because there is a *necessary* connection between action (vaccination) and outcome (immunisation and hence reduced risk of outbreak) that remains the case regardless of whether the rule is followed or not. The connection between action and outcome is not to be found *in the rule*. Rather, it is an objective and inescapable part of the action situation. Similarly, in moral-political contexts, the connection between rule and action does not depend on the law itself. If something is the right or wrong thing to do, then it remains right or wrong regardless of what legal consequences are attached to it. The use of marijuana for medical purposes is not morally wrong by virtue of being illegal. Either it is wrong or it is not and the law does not change this ontological truth, which is part of what defines the action situation.

If these were the only types of situation we had to deal with then it is difficult to see how social systems in the Parsonian sense could arise. The legitimacy of law in these areas has a very direct connection to a communicatively structured consensus, which makes the idea that formal rules could link up to create *autonomous* social systems that are beyond human control look very implausible. To the extent that systems made of technical and moral-political rules exist, they would in principle be rationally justifiable. If they were not, the ontological truth would remain accessible independently of the formal rules. If a 'truth gap' were to open up then sooner or later rules would be brought back into line with objective or social reality. The only way to prevent this happening would be brute force because the legitimacy that is by far the more important foundation of order would be missing.

Contractual-Administrative Rules: Stabilising Money and Power Steering

There are other types of rule, however, that *create* a connection between action and consequence where one would not otherwise exist. We can call these contractual-administrative rules and directives. There are two basic models for this type of rule: the contract of exchange and membership in voluntary associations (Cradden, 2005).

There is no intrinsic connection between a transfer of money from one actor to another and the transfer of goods or services in the other direction. The connection is created by the exchange, which, once agreed by the parties, becomes legally enforceable. The connection between action and outcome only exists because the actors involved agree that it should. There is no ontological truth of the matter to which to refer as a means of assessing the rightness or efficacy of the rule. To use Parsons's terms, actors are pursuing the value of *utility* and their agreement to exchange is based on the application of the rationality criterion of *profitability*. The simple fact that the exchange is agreed and goes ahead means we assume it is profitable for both parties. The bare fact of compliance allows us to infer the legitimacy of the contract, something that we would usually describe as its fairness. The 'is' and the 'ought' of the situation are inseparable.

Similarly, the ontological and judicial truths of the matter with respect to the internal rules of a private voluntary association like a sports club are not analytically separable. Actors agree to abide by the rules of their sport and of the club itself. Critically, this involves accepting the authority of the club's office-holders as long as this remains within the mandate given to them by the rules. Compliance with the directives and rulings of office-holders only makes sense if all the actors involved have agreed that doing so is an effective means of realising goals that they all share. In Parsons's terms, actors pursue the value of the *effective realisation of collective goals* (participating in sport) based on the application of the rationality criterion of the *sovereignty* of the club's office-holders (team captain, president etc). There is nothing intrinsically valid about some particular way of organising competitions or the access of members to club facilities or the administration of membership dues. They only make sense in the context of each actors' desire to participate in the sport and their recognition of certain organizational and administrative prerequisites for that. As long as they remain as members of the club, it makes sense to assume that they freely accept the authority of the office-holders who decide on the club's systems and procedures. Authority only exists as long as all involved accept that its exercise permits and facilitates the participation of all of the members of the club in an activity they value. To the extent that compliance is a cost to members, it is an acceptable trade-off given what they gain from their participation. If it were not, they would simply leave the club. Again, the fact that the members of the club remain members entitles us to believe that the order of the club is legitimate; a *normative* evaluation is implied in the simple *cognitive* step of noting the existence of the association.

Clearly, these two situations are in themselves commonplace and unproblematic, but this is because we have direct information about the motives of the participants. The difficulty only arises if we assume that the values of utility and the effective realisation of collective goals can be *generalised*, that is, can be presumed to motivate or bind all actors in the same way at all times and places. If this is the case, all institutional forms of social order similar to markets and organizations can be explained by the participants' adherence to these values. We make the leap from observing order to explaining it on the basis of the validity of certain norms. This methodological step, as we saw above, allows us to adopt a systems perspective and opens the possibility of positivist analyses. In taking a systems perspective, we can explain empirically observed, actually existing social order like markets and organizations as the result of the pursuit of generalised values that lead to consistent and predictable responses to particular kinds of social interaction. Once we make this 'methodological objectification', as Habermas calls it, systems can become part of the definition of action situations, appearing as autonomous social phenomena with fixed characteristics.

Let us suppose that we are considering introducing some formal rule intended to give rise to rationally desirable outcomes in term of wages and employment. We need to be able to show that any eventual rule bears a rational relation to the action situation such that it will lead to the consequences we want. If we conceive the action situation as a labour market by assuming that wage levels are the result of a generalised adherence to the value of utility, this implies that the value of utility is recognised as legitimate by all the actors involved, in this case employers and workers. The judicial truth implied in any eventual regulation is that utility is the only generally legitimate value in this situation; the only one required to explain action. Thinking in terms of a labour market is simply a way of grasping the overall effect of a generalised adherence to utility in setting the exchange value of labour. The functional characteristics of the labour market allow us to predict the result of certain inputs and thus to formulate a formal rule that will produce desirable results, but these characteristics are themselves deduced from the assumption that actors are utility maximizing. If the legitimacy of a formal rule depends on its having the desired results, then in the case of the labour market this can be logically reduced to whether the value of utility is generally adhered to in wage setting. But since any formal rule (or directive) will ultimately be enforced via incentives and sanctions, it *creates* the factual adherence to the generalised values that the logic of the contractual-administrative situation says is simultaneously an evaluation of their normative validity. From the point at which we adopt a systems perspective, any rule consistent with the assumption of the validity of generalised values creates its own justification. There is no analytical distinction between ontological and judicial truth. As Andrini puts it, "the juridical model tends more towards *constructing* the world rather than *recognizing* it" (2004, p. 147; emphasis in original).

In the labour market case, we could decide to make individual bargaining mandatory on the grounds that collective bargaining leads to wages that are higher than the long-run competitive equilibrium level and hence to unemployment. Enforcing this rule will only reduce unemployment if all actors are consistently individually utility-maximising in the way that neoclassical labour economics says that they are. However, preventing collective action obliges workers to adopt an individual utility-maximising strategy. In this sense, the rule is its own justification. The formal rule is not legitimate because the action situation is as it is, but because the action situation is as the rule makes it. The argument for the legitimacy of the rule ultimately depends on the legitimacy of the rule.

This circularity cannot be resolved from the perspective of the individual actor because the only way to resolve it would be to *know* that generalised values are legitimate (or not legitimate); to know that all exchange values have been freely accepted by both parties and that all organizational rules have been freely accepted by members of those organizations. The rationality of action depends on the simultaneous choices of a large number of other actors who are not present and whose identities are not even known.

The Limits of Formal Pragmatics

This is where Habermas draws the logical limits of his 'formal pragmatics', arguing along with other systems theorists like Parsons and Luhmann that there is a point in the development of contractual-administrative rules at which we pass into a situation where all actors can do is respond to structural requirements (incentives and sanctions) on the basis of whatever room for manoeuvre their material circumstances leave them. Coordinated social action becomes literally meaningless, neither legitimate nor illegitimate, with compliance falling into something like Weber's intermediate category of unthinking custom or habit. As Habermas puts it, "formally organized domains of action emerge that—in the final analysis—are no longer integrated through the mechanism of mutual understanding, that sheer off from lifeworld contexts and congeal into a kind of norm-free sociality"(1987, p. 307). From the perspective of individual actors, these structures are not tools to facilitate certain kinds of coordinated social interaction whose form is contingent and that can be reshaped to suit changing needs, but autonomous, objective forces that direct and limit behaviour. In markets and bureaucracies, argument is not available as a means of resolving disagreements about what we should do and how we should live. The processes of market exchange and public and private policy development and the rule-making that follows lock down the argument, leaving behind a structure of fixed relationships based on interactions with more or less predetermined outcomes. Although in principle the rules can be re-written, this is not a solution available to those involved in day-to-day interactions, even where all involved would in principle be willing to do things differently.

Conclusions: Back to Institutionalism?

Having got to this point, we might reasonably wonder whether Habermas has not simply confirmed the basic intuition of neoclassical economics. He has given us good reason to believe that the normal processes of social action coordination cannot lead to a secure agreement about coordinated action in systemic contexts. Instead, action is steered by media, which is to say financial incentives, organizational rules and the directives of office-holders. For Habermas, this is not an empirical observation but a conclusion derived from the philosophy of language. His solution to the problem of structure and agency is to draw a line between different spheres of action, arguing that different theories of action are appropriate in each sphere. System and lifeworld have become 'uncoupled'; the validity basis of action proper to each sphere has little or no purchase in the other. In taking this approach, he seems tacitly to reject the alternative, which is systematically to address the question of the extent to which social action in any given situation is steered by money and/or power as opposed to being taken on the basis of a communicatively-achieved consensus. To cite Mouzelis (1997), he assumes that in systemic (administrative) contexts, "the co-ordinating role of communicative understanding is peripheral or subordinate to that played by the steering media" (p. 115); he does *not* address "the substantive empirical issue of how important steering and non-steering mechanisms of co-ordination are in each institutional sphere" (pp. 115–16).

In fact, he does address this issue. It is just that he has no theoretical insight to offer with respect to the balance between achieved consensus and steering. Habermas is perfectly aware that communicative understanding remains vitally important within organizations: "if all processes of genuinely reaching understanding were banished from the interior of organizations, formally regulated social relations could not be sustained, nor could organizational goals be realized" (Habermas, 1987, p. 310). He even takes Luhmann to task for turning the vision of the totally administered world that for Adorno was a "vision of extreme horror" into "a trivial presupposition" (ibid., p. 312). For Habermas, the fact that organizations are made of formal rules means not that action *is not* or *cannot be* coordinated on the basis of communicatively-achieved agreement, but that it *need not* be. He argues that steering mechanisms do not replace communicative action within organizations, but disempower it by providing the opportunity for certain actors to decide that agreement is *not* required before action goes ahead. To put it another way, managers can seek to coordinate action via consensus if they wish, but formal hierarchy means that there is no need for them to do so. Having offered this insight, however, Habermas can take us no further:

> There is no doubt that the coordinating mechanism of mutual understanding is put partially out of play within formally organized domains, but the relative weights of social versus system integration is a different question, and *one that can be answered only empirically.*
>
> (ibid.)

Having started with Parsons's quest for a more theoretically satisfactory alternative to institutionalism, we seem to have arrived back at the point at which we can offer no a priori indication of the extent to which a systems approach is likely to give an accurate picture of industrial life.

Notes

1 Parsons defines 'normative' as follows: "the term normative will be used as applicable to an aspect, part or element of a system of action if, and only in so far as, it may be held to manifest or otherwise involve a sentiment attributable to one or more actors that something is an end in itself, regardless of its status as a means to any other end (1) for the members of a collectivity, (2) for some portion of the members of a collectivity or (3) for the collectivity as a unit" (1949, p. 75).
2 This is the epigraph to Bourdieu's *Social Structures of the Economy* (2005).
3 As well as Quiggin's recent work on 'zombie economics' (2012), classic critiques include (Bourdieu, 2005; Green and Shapiro, 1996; Sen, 1977). Specifically with respect to industrial relations, Kaufman's (2010) paper does a splendid job of debunking neoclassical approaches to labour economics.
4 Mercier and his colleagues have identified a great many factors that could mean that individual and collective decision-making processes may not reproduce the deliberative ideal (Mercier and Landemore, 2012; Mercier and Sperber, 2011).

5 Frames of Reference

In this chapter I want to suggest not only that there is a relatively simple way to solve the problem with Habermas's approach that we encountered in Chapter 4, but also that the solution is to be found within the theoretical tradition of industrial relations. The concept of frames of reference is a way of explaining how we grasp work and work relationships in a way that simultaneously recognises the autonomy and objectivity of system requirements and their fundamentally normative character. Frames of reference provide a structure for analysing the balance between structural requirements and substantive normative choice as the antecedents of action at work. It allows us to show how this balance varies systematically between different industrial relations contexts depending on how actors see and understand their circumstances.

Grasping Systems From an Action Perspective

Perkmann (1998) argues that Habermas is mistaken to draw a sharp line between different contexts of action, with the economy and political-administrative systems on one side and culture, convention, morality and socialisation on the other. Rather, system and lifeworld are entangled and intertwined because of the ability of social actors to perceive and thematise structural phenomena in argument. A glance at any economic or social policy argument would quickly confirm that markets and regulatory systems are ubiquitous subjects of debate and discussion. It is entirely commonplace to treat systems as if they were objective aspects of the action situation with fixed and knowable functional characteristics. But we also treat systems as phenomena with a normative character. We constantly evaluate whether taking up some market opportunity is or was the right thing to do, whether avoiding transactions involving what we see as unfair market relationships or simply being satisfied with the price and quality of something we have just bought. Perceptions of the fairness and effectiveness of systems influence not just what we buy but how we vote,[1] whether we go on strike and how we react to change at work. This is true at least as much on the political level where, as we saw in Chapter 2, the same type of judgements are made as a prelude to designing law and policy. The conflict and cooperation assumptions are precisely evaluations of the normative character of the economic system.

However, as we have seen at various points so far in the discussion, the question of what counts as evidence for making these evaluations is highly political. As Fischer and Gottweis put it, "Policy making is fundamentally an on-going discursive *struggle* over the definition and conceptual framing of problems, the public understanding of the issues, the shared meanings that motivate policy responses and criteria for evaluation" (2012). In Chapter 2, for example, I argued that the discursive struggle over collective industrial relations took a turn in favour of capital when the idea took hold that collective bargaining can only be supported as a policy position on the basis of quantitative empirical evidence.

Habermas's formal pragmatics provides a compelling account of why this should be so: of why the ontological truth of contractual-administrative action contexts is so elusive and hence so political. On his reading, it is strictly a question of logic. The circularity between the legitimacy of rules of action and the aggregate outcomes of action cannot be resolved, which means that there is ultimately no way of settling the issue one way or another. However, what Habermas does not consider is that on the basis of culture, socialisation and experience, actors may be *predisposed* to believe certain things about the market economy and business organizations. They may already believe that prices and wages are generally fair or generally unfair. They may already believe that compliance with organizational rules generally leads to the effective pursuit of shared goals or generally does not. In other words, they may approach decisions about action already equipped with a *frame of reference*; with certain beliefs about the characteristics and normative character of the social structures and institutions in the context of which that action will take place. Frames of reference, on this reading, supply a presumed ontological truth about the fairness of exchanges and the legitimacy and effectiveness of structures of coordination and authority that can be compared with the judicial truth implied by the rules and directives governing work.

If we take some further liberties with Habermas's formal pragmatic analysis, we can apply it not just to individual rules or directives but to economic and organizational systems in their entirety. We can treat system requirements as if they were the statements of a communicative actor. Actors' reactions to signals from the system would then be based on whether they accepted the following validity claims:

the generalized values characteristic of the system and the means by which they are pursued are legitimate in a moral and political-ethical sense;

the structure of social organization involved in the pursuit of these values is an objectively effective means of pursuing the ends of the system;

the formal organization of action has no purpose other than the realization of the values it is intended to realise.

Accepting the first claim involves the recognition that, within certain limits, it is acceptable for individual actors to be utility-maximising and for groups of actors to pursue whatever goals they define for themselves. It also involves the recognition that the means of action that systems provide—markets and organizations—are built from basically legitimate forms of social relationship. Accepting the second claim means recognising that systems are useful means for the pursuit of legitimate ends. Markets and organizations are seen as technologies of social coordination that expand human capacities rather than limiting them. Accepting the third claim, the systemic equivalent of the sincerity of the communicative actor who says what she says and nothing more, is a recognition that the possibility of pursuing individual utility and legitimate collective goals via systems is not illusory. Systems do not have a hidden 'real' purpose separate from that which they are nominally intended to achieve.

If all of these systemic validity claims are accepted by actors, then system requirements will have something of the rationally motivating power of 'the better argument'. Actors will recognise system requirements as a positive social force and the risk of sanctions for non-compliance will add little to the overall decision to comply. If any of the claims are rejected, the opposite will be the case. The risk of sanctions is then the primary factor motivating compliance. The system represents a negative social force and its requirements will be considered coercive. If actors are unable to determine whether the validity claims are or are not acceptable, then system requirements are neither positive nor negative but meaningless. They are simply objective elements in the action situation that demand a response.

Positively Evaluated Systems

A positive evaluation of an economic or organizational system implies that, in the absence of any immediate evidence to the contrary, conformity with the role behaviour required by the system is a valid end in itself rather than simply a means to avoid sanctions or seek rewards. In the same way that we accept that there is no effective difference between a properly licensed medical practitioner (judicial truth) and a technically competent medical practitioner (ontological truth), actors are predisposed to believe that there is no significant difference between the incentives, constraints and obligations arising from a system and coordinated action taken on the basis of a communicatively achieved consensus.

Where systems are accorded this kind of positive value status, then from the political-ethical standpoint, resisting the required role behaviour is a culpable failure to fulfil a duty to the organizational community. For example, to challenge or resist the authority of an office-holder in an organization outside any structures that exist to resolve differences of opinion, is to put oneself in opposition to the organizational community as a whole; to oppose a community to which one owes a duty of loyalty. Given that the aims and goals of the community have been determined via legitimate procedures, the only acceptable attitude is cooperation. Similarly, exchange values *ought* to be in some rational relation to market prices. Actors owe it to other market participants to take up the guidance that prices offer in order to maintain the integrity of the system.

Negatively-Evaluated Systems

It may be that actors perceive a permanent, unbridgeable gap between system requirements and their own interests or those of the wider community. The only reason to comply with those requirements is the fear of sanctions and this will be experienced as coercion. There is no trace of the freedom characteristic of situations in which actors recognise themselves as the rational authors of the law.

From the normative perspective, a negative evaluation means that the values the system is intended to realise are not recognised as generalizable. The requirements of the system are not universally legitimate objects of collective action, either because they are straightforwardly morally wrong, because they represent the interests of only a limited group of actors or because, despite being taken in pursuit of otherwise defensible goals, they represent actions which are in themselves morally indefensible.

From the perspective of the objective effectiveness of coordinated action, a negative evaluation means that although the values the system is intended to pursue may be recognised as legitimate, the structural means of pursuing those values is technically questionable. Actors may be predisposed to believe, for example, that bureaucracies are inherently ineffective structures that hinder rather than help the realisation of collective goals.

In terms of whether the system has a hidden purpose like the preservation of the power or wealth of certain groups—the analogue of the subjective truthfulness of the communicative actor—the most important indicator that a negative evaluation is appropriate is the absence of any procedural means of closing the gap between judicial and ontological truth. This is discussed in more detail below, but for the moment, we can say that if actors are not free to adjust their behaviour in the attempt to change system outcomes from the inside, then they are not participants in the system but merely its objects. From the perspective of the intentions behind the system, this implies the existence of a 'them' whose interests conflict with those of an 'us', and who have the social power to pursue those interests at the expense of other groups.

There are two possible rational responses to negatively-evaluated systems. These correspond roughly to the revolutionary and reformist strategies we identified earlier when we were discussing IR policies arising from the conflict assumption. Participants may directly attack or try to overturn the entire system via sabotage, public protest, attempts to organise a revolution or some other means of direct or indirect opposition to 'them'.

Alternatively, participants may decide to leave the system in place but to attempt to correct its negative outcomes from the outside by constructing a countervailing social structure that places empirical constraints on the extent to which 'they' are able to pursue their interests as they see them. Any relaxing of these constraints depends on negotiating an acceptable accommodation with the actors who have evaluated the system as negative. The coercive aspects of the system are defused by the addition of a second system intended to extract compensation for these negative effects from the 'owners' of the original system.

Meaningless Systems

Where social systems are deemed meaningless, it is because the idea that there could be a gap between judicial and ontological truth does not make sense. Actors do not recognise the system as being something that is susceptible to normative evaluation and comply simply because they have no real option but to do so—because of what Habermas calls the 'empirical motivation' of physical force or material need. From this perspective, social systems appear to actors with the same status as physical necessity. The system is assumed to be prior to and separate from immediate decisions about coordinated action rather being an emergent property of that action. Compliance with the required role behaviour is simply a question of survival and can be understood neither as an end in itself nor a capitulation in the face of powerful groups pursuing their partial interests at everyone else's expense. To grasp a system as meaningless means that resisting system requirements is as inappropriate a response as positive and active cooperation. Conflict is not a rational response, but neither is anything other than passive, minimal compliance.

Normative Choice and Social Systems[2]

It is all very well to propose that positive and negative evaluations of economic and organizational systems are possible, but it causes theoretical problems that we do not yet have the resources to resolve. Habermas's dilemma is that if a system is really a system then our response to its requirements is not a choice but a simple adaptation to objective circumstances. On the other hand, if there *is* real choice involved in decisions about action coordination, including the choice to resist what the system requires, then we cannot in fact call what is going on a system. This is why Habermas ends up concluding that there are two separate spheres of social action: system, in which normative choice is not possible, and lifeworld, in which it is.

The concept of the frames of reference implies that actively accepting or rejecting system requirements on normative grounds is possible, but in Habermasian terms, this is like having your cake and eating it too. The situation is reminiscent of the old joke about the stopped clock telling the right time twice a day. As long as what the system requires us to do happens to coincide with what we think is right or what we think is wrong, then everything is fine. We can cooperate or resist as we like. But what if our frame of reference involves a positive system evaluation and yet what the system requires of us is something we cannot help but think is wrong? Or what if the system appears to be demanding that we do something that looks like the right thing to do, even though we believe that what it requires is generally wrong?

The question may seem like an obscure point of theory, but resolving it is critically important to the possibility of achieving a consensual capitalism. If we cannot show that the possibility of choice in economic and organizational contexts is real, then the very idea of consensuality makes no sense. We would be wiser to listen to those who argue that we must never accept the legitimacy of business and the market, even as a possibility, in order to preserve the maximum capacity to refuse its demands when necessary.

If we want to avoid this, the question we need to answer is how to connect system requirements with normative choices about action. At the moment, we cannot say that frames of reference are anything more than a dogmatic or ideological will to believe one thing rather than another. We need to show how we can be in a position to judge whether market and organizational relationships are or are not substantively legitimate on the basis of good reasons that are potentially acceptable to all involved. If we can do that, then we will also understand what we can do to make them legitimate where they are not.

Positive and Negative Economic Systems

We are so used to thinking of markets either as an objective reality we simply have to live with or as social forces we should try to resist that it can be difficult to grasp how they could be perceived positively. Market 'imperatives' are frequently depicted either as no more than a disguise for the partial interests of the owners of capital, or as normatively neutral survival imperatives to which 'There Is No Alternative'. To argue that market forces potentially represent politically and ethically *legitimate* guidance on decisions about action seems to be not only counterintuitive but also difficult to defend on an intellectual level. In truth, as Habermas and other systems theorists have recognised, the question is at least as pertinent when it comes to negative assessments of market forces. The theoretical problem is that we do not seem to have the information needed to make any kind of normative evaluation of markets, whether positive or negative. And yet, we do it all the time.

As we saw in Chapter 4, the normative logic of enforceable contracts centres on the assumption that exchange is fair. From a strict systems perspective, the mere fact of exchange is all the guarantee of fairness that is required or is even possible. Only the participants are in a position to judge the utility of what is on offer and hence whether an exchange is profitable. How, then, can we say that it is possible to recognise the market as something that carries or transmits norms that have some substantive legitimacy—or illegitimacy—beyond the immediate participants in an exchange?

When Is Exchange Legitimate?

There is no need to take a course on Hayek and Friedman to appreciate that a single exchange or price can be *fair*; that it reflects a reasonable balance between the interests of each party. This is commonplace and comprehensible. Cut down to its essentials, exchange or trade is a perfectly defensible social practice. If someone has more of some useful thing than she can use, and her neighbour has none but could use some, then there are two things she can do. She can either just give her neighbour the spare goods or she can trade them for something that she needs but does not have. The two ethical questions that arise are these: when it is okay to trade as opposed to just giving, and what makes for a *fair* trade?

Imagine a situation in which two neighbours are both competent amateur gardeners. They each grow a different range of fruit and vegetables and usually produce more in their gardens than they can consume themselves. The obvious thing for them to do with their surplus produce is to trade it. In fact, it is so obvious that we would think it very odd if one neighbour gave the other a bag of carrots but got nothing in return, even though their neighbour also had surplus produce to dispose of. There is a default expectation of *reciprocity* in this situation. If fulfilled, it puts a social seal on the relationship. By exchanging comparable amounts of produce, the neighbours have done the right thing by each other. Other members of society are likely to look positively at that relationship.

The major qualification here is that this kind of direct reciprocity is not always a reasonable thing to expect: it depends on the circumstances. If one neighbour was elderly and was finding it difficult to keep up her garden, then it would clearly be unreasonable for the other to stop bringing her their spare produce. Trade always takes place in the context of a social relationship, and the 'rightness' of trade has to be judged in relation to that relationship; in relation to one person's situation as compared to that of another. The exchange of fruit and vegetables is saying that both neighbours are independent, capable people who treat each other as such. The trade reflects a relationship of equals, with neither party condescending to the other or trying to exploit the situation to their exclusive advantage. Most importantly, the relationship takes into account the fact that the two participants are able to make a similar physical or material contribution to the relationship.

Similarly, once it has been established that trading is acceptable, the assessment of the fairness of a specific exchange is not a question of finding some permanent substantive equivalence of value between, say, cherries and carrots. The nature and scarcity of the goods exchanged are certainly relevant, but so are the circumstances of the participants. Fair exchange has both a material and a social component. It is not just about price but also about price *in the context of* a set of material and social facts.

For example, if by some random good fortune an individual has ended up being the only vendor of some commodity that is of little use to her but is very useful to others, then to sell it for a high price seems unreasonable. But if she has the commodity because she worked harder or smarter than other people, and if there is no reason why other people could not have worked in the same way if they had wanted to, and if the people who want the thing are in a position to pay a high price for it, that makes the situation rather different. In this case we could argue that a high price is a fair price, because the vendor is not exploiting any unearned advantages that she has. Those who pay the high price could do so in the recognition that that price maintains an acceptable relationship between them and the vendor; that the vendor, for example, is not simply exploiting her monopoly position to extract an advantage from other market actors. So, the fairness of an exchange depends on how one participant's situation compares with the other participant's situation.

How Do Fair Exchanges Add Up to a Market?

We can think of markets as a pool of knowledge about exchange relationships. It may be that our two gardening neighbours are well known in their local area as talented horticulturalists who grow decent produce, and as generally fair and reasonable people, able to look after themselves and likely to treat each other with respect. For this reason, the exchanges that they make may be used as a point of reference by other gardeners looking to exchange the same vegetables. The gardeners in the area recognise that the exchange value implied in the trade is not arbitrary. Rather, it is fair not just because it was agreed by the participants but because it was based on a healthy social relationship and as such can act as a standard for other deals. It is a relatively simple to make adjustments based on perceptible physical differences between the goods in the standard exchange and those in some later deal. Therefore, if the original trade was carrots for cherries, someone swapping parsnips for cherries might agree to accept fewer cherries for the same weight of parsnips because even though the two kinds of vegetable are otherwise very similar, fewer people like parsnips. In this way, the fairness of the original deal is transmitted through subsequent deals as long as everyone continues to behave reasonably. Once a certain point is passed, the original standard deal gets lost to view amid the plethora of fruit and vegetable trades that are going on, and instead the standard becomes all the deals that have recently taken place. Or rather, the standard becomes a rough average of all of these.

Recognisable markets only appear after barter is replaced by a medium of exchange. If five hens are worth two piglets, and a piglet is worth five kilos of cheese, then a hen is worth two kilos of cheese. To say that cheese goes for €5 a kilo, hens cost €10 and piglets €25 expresses the same set of exchange values but makes the range of actors who can participate in trades much wider and makes getting a grip on the available information about exchanges a lot easier. First of all, if an actor wants carrots and has cherries, she does not have to find someone who has carrots and wants cherries. All she has to do is find someone who *wants* cherries and someone who *has* carrots. They no longer have to be the same person. Secondly, instead of a confusing record of swaps involving relationships between different quantities of different kinds of commodities, the information you get from the market (which starts up when someone uses an existing fair exchange as a point of reference for agreeing a second exchange) is just a series of prices for a given quantity of each type of goods. It becomes very easy to understand what each product is worth in relation to other products that are available.

While all this might be fairly plausible as an explanation of how markets come about, it is more difficult to see how we can say that deals are fair or not fair once a market exists and exchanges are settled by reference to the purely statistical phenomenon of market prices rather than known, specific exchanges. Markets make relationships of value between different commodities very easy to understand, but they also insulate us from the social component of exchange values; from the *people* we are dealing with. If the long series of exchanges of which the market provides an aggregate picture are all fair, then market prices are fair. This is the judicial truth of the complex of contracts that comprises the economy.

Yet, in a typical market transaction, the ontological truth of the situation is obscured. All that is known is the price (and how that price relates to other prices, whether of similar or different goods) and the characteristics of the product (its usefulness, desirability etc). We know little if anything about the way the product was produced, about who else was involved, or about whether any of the intermediate exchanges were themselves fair. The situations of the individuals involved and the social processes that led to some product or service arriving on the market are in most cases entirely hidden. But of course, there are any number of ways that markets can be unfair and market actors can behave unfairly. Information about unfair exchanges within a market will be transmitted via price signals in exactly the same way that information about fair exchanges will be transmitted. Any significant incidence of unfairness in a market means it is no longer a reliable guide to fair exchange values.

Deciding to Know More

In fact, the answer to our dilemma is quite simple. All we have to do is go looking for evidence about whether exchanges in the market in which we are participating are fair. It is no more than a question of finding evidence to corroborate the implied claim that the market price is a fair price. Arriving at an evaluation of the normative character of markets is above all a question of deciding that evaluation is possible; of rejecting the studied and deliberate ignorance of the social reality of exchange typical of neoliberalism and instead keeping a grip on what the market is for. In markets, the ontological truth of the matter exists only as an outcome; as a hypothesis that has to be continually tested rather than something that can be assumed to be true before any coordinated action takes place. What we have here is a *methodological inversion of neoliberalism*. Rather than being an initial assumption, the fairness of exchanges is a contingent summative judgement made on the basis of empirical evidence about the outcomes of action in the context of a socio-culturally established standard of fairness. The market is *supposed* to improve the distribution of material goods. It is *supposed* to make work and investment as efficient and effective as possible by allowing individuals to pursue their own interests in the context of a social force that orients individual actions towards socially useful ends. Finding out whether this is actually happening means asking whether money and time are being invested in useful, sustainable ways, and whether (as a consequence) the world is becoming fairer. If it is not, then the market is getting it wrong. Somewhere along the line, someone is taking an *excessive profit*, for example on account of having an effective monopoly position or because they manage to externalise some of the costs of production, but the feedback processes that mean that this should be corrected are not working. Certain market participants are being forced to accept the terms of exchange rather than being free to accept or not accept them as they wish; and society is subsidising the costs of certain types of production, making businesses viable that ought not to be.

Evidence

If we choose to consider it, evidence about the general level of fairness or unfairness of market exchange is readily available. There are two sources of information: qualitative evidence from specific exchange situations and about the detail of regulatory impact,; and quantitative information about the aggregate outcomes of market economic activity.

   The first kind of evidence relates to whether institutional structures are in place that allow all the actors in the system to participate in the evaluation and re-evaluation of outcomes required to maintain the system in a normatively positive state. Does it seem plausible that workers have freely chosen to work under conditions they do? Are workers free to offer their services to other organizations? Are they free to act collectively to negotiate their pay and conditions with the businesses they work for? Are companies that own brand names using their monopoly power to put heavy downward pressure on prices which is then passed on to workers via low pay and poor working conditions? Are there government subsidies to producers in certain countries that mean that producers in other countries are at a disadvantage in the international market? Are international trading rules being settled based on what works for everyone, or are they the result of geopolitical jostling and the lobbying of multi-national corporations?

The second kind of evidence is about the material outcomes of systems. Among the most relevant statistics are the labour share of national income, the proportion of the price consumers pay for a product that ends up in the hands of the workers who produce the goods, the proportion of workers who earn below a living wage, ratios of the salaries of chief executives to those of ordinary workers, the movement of indicators, like the Gini co-efficient that measures the (in)equality of distribution and so forth.

Certainly, ordinary market actors will rarely think in these rather formal terms about the information on which their frames of reference are based. Nevertheless, the point is that information is available, is potentially accessible to everyone and can become part of the normally unquestioned background to action.

Positive and Negative Organizational Systems in the Market Context

It is rather more intuitively comprehensible to say that organizational systems can be the subject of normative evaluations. The 'order' of the organization is what workers live every day, which means that the experience of rules and authoritative directives takes place closer to their origin. Although organizational systems are made up of 'static' internal rules as well as ad hoc directives issued by office-holders, I want to focus on the standard situation of the issuing of an enforceable order or ruling by a member of the organization who, on whatever formal basis of justification, is within their rights to do so. This is the much-discussed issue of the legitimacy of authority.

As we saw in Chapter 4, when an office-holder in an organization issues a command backed by sanctions this will not be experienced as coercion as long as the addressee of that command recognises that there is good reason to believe that compliance is an effective means of realising legitimate shared goals. In the general case of coordinated social action, there are two parts to this: the recognition of the legitimacy of goals and the recognition that coordinating action via authoritative directives issued by office-holders is an effective means of realising these goals.

Just like the idea that an exchange can be fair, the idea that conditions of this kind can be fulfilled is perfectly comprehensible. A person who comes across the scene of an accident and is asked to help by someone who plausibly identifies herself as a doctor is likely to willingly cooperate with any instructions the doctor gives. The shared goal of saving lives and reducing suffering is unquestionable and closely following the instructions of a medical professional is an effective means for someone with no training or experience in the field to contribute to realising that goal. Because these conditions are fulfilled, there is no sense in which the helper is subject to a relationship of domination, even though he puts himself entirely at the disposal of the doctor. It would be reasonable to say that in a very strong moral sense, that person *ought* to do what the doctor asks. In certain jurisdictions, for example in France, a passer-by in this kind of situation who does not help when asked to do so might even find themselves charged with a criminal offence.

However, action within organizations whose goals are set by reference to the market is different from the general case of coordinated social action in that it is subject to the economic as well as the organizational systems. This is a well-established theoretical commitment in the field of work and employment, whether we think in terms of Marx's distinction between the exchange of labour power and the labour process, the line drawn by Commons between the market transaction and the managerial and rationing transactions, Flanders' identification of market and managerial relations, or the argument in transaction cost economics that employment is at once an exchange and a power relationship. The legitimacy of authority in the work relationship depends not just on the organization itself but on the normative character of the economic system in two senses: the legitimacy of the organization's overarching market goals and the preservation of an acceptable equivalence between the individual contribution of the worker and their wage, that is, the fairness of the exchange of labour for money.

Organizational Goals in the Context of Different Evaluations of the Economic System

If the economic system is evaluated positively, then legitimate market goals are those that have the quality of consensual choices. However, as we saw above, that quality can only be maintained if appropriate processes are in place to allow actors to adjust their behaviour in response to the outcomes of market action. The criteria for any such adjustments will have a normative component focused on the maintenance of fair exchange relationships, whether those entered into externally with suppliers and customers or internal relationships between workers and the organization. This means that the relation between prevailing labour market rates and actual pay rates within an organization has to be the subject of free, positive agreement between the organization and all its worker members on the basis of whatever criteria and whatever institutional machinery are universally agreed to be appropriate. It also implies some institutional procedure for ensuring that that decisions about participation in product and finance markets are validated by all the actors involved and, again, that there is some means of reviewing and changing these decisions in response to assessments of the achievement of goals.

Where an economic system is evaluated negatively, actors will recognise that the organization cannot have a single overarching goal or set of goals arising solely from the market. The market is not a neutral point of reference, but a guide to the interests of one group in particular, the owners of capital. The legitimacy of organizational goals is therefore a question of the degree to which some set of intermediate objectives can be identified that represents a rough balance between the interests of capital and those of labour. Logically, this can only be a process of negotiation since it is clear from the outset that the two groups have no common interests. To the degree that product and finance market objectives are thought to impact on the interests of labour, these too may be the subject of negotiated intermediate objectives.

If the economic system is thought to be meaningless, then the market goals of the organization are not *chosen* but merely *identified* in a strictly technical process of interpreting price signals. The positivist epistemology of market action demands that goals are determined by experts. They can be communicated and explained to other actors, but the idea that unqualified individuals should participate in decision-making makes no sense. This applies equally to labour, product and finance markets. Consultation with non-experts may well be appropriate, but this cannot be allowed to gainsay the technical decision-making process. Perhaps most notably, the right wage is that which is set in a technically effective relation to prevailing labour market rates. This precludes the participation of non-experts in wage setting. Workers are free to choose whether to accept the exchange value on offer, but rejecting it means leaving the organization.

Authority Relationships and Organizational Systems

Although the grounding of legitimate authority in organizations depends on evaluations of the value status of the economy, there is also scope for it to vary independently of market goals. We can understand this variation as arising from different evaluations of the normative quality of relationships within the organization itself.

Where the organizational system is evaluated positively, every binding directive is seen to be backed by with good reasons that could in principle be explained before action takes place. These reasons extend to why there must be office-holders at all and to why a particular organization member at a particular point in time should have the right to issue binding directives. The justification for organizational hierarchy must be continually renewed. It may be that good reasons for compliance with directives are immediately evident, but past a certain level of organizational complexity, directly accessible reasons can be substituted with institutional procedures that provide actors with a warranted belief that good reasons could be supplied if necessary.

Negatively-evaluated organizational systems cannot give rise to stable IR as actors will not recognise binding directives as anything other than coercion, even where the economic system is seen as the source of legitimate goals. Legitimate authority cannot exist because actors will understand the entire legal and institutional structure of the work relationship as a means for a limited group of 'others' to control organizations for their own gain. Organizational hierarchy within the framework of contractually governed work relationships will be seen as an illegitimate form of coercion under any and all circumstances.

Meaningless organizational systems are those in which authority relationships will be seen as a purely pragmatic mode of action coordination that can be specified from a technical perspective. It is assumed that the design of effective systems is a matter of the application of expert knowledge and that the justification of authority rests on the technical competence of office-holders.

Evidence

As with the economic system, actors can draw conclusions about the normative status of the system on the basis of evidence about specific incidences of the authority relationship and associated regulatory structures (the quality of jobs, wages, working conditions and so forth) together with evidence about the outcomes of the organizational system—whether the substance of coordinated activity adds up in practice to the realisation of organizational goals. The evidence counted as relevant in this respect will depend on what organizational goals are thought to be. In the context of negative evaluations of the economic system, for example, increased sales or profits or other evidence of market success is at best only partial evidence of the realisation of the organization's goals. At least as relevant are the individual and collective outcomes for workers.

All of these possible evaluations are particularly susceptible to being made on the basis of cultural knowledge, but as Fox cogently argues, the lived experience of work and the face-to-face relationships it involves will orient actors towards an opinion that is coherent with their personal experience

Positively Evaluated Systems and the Democratic Imperative

The very short version of our argument about normative choice in systemic contexts is that it is only really possible if there is a degree of democracy in decision-making. If systems are evaluated as normatively positive, then in Habermas's terms this means the appropriate form of action is *communicative* rather than *strategic*. Although Habermas rightly argues that the validity basis of communicative action is ultimately insecure in systemic contexts, this does not mean that actors cannot approach action with a communicative attitude. They may have a perfectly sincere intention to seek consensus on courses of coordinated action. Whereas a strategic actor will simply accept the most profitable deal on offer or comply with any legal command, regardless of the conditions surrounding it, a communicative actor will seek to offer and accept only substantively fair exchanges and to formulate and comply only with substantively effective rules and directives. This may involve a rejection of what the system objectively appears to require in favour of what actors believe it *ought* to require on the basis of evidence about the social conditions of the exchanges and organizational relationships that have taken place prior to the immediate decision about action.

If it looks to actors that compliance with system requirements is not the right thing to do, the system can only maintain a positive normative status if actors are free to act differently with a view to bringing action and desired outcome back into alignment. For example, they might change the price asked or offered for some commodity, or question the effectiveness of some organizational plan or strategy. If one actor or a group of actors is in a position to prevent this kind of adjustment for its own reasons, the entire system is rendered illegitimate. A communicative actor, one oriented towards mutual consensus, would not bring the discussion of action to an end before agreement was reached because the validity basis of action has not been secured. The act of closing discussion, of preventing adjustment of responses to system requirements, involves the use of power to impose a course of action even though there is no consensus about its legitimacy. This means that positive evaluations of systems imply the existence of institutional mechanisms to ensure that the legitimacy of contracts, administrative rules and directives can be established. These mechanisms must themselves respond to the rationality criteria of legitimacy, effectiveness and institutional sincerity. This in turn points to an inherent connection between positive system evaluations and coercion-free forms of governance based on consent and accountability. In the context of exchange, this implies that there must be some way of maintaining a balance of power between the parties. In the organizational context, it implies that plans, strategies and directives must have the consent of all those to whom they are addressed. This consent could be given on the basis of an advance of trust to officer-holders, but only as long as organization members have the effective right to withdraw it at any time. In short, there is a direct connection between positive system evaluations and democratic forms of governance. The absence of democratic governance is a strong signal that a system should not be evaluated positively.

The Content of Frames of Reference

Each frame of reference simultaneously involves an evaluation of the normative character or quality of the economic system and that of the organizational system. Given that the validity of market goals and systems of action coordination can be evaluated separately, we can point to nine different frames of reference, as set out in table 5.1 below. The six frames that give rise to the possibility of stable IR systems are the four variants of unitarism and the two types of pluralism. Table 5.2 shows how Fox's categories map onto the new classification.

Each frame of reference has two aspects: an action aspect that we can call a narrative of agency and a structural aspect that we can call a conceptual

Table 5.1 The Frames of Reference

		Organizational system		
		Positive	Meaningless	Negative
Economic system	Positive	Democratic unitarism	Bureaucratic unitarism	Anarcho-capitalism
	Meaningless	High-commitment unitarism	Low-commitment unitarism	Anarcho-syndicalism/ Workers' control
	Negative	Integrative pluralism	Adversarial pluralism	Revolutionary anti-capitalism

Table 5.2 Mapping Fox's Frames of Reference onto NTIR Categories

		Organizational system		
		Positive	Meaningless	Negative
Economic system	Positive	Unitarism		
	Meaningless			
	Negative	Pluralism		Radicalism

model of the organization. Together these aspects imply the outlines of an industrial relations policy model and the institutional structures required to put it into operation. They also imply what we can call an epistemology of organization and worker behaviour, that is, approaches to the development and testing of knowledge about actors and systems. I will sketch the characteristics of each frame of reference in some detail in Chapter 6. In the rest of this chapter, I want to outline the different aspects of the frames of reference and how these relate to agency and structure, and, as a consequence, to policy and epistemology.

Narratives of Agency: Normative Evaluation and Worker Engagement

Although sociologists working in the Weberian tradition tend to take the connection between norms and action for granted, the literature on work and organizational psychology shows that there is a well-established connection between different evaluative judgements of the rightness of social situations and individual attitudes and motivation. Research on 'employee engagement' confirms not only that motivation has an important normative component, but that the antecedents of motivation can be categorised into factors relating to collective organizational life on the one hand and, on the other, the individual exchange relationship.

For Maslach and her colleagues, engagement is a psychological state characterised by energy, involvement and efficacy (2001, p. 416). An associated group of researchers have described it as "a persistent, positive affective-motivational state of fulfillment in employees that is characterized by vigor, dedication, and absorption" (Maslach et al., 2001, p. 417). Saks identifies two types of definition that are more specifically related to the relationship between individuals and organizations, those that stress emotional and intellectual commitment to the organization and those that focus on discretionary effort (2006, p. 601). Compatible with all of these definitions is the idea that this kind of positive psychological orientation towards the organization arises when there is a high degree of compatibility between job roles and the person, an idea frequently known as job-person fit. Drawing on the work of Goffman among others, Kahn draws a distinction between individuals and social roles, and proposes that people's attachment to or detachment from social roles can vary. Playing a role can be experienced positively as an affirmation of the self, or negatively as a denial of the self. For Kahn, engagement is what you get when a job role is experienced positively. It is "the harnessing of organization members' selves to their work roles" (1990, p. 694). He explains the underlying process as follows:

> [P]eople have dimensions of themselves that, given appropriate conditions, they prefer to use and express in the course of role performances. To employ such dimensions is to drive personal energies into physical, cognitive and emotional labors. Such self-employment underlies what researchers have referred to as effort, involvement, flow, mindfulness and intrinsic motivation.
>
> (1990, p. 700)

The most-cited authors in the area seem to concur on two things. First of all, the 'job' aspects of job-person fit have to be defined much more widely than simply in terms of the specific tasks involved. The larger situation or organizational context has also to be taken into account. So as well as the details of the job task, Kahn argues that engagement is contingent on the status, influence and dignity that accompany work roles together with group and intergroup dynamics, management style and process and organizational norms (1990, p. 705). As well as workload and control, Maslach et al point to the importance of intersubjective perceptions of community and fairness and the perceived legitimacy of the organization's values (2001).

The second point of consensus is that the larger situational context of a job involves the returns that the employee can expect from his or her work; his or her individual interest in the work relationship. As Saks puts it, "the amount of cognitive, emotional and physical resources that an individual is prepared to devote in the performance of one's work roles is contingent on the economic and socioemotional resources received from the organization" (2006, p. 603). Kahn suggests that it can be useful to think of the existence of a 'contract' between person and role, while Maslach et al refer to Rousseau's well-known work on the psychological contract, arguing that fit or misfit can be described in terms of "the enduring working relationship people have with their job" (2001, p. 413). The emphasis on resources received from the organization and the metaphor of contract strongly suggest that engagement is fundamentally a question of rational reciprocity. The recognition that participating in organizational life is a legitimate pursuit—that it is the right thing to do—is what leads to engagement.

The literature on engagement amounts to a useful confirmation that Fox's intuitions about frames of reference and worker motivation were broadly accurate. However, what neither Fox nor the organizational psychologists manage to do is to connect the different possibilities for interpreting the work relationship with different types of substantive 'content' for engagement and different attitudes to work tasks themselves. The dimension of engagement vs. lack of engagement conflates perceptions of the possibility of agency with perceptions of the overall legitimacy of the work situation. It does not recognise that the evaluation of the work situation as illegitimate does not point to passivity ('burnout') but to active opposition, which is another form of agency. Passivity—the absence of agency—arises from the inability to make a normative evaluation of the work situation, not from a negative evaluation.

We can refer to the frames of reference as they relate to individual motivation as 'narratives of agency'. Seen from this perspective, frames of reference tell us what kind of action will make sense to the worker, whether cooperation with structural requirements, passive acceptance or active conflict and resistance. A worker who sees an organizational system as negative, as characterised above all by illegitimate forms of coercion, might conduct herself with energy, involvement and efficacy in her attempts to win battles with management. She might be fully absorbed in and passionate about this struggle, experiencing the emotional fulfillment that arises from feeling that one is doing the right thing. However, she will approach her actual job role with the aim of doing the minimum necessary to remain in employment and indeed will see it as her duty to resist and frustrate managerial direction wherever possible.

A worker with a pluralist (exchange) outlook might display 'vigor, dedication and absorption' while participating in good faith collective bargaining and the processes of consultation and discussion that go with it. Unlike the radical worker, however, she will approach the proper performance of her job as something that is *owed* to the organization and, as long as tasks and managerial direction are consistent with substantive and procedural collective agreements, will willingly perform to the agreed standard. On the other hand, she will not feel any moral or political-ethical duty to help her employer pursue his goals beyond her defined contribution, even when such discretionary effort would clearly help to realise those goals. Indeed, she may feel ethically constrained *not* to contribute discretionary effort out of a sense of solidarity with her co-workers on the grounds that it would upset the collectively agreed balance of work for wages.

For workers who believe that employment is best characterised as a relationship of membership in a social group with a single set of collective goals, engagement involves devoting all of their intellectual and emotional energies to their jobs themselves. The better they are able to do their jobs, the better they feel.

Conceptual Models of the Organization and IR Policy Models

For every narrative of agency, there is a corresponding conceptual model of the organization in its market environment that captures the nature of the organization and how it is thematised in arguments about action. Conceptual models allow actors to grasp the organization and the functional characteristics of the organizational system in such a way as to draw conclusions about the likely outcomes of different system inputs and how changes to institutional structures might affect these. The unitarist frames of reference, for example, all conceive the organization as a social group with a single—or unitary—goal. From this perspective, institutional structures that mandate or strongly encourage collective bargaining make little sense because they introduce a confusing and arbitrary division between worker and employer interests that would not otherwise exist. By giving workers an effective right of veto over certain aspects of organizational decision-making and by encouraging them to believe that they can use this leverage to pursue their own interests however they choose to define them, collective industrial relations as seen from this perspective guarantees that organizational performance will be suboptimal. An organization's scope for responding to market signals will be limited by workers' pursuit of non-market values. In terms of IR policy, institutional structures should be geared towards some form of control-oriented people management. As we will see in Chapter 6, there is significant scope for variation within the unitarist 'zone' of the frames of reference and different types of COPM can be radically different from each other, but this essential characteristic is shared by them all.

By contrast, from the perspective of the pluralist frames of reference, the organization is a structure animated by the pursuit of a plurality of interests. Organizational performance is a question of negotiating the compromise that maintains the organization in a viable state while at the same time maximising the satisfaction of the interests of each group to the extent that this is compatible with a similar ambition for all the others. Finding this compromise *demands* a structure of collective interest representation. Refusing to allow it is not only straightforwardly wrong, it is also counter-productive from a wider economic perspective. Collective industrial relations, then, is the only policy model that makes any sense.

The Epistemology of Worker and Organization Behavior

The epistemology of worker and organizational behavior implied in each frame of reference is a question of the extent to which the evaluation of the economic and organizational systems is thought to be positive or negative as opposed to meaningless. The most relevant dimension is agency-structure rather than positive-negative. Positive and negative evaluations imply that workers have or could have agency; that they are reacting to system requirements as if in a communicatively structured situation. The greater the capacity of system actors to choose, the more the economic and organizational systems lose their autonomous and predictable character. They stop becoming *forces* and start becoming *tools* that can be used in whatever way actors choose rather than having their use predetermined. The consequence is that positivist approaches to the collection of evidence and to policy development have less and less purchase the more actors are either actively cooperating with or fighting against system requirements. From the perspective of the frame of reference with the least normative content, low-commitment unitarism, we would expect positivist policy models to make reasonably accurate predictions, for example about the effect of minimum wages or employment protection legislation on wages and employment. The closer we get to the frames with the most normative content, democratic unitarism and revolutionary anti-capitalism, the less likely it is that an external, objectivising perspective on action will be able to tell us anything useful at all about how workers and hence organizations will react to this or that economic development or policy change.

Conclusions: The Theoretical Significance of the Frames of Reference

Frames of reference are a solution to the circularity that arises when actors try to assess what is the right thing to do in response to the incentives, obligations and constraints arising from market and organizational systems. As we saw in Chapter 4, there are contexts of action in which rules and directives do not recognise objective or normative relationships that exist already, but are self-referential in the sense that they are intended to create some desirable situation and are justified on the basis of the assumption that that act of creation will be successful. From the perspective of the individual actor, the normative rightness of any action in response to the requirements of the system depends on the ultimate outcome of the actions of all those responding to these same requirements. Since that outcome will change depending on how all the actors involved respond, it is only by making a series of assumptions about what other people will do that the rationality of compliance can be evaluated. This involves what Habermas argues is a "counterintuitive analysis from the standpoint of an observer who objectivates the lifeworld" (1987, p. 232). This in turn involves the creation of a kind of baseline ontological truth about social structures and institutions to set alongside and compare with the judicial truth implied in the structural requirements of the system. The ontological truth about systems can be grasped as a series of social scientific 'laws' that allow us to relate inputs (action) to outcomes on the basis of theoretical propositions about the validity of the two generalised values: utility and the effective realisation of collective goals.

I have argued that Habermas underestimates the extent to which beliefs about the nature and characteristics of systems—frames of reference—can become part of the shared background knowledge drawn on by actors. At the same time, he is correct to say that this kind of constructed knowledge about systems ultimately lacks an anchoring in objective or normative knowledge whose validity can be established independently of any reference to means-end calculations. Although this does not mean that it has no impact on action, as Habermas sometimes implies, it does mean that it is a contingent form of knowledge that is vulnerable to *re*-construction in the reflexive circle of social scientific explanation, policy-making, institution-building and collective self-understanding. What we believe about the characteristics of economic and organizational systems implies a certain logic of action, which, on the aggregate level, results in those economic and organizational systems. The logic of action will change depending on what we think those characteristics are. This in turn has an impact on the outcomes of action in the sense of the actual empirical characteristics of systems.

This is in line with the insight shared by authors as diverse as Parsons, Dunlop and Bourdieu that there is an intersubjective ideological or normative foundation to what appear to be the most individualistic of calculations. It is remarkable how closely Bourdieu's and Parsons's views on the subject are.

> Everything economic science posits as given, that is, the range of dispositions of the economic agent which ground the illusion of the ahistorical universality of the categories and concepts employed by that science, is, in fact, the paradoxical product of a long collective history, endlessly reproduced in individual histories, which can be fully accounted for only by historical analysis: it is because history has inscribed these concomitantly in social and cognitive structures, practical patterns of thinking, perception and action, that it has conferred the appearance of

natural, universal self-evidence on the institutions economics claims to theorize ahistorically.

(Bourdieu, 2005, p. 5)

Parsons's commentary is less elaborate, but his point is precisely the same:

'economic motivation' is not a category of motivation on the deeper level at all, but is rather a point at which many different motives may be brought to bear on a certain type of situation. Its remarkable constancy and generality is not the result of a corresponding uniformity in 'human nature' such as egoism or hedonism, but of certain features of the structure of social systems of action which, however, are not entirely constant but subject to institutional variation.

(Parsons, cited in Joas and Knöbl, 2009, p. 37)

Thinking of the intersubjective components of action as frames of reference made up of normative evaluations of systems allows to make a number of propositions that contribute the essentials of our new theory of industrial relations.

The first proposition we can make is that the addition of the idea of frames of reference allows us to categorise action situations according to the most fundamental beliefs of the actors. We can go beyond the specifics of each situation to identify certain basic characteristics shared across sectoral and national contexts and across time. Those beliefs indicate how actors will respond to the forces of the market and the more immediate structures of the organizational situation.

The second proposition is that one possible response to 'the structures of the situation' is exactly the kind of passivity assumed by comprehensive systems theories like Luhmann's. Habermas uses Searle and Austin's language philosophy to brilliant effect, showing how the ontological truth of the matter in systemic action contexts cannot be definitively established and that, as a consequence, no judgement can be made about whether the sanctions and incentives that construct the judicial truth are legitimate or illegitimate. Actors can quite literally be unable to say whether they are the rational authors of the law. If actors lack the cognitive resources to make a normative judgement, active resistance is as illogical as active cooperation. All that is left is passive, instrumental compliance. This adds a third possibility to the traditional dichotomy of conflict and cooperation.

The third proposition is that what Cox calls 'ideological analysis', i.e. the attempt to understand the frames of reference with which actors are working, allows us to make some predictions about the likely accuracy of positivist systems models. If actors respond passively to incentives and sanctions, for example, rather than either resisting the coordinated activity they are designed to prompt or responding with the cooperation born of a recognition of its legitimacy, this increases the chance that systems models will give an empirically realistic picture of the likely outcomes of policy measures or managerial plans.

The fourth proposition is simply that normative choice is possible in economic and organizational systems. I have argued that by drawing on evidence about the fairness of markets and the effectiveness of organizational action from beyond the immediate context of action and the very limited, formalised information it supplies, actors are able to make a global judgement about the normative status of system requirements. This judgement allows them to adjust their response to system requirements in a way that preserves or restores fairness and efficacy in those cases where the evidence suggests that errors or injustice elsewhere in the system are being transmitted via systemic signals.

Notes

1 More than 20% of voters in the first round of the 2017 French presidential elections voted for radical anti-capitalist parties.
2 A more detailed version of the argument in this section is presented in Cradden (2005), chapter 5.

6   A New Theory of Industrial Relations

In this chapter, I want to pull together the threads of the argument made in Chapters 3, 4 and 5 to finally propose the new theory of industrial relations that is the point of this work. In the first part of the chapter, I will outline the basic elements of the theory, while in the second I will provide a sketch of each of the nine possible frames of reference it implies.

NTIR: An Overview

The new theory of industrial relations (NTIR) is a critical theory of the governance of work under capitalism. 'The governance of work' refers to the structures of incentives and sanctions, authority, accountability and direct and representative participation within and beyond the workplace by which decisions about the content, conditions and remuneration of work are made, applied, challenged and revised.

My aim with NTIR is not only to explain existing patterns of industrial relations but also to show what needs to change to make work relationships consensual. A consensual system of industrial relations would be one in which organizations are under the collective control of their members, both those who contribute capital and those who contribute labour. Work will be consensual when the governance of work is substantively legitimate. The analytic purpose of NTIR is therefore to specify the different possible conditions under which this will be the case.

I deliberately avoid using the terms 'employer', 'employee' and 'manager', instead talking in terms of organizations, actors or workers, and office-holders. This is because the idea of the necessity of subordination is indissociable from the conventional vocabulary of industrial relations. I refer to 'the work relationship' rather than 'the employment relationship' because NTIR is intended to be applicable to any relationship in which a worker is dependent on an organization for their work and is obliged to accept direction from it. It therefore includes all forms of informal and non-standard employment, as well as triangular employment situations in which production is distributed across a chain or network of organizations rather than taking place within a single organization. The only situation not covered by the framework is genuine self-employment, in which an individual has all the competences of an organization in terms of the determination of the work process and is responsible only for the product or service produced.

The work relationship is defined by an obligation to accept direction. However, this does not in itself imply domination but merely a situation in which the individual worker takes on a role that is one part of a coordinated system of roles designed to achieve certain collective goals. The worker is subject to the collective authority of the organization in a way that is analogous to the citizen being subject to the legal authority of the state. The obligation to accept direction implies nothing about how collective goals are set or work processes designed. Just as citizens may or may not be entitled to participate in the governance of the state, workers may or may not be entitled to participate in the governance of work. Just as democracy can take many different forms, so worker participation in the governance of work can take many different forms.

In line with both the IR theoretical tradition and contemporary social theory, NTIR takes structure and agency equally seriously. I follow Cox in explaining the different aspects and outcomes of the governance of work in terms of the interaction between:

- objective structural forces (the substantive requirements and benefits of the work relationship arising from the demands of market economy and of the organization);
- the intersubjective cognitive and normative orientations to organizations and the work relationship that actors bring to work ('frames of reference'); and
- the legal-institutional form of organizations themselves together with the external administrative and judicial processes relevant to work relationships.

Workers will respond to the objective demands of the market and organization cooperatively, passively or conflictually depending not only on the substance of those demands but on how they understand the nature of work and the organization—their frame of reference. However, since the economic and organizational systems are nothing more than complexes of action, worker action in response to system requirements is part of the process that ultimately gives rise to system requirements. The demands of the system therefore depend on actors' frames of reference. But frames of reference also depend on the demands of the system. If frames of reference are not cognitively adequate in the sense that they give rise to expectations about the objective aspects of the work relationship that are consistently contradicted by the lived experience of work, they will ultimately change. Frames of reference depend on the demands of the system, which depend on frames of reference.

The legal-institutional form of industrial relations stabilises this feedback relationship by privileging one particular frame of reference in the form of an IR policy model and the regulation derived from it. Depending on enforcement practices, this regulation will limit the degree to which system requirements can adapt. IR systems, intended in the non-theoretically-loaded sense of the ensemble of law and practice relating to work relationships in any specific context, are therefore made up of these three components: objective, subjective and institutional. Stability requires that the components are more or less in phase with each other; that system requirements are more or less as expected and that institutions support responses in terms of action that maintain the system more or less as it is. Change and transformation of IR systems comes about as the result of what Cox calls "actual or potential disjunctions among [the objective, subjective and institutional] aspects" (1987, p. 17).

The Economic and Organizational Systems: The Objective Requirements and Benefits of Work

The objective aspects of work are the substantive, unavoidable demands for conformity associated with each work role, and, on the other side of the balance, the material rewards in terms of wages and near-wage terms and conditions. Conformity is intended in Fox's sense of completing work tasks but also performing duties and responsibilities towards the organization, meeting expected standards of behaviour and so forth (see Chapter 3). These requirements are the consequence of external and internal structural forces which correspond to the demands of what Parsons and Habermas call the economic and administrative systems. The economic system is made up of product, labour and financial markets and is external to the organization. In Parsons's scheme, the administrative system encompasses the entire political-bureaucratic and legal apparatus of a society, but we are interested only in those society-wide aspects that have a bearing on organizational action and on the internal systems of organizations. Rather than the administrative system, then, NTIR refers to the organizational system. The forces articulated via the organizational system are partially external in the sense that they include national law and other forms of regulation and policy having their origins beyond the organization. However, their immediate presentation is as the *enforceable* demands on actors arising within the organization, i.e. those with which actors have to comply to avoid facing sanctions.

According to Parsons, where action falls fully under the economic system, actors' choices are 'steered' or directed by money. Actors are utility maximising and will always choose the most *profitable* available offer. Where action falls under the organizational system, choices are steered by power. Actors "hold in abeyance [their] own critical faculties for choosing between alternatives and use the formal criterion of the receipt of a command or signal as [their] basis for choice" (Simon, 2013, p. 179). Actors will comply when an office-holder is able to establish their *sovereignty* or legal right to command. This demands that they have already accepted as a generally valid proposition the implied claim that the decision-making structures of the organization are such that there is good reason to believe that what organization members are required to do represents an effective means of pursuing legitimate collective goals. 'Power' is understood here in the non-evaluative sense of an actor being subject to enforceable rules, including most importantly those rules that define the scope of the formal authority of office-holders, that is, the right to direct the day-to-day activities of workers. It is not intended to imply either legitimacy or the absence of legitimacy.

Central to NTIR is the proposal that the governance of work falls under both the economic and organizational systems at once. There are two senses in which this is the case. Workers exchange their labour power for money at a rate that is determined by reference to a labour market. This contractual exchange makes the worker a member of the organization and hence subject to its internal rules. The requirements of work in Fox's sense of the structures of the situation arise from the organizational system but gain their imperative quality from the financial incentives and sanctions that organizations have at their disposal via labour market exchange. The second sense in which the economic and organizational systems are jointly implicated in the governance of work is that decisions about the substance of organizational action are taken with reference to the demands that the economic system makes on the organization. The collective goals that are pursued via the organizational system are determined by reference to the market.

Where NTIR parts company with Parsonian systems theory is in proposing that although it is possible that the generalised values of utility and the effective pursuit of collective goals bind a group of actors in the same way at all times and places, they need not do so. Certainly, it is perfectly possible that actors continually monitor the strictly individual balance of the costs and benefits of a particular work relationship in relation to the other possibilities on offer and consistently choose the most profitable available. This goes for office-holders as much as workers. It is also possible that workers simply accept whatever is demanded of them and passively comply with whatever work tasks they are given along with any other requirements of their particular situation—within the limits set by the overarching aim of maintaining a profitable exchange. However, whether and to what extent actors actually do behave in this way depends on their frame of reference.

Frames of Reference

The subjective aspects of work are what actors think and believe they are doing in responding to the demands of the economic and organizational systems, whether this response involves cooperation, bare compliance or active resistance. NTIR follows Fox in calling these ways of thinking or forms of understanding 'frames of reference'.

As we saw in Chapter 3, Fox defines a frame of reference as "a distillation of the observer's background, experience, values and purposes" (1974b, p. 77). Frames of reference arise from:

- the norms, conventions and values held to be valid in actors' immediate social environments, whether within the workplace or outside it;
- beliefs about the state of power relations in industry and the balance of interests in the economy;
- general socio-cultural attitudes arising from normal socialisation processes; and
- lived experience in the workplace.

Frames of reference thus arise from that part of the person that has its roots in socialisation processes and lived experience rather than in (for want of a better term) 'hard-wired' personality structures. They are the result of processes of communication and consensus-formation, whether explicit or implicit, tacit or open. Frames of reference are built on beliefs about the normative character of economic and organizational systems.

Frames of reference represent the understandable subjective meaning of the work relationship, allowing us to explain from the internal perspective of the actor the observable statistical uniformities that, from an external perspective, appear as the economic and organizational systems. They represent both narratives of agency and conceptual models of the organization in its environment. Narratives of agency are normative accounts of the nature of action within the organization; of the scope for actors to make genuine choices within work relationships and the criteria for determining *the right thing to do* in the face of the objective requirements of the work relationship. Conceptual models of the organization allow actors to grasp the kind of social action that is going on; to understand what kind of structure of action the organization represents. These aspects of each frame of reference both imply and are implied by the other.

Frames of reference can be categorised deductively into nine different ideal types on the basis of the degree to which structural forces are understood by actors as susceptible to normative evaluation, and of the 'sign' of that evaluation—either positive or negative—if it is thought to be possible. Where structural forces *are* thought to be susceptible to normative evaluation, actors recognise them as the result of human agency and hence recognise the possibility of making a judgement about the legitimacy of the required action. As we saw in Chapter 4, frames of reference resolve the circularity that arises when we attempt to evaluate the legitimacy of contractual-administrative rules in the same way that we decide whether technical and moral-political rules are just and worthy of support.

Where structural forces are thought to give broadly legitimate direction to action, actors will react with a positive acceptance and ownership of structural requirements (cooperation). Where structurally required action is thought to be illegitimate, the result will be some kind of opposition (conflict). Where no evaluation is thought to be possible, structural forces will be seen as meaningless in Weber's sense of having no social signification. Actors will react passively to structural forces, complying to the extent that it is unavoidable but not engaging in active opposition or resistance.

The normative character of economic forces and that of organizational forces are grasped separately. The combination of the different possibilities for evaluation (positive, negative or meaningless) on the two structural dimensions gives rise to nine ideal-typical frames of reference. This opens up the possibility that conflict on one dimension may coexist with cooperation on another. In some circumstances, this may allow the cooperative resolution of conflict via agreed institutional mechanisms.

Frames of reference are neither true nor false in themselves. Rather, they are global interpretations of the work relationship that in the abstract are equally valid; they all *could be* accurate accounts of social relations at work. Arguments that directly confront different frames of reference conceived as essential and necessary characterisations of work cannot be resolved. However, as Fox argues, it is perfectly possible that frames of reference give rise to expectations about work that are not borne out by the evidence. This means that actors will tend to revert to a pattern of beliefs that makes sense of their actual experience of the work relationship in the context of wider sociocultural beliefs about work. This does not mean that the same set of objective factors cannot be understood in more than one way, but it does limit the range of possibilities. Narratives of agency and conceptual models of the organization must be broadly coherent with the evidence arising both inside and outside the organization. Frames of reference imply that certain outcomes will be the result of particular types of action at work. Persistent exposure to evidence that these outcomes do not arise in practice will put the frame of reference itself in question and is likely to lead to change.

Significant change in frames of reference will also lead to change in the functional characteristics of the economic and organizational systems. Since the responses of actors to system requirements will vary depending on their frames of reference, the complex of action that on the aggregate level comprises the system will have different characteristics—the same inputs will lead to different outputs—according to the frames of reference of the actors involved. Frames of reference and system requirements are therefore connected in a process of mutual feedback. While it is possible for this feedback process to be self-stabilising in the sense that frames of reference prompt responses to system requirements that are coherent with the existing state of the system and serve to reproduce it as it is, the scope for destabilising reactions is significant. These could either come from change in system requirements that demands change in frames of reference, or change in frames of reference that leads to change in system requirements. Destabilisation can also be the result of forces exogenous to the system itself like technological innovation or sociocultural change.

The different frames of reference are not just ways of seeing. Rather, they imply different degrees of autonomy for economic and organizational systems and correspondingly different degrees of agency for the actors within them. This is true not just as a question of how actors understand systemic forces, but as how those forces objectively *are*. The more scope there is thought to be for agency within a frame of reference, the less autonomous systems will be and the more control actors will have in reality over their organizations. NTIR therefore follows Cox in proposing that the 'real or essential structure' of social relationships at work is determined by "objective and subjective factors . . . *in their reciprocal interaction*" (1987, p. 26).

Frames of reference therefore also imply an epistemology of worker and organization behaviour. The actions of workers who react passively to the requirements of the economic and organizational systems will link up into a system of action that is autonomous and beyond control in the way assumed by neoclassical economics and Parsonian or Luhmannian systems theory. Consistent system inputs will lead to consistent outputs. Positivist models and modes of analysis are likely to give rise to more or less accurate predictions of the consequences of different policy measures. Workers who believe they have agency, however, will evidently not react passively, either resisting structural requirements or acting to maintain a system in a normatively positive state. Exactly what action will be taken will depend on the concrete historical circumstances of the work relationship. Comparatively little generalisation will be possible. Interpretative modes of analysis will be required in order to understand the types of behaviour that are likely to arise.

Institutional Structures

NTIR's emphasis on the real structure of IR is in contrast to the traditional focus on the third element in the industrial relations system, the formal legal-institutional structure of organizations and industrial relations. The institutional structure is an attempt to model one particular frame of reference as enforceable law and practice; to constrain the behaviour of actors at work within certain limits and thus to avoid the potential for the drift of work relationships towards a different model because of feedback effects. These relationships are shown graphically in figure 6.1. The objective and subjective aspects of the IR system are in a dynamic relationship of mutual influence, while the institutional structures of IR attempt to stabilise that relationship from the perspective of a particular frame of reference.

There are two aspects to each institutional structure, corresponding to the economic and organizational systems respectively: the establishment of

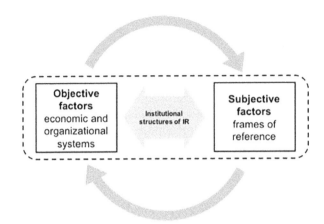

Figure 6.1 The Relationship Between the Objective, Subjective and Institutional
Aspects of the IR System

the exchange value of labour, together with the associated terms and conditions of the employment contract; and the establishment of the rules for the appointment of office-holders in the organization together with the conditions under which they have the right to issue and enforce binding directives. The role of the institutional framework, then, is to specify decision-making rights, which is to say the formal procedural conditions under which the claims of the organization on its members and the claims of members on the organization are legally enforceable.

Just as with political institutions and technical decision-making bodies, IR institutions are intended to be the source of a warranted belief in the overall legitimacy of organizational decision-making. What institutional structures are credible in this respect will depend on the frame of reference. Frames of reference involving the conflict assumption, for example, point to the need for some means of interest conciliation involving representation from both workers and the owners of capital. Frames of reference involving the cooperation assumption demand decision-making procedures that establish a connection between action and legitimate collective goals. Each frame of reference implies an IR policy model, which in turn implies a distinctive complex of formal rules to maintain and stabilise the systems of work relationships that appear appropriate from the perspective of the frame.

Cox argues that the institutional framework does not determine the nature of the IR system, but may nevertheless have a role in legitimising the real structure of work relations. Since the policy models that specify the basic structure of the institutional framework are derived from frames of reference, institutions do tend to reflect the dominant frame of reference in any system. However, as Cox also points out, there may be "a hiatus between the formal institutions and the real structure of relationships" (1987, p. 26). He gives the example of a formal structure based on bipartite interest representation that 'hides' a corporatist relationship in which senior officials on each side collude to determine outcomes based on basically shared goals. What is more, formal institutions may not be adequate to the task they are on the surface intended to accomplish. As we saw in Chapter 2, the ILO/common law policy model is intended to provide a warranted belief that those workers who wish to act collectively can do so, but in practice does no such thing. As Kannankulam and Georgi put it,

> institutions cannot be analysed without analysing the shifting relationships of forces in a society. But in order to analyse relationships of forces, we must also analyse institutions, because the existing configurations of institutions are material condensations of earlier relationships of forces, and thus pre-structure the terrain on which societal conflicts are fought out.
>
> (2014, p. 62)

The Nine Frames of Reference

We have finally arrived at the point where I can describe the nine frames of reference that arise from the interaction of the different possible normative evaluations of the market and organizational systems. Frames of reference are simultaneously normative and cognitive. Each has an action aspect and a structural aspect that both imply and are implied by each other. The action aspect represents a narrative of agency at work and the structural aspect a conceptual model of the employing organization. Each frame of reference has implications for the epistemology of social behaviour and for IR policy. IR policy in turn dictates the design of the institutional structures that should stabilise one particular vision of social relationships at work. For each frame of reference, I provide an outline description which is not intended to be exhaustive but to highlight the most pertinent and distinctive features. The features of the six frames of reference involving non-negative evaluations of the organizational system are detailed systematically in the comparison table (table 6.1, below). The three frames in which the organizational system is negatively evaluated cannot logically give rise to IR policy models as from the perspective of these radical viewpoints the organization is incorrigibly oppressive. No progress is possible without overthrowing the existing system, either the organizational system or both the organizational and economic systems. But it is the organization that is the primary obstacles to progress. The work experience is necessarily dissonant with reality in the sense that the organization itself is thought to be illegitimate. Stabilising such a belief through institutional design makes no sense. For this reason, I only give very brief sketches of the frames of reference in which the organization is negatively evaluated.

Democratic Unitarism

Democratic unitarism is the frame of reference that arises when both the market and organizational systems are given a positive normative evaluation. It represents the theoretical outer limit for the positive normative content of paid work and to this extent is barely distinguishable from an informal or voluntary action context. Members of organizations (or other types of production systems) will approach their work with a basically communicative attitude. DU is the logical outcome of the meeting of the principle of democratic worker representation and the recognition that market imperatives do not necessarily embody only the partial interests of capital.

In its ideal incarnation, democratic unitarism is the vision of a kind of organizational nirvana. Every member of the organization recognises that their fulfilment of their work role to the best of their ability is an effective contribution to the realisation of collective goals whose legitimacy they unreservedly accept. More importantly, this is the case *because* every member has an equal role in defining both the action situation and the rational response to it, given the organizational goals to which all members have freely signed up. To the extent that action is coordinated hierarchically via a structure of office-holders, those organization members who take direction from others accept that their taking direction is justified on the basis of its technical validity (for example, demonstrated or externally-validated scientific competence) or its normative validity (for example, the mandate of a legitimate organizational governance structure). In effect, the possibility of being subject to discipline for non-compliance is not a significant contributing factor in worker motivation.

The collective goals of the organization are set in relation to the market environment and the broad direction given by the market is recognised as legitimate. Similarly, wages are set in relation to prevailing labour market levels. Nevertheless, actors are aware that market signals should be treated with reserve. They believe that the market is a useful and generally valid guide to action, but also that it is not perfect; that there may be a gap between the judicial or systemic truth of the empirically determinable market price and the ontological truth of the price that maintains a fair relationship between buyer and seller. From the perspective of democratic unitarism, market signals must be deciphered with a view towards maintaining the normative integrity of the system as well as the strategic advantage of the organization. For example, even if a supplier was willing to accept it, a democratic unitarist organization would not agree a contract with a supplier in which the supplier's margins were so thin that it could not pay a living wage to its workers. Neither could a democratic unitarist organization adopt strategic objectives that contradicted the fundamental values and beliefs of its members. Given that the market and organizational systems are recognised as tools for the maintenance of *legitimate* relationships, and since no actor or group of actors can claim a monopoly on the definition of legitimacy, all decision-making processes are ultimately subject to democratic control.

The policy model arising from democratic unitarism is, of course, industrial democracy. No specific institutional structure of democracy is indicated and a wide array of different approaches could be acceptable. The three critical elements are that office-holders within the organization are accountable to its (democratic) governing structure, that this structure gives representation to both workers and shareholders by some mutually acceptable formula and that organizational discipline is not in the hands of office-holders but is applied via a system of peer tribunals. These three institutional features ensure that power is exercised in the interests of the organization as a whole rather than that of the owners of capital or a permanent hierarchy of office-holders. It guarantees the possibility of feedback processes that allow responses to structural imperatives to be adjusted on the basis of an assessment of their outcomes. The strong emphasis on organizational democracy puts a question mark over the need for independent worker organization. Rights to representation are built into the most basic institutional structures of the organization and it is difficult to see what logical purpose another layer of democratic organization of non-office-holding workers within the organization would have. On the other hand, and all idealism aside, DU opens up a whole new range of possibilities for organizational dysfunction along the lines of the 'tyranny of the majority' that could put the rights and well-being of actors at risk. It may be that independent organizations of workers, particularly if they existed beyond business organizations, could have a role to play in providing protection. They might also act as repositories of information and expertise about different methods and structures of democratic organization.

Although establishing democratic unitarism would in most jurisdictions require significant changes to company law as well as employment law, there are a number of existing organizational models that approach it in principle. On the one hand, small ethically-oriented businesses, social enterprises of various kinds, early stage 'start-ups' run by groups of partners and family-run businesses with deep ties to their communities have some of the characteristics of DU in the sense that they do not seek to 'do business' for its own sake and are self-consciously oriented towards maintaining respect for certain values and principles. On the other, businesses with unconventional governance structures like the Mondragon cooperatives in Spain or the Brazilian company Semco Partners show how workable institutional forms of industrial democracy can be operated even in large businesses.

The high level of normative content and communicatively structured interaction that is the defining characteristic of DU mean that positivist modes of analysis are likely to be of little value in understanding or predicting the actions of organizations. The aims and values of organizational actors are likely to vary considerably between different historical and sociocultural contexts. The likelihood that standard organizational techniques and strategies will be adopted is low. In short, it is very hard to say what businesses of this kind might end up doing. Research aiming to shed light on worker and organization behaviour would have to be largely qualitative and hermeneutic.

High-Commitment Unitarism

High-commitment unitarism is the frame of reference in which a positive evaluation of the organizational system coexists with the view that the economic system is meaningless. This maps onto the various paradigms of work organization that stress the personal engagement of workers in a technically-conceived 'high road' response to market imperatives: the high-performance workplace or work system; the high wage, high skills equilibrium; 'soft' strategic human resource management and so forth.

Work relationships within the HCU organization, including authority relationships, are fully legitimate (and hence positively evaluated) but legitimacy is grounded on technique rather than democracy. This is because the organization derives its goals from a *meaningless* market; a market which can and must be treated as an objective phenomenon with functional characteristics that can be known via positivist methods. These methods are in turn properly understood only by qualified professional experts. A permanent technical hierarchy is therefore required to ensure that decision-making remains in line with market demands. It may be that these imperatives are difficult for workers to accept.

A metaphor for this frame of reference might be the team of medical professionals and technicians working together to treat patients under the leadership of the most qualified and experienced professional. Hierarchy within the team is permanent and superiors are not directly accountable to subordinates. The consequent relationships of subordination are nonetheless legitimate because that hierarchy is strictly technical, based on certified expertise and experience. The reason why the team leader occupies that position of authority is that in the end they are the best placed to judge the optimal strategies for achieving collective goals.

From the HCU perspective, appropriate techniques of management are centred on communication and education. The coordination of action within the organization demands that workers accept the technical basis of authority and the claim that organizational action is only ever that which is demanded by the market. Office-holders do not make free, self-interested or political choices, but *technical* choices. However, making technically optimal choices also means gathering all the relevant information and taking account of the opinions of subordinate actors who have relevant experience and expertise. As extensive and open a consultation with other actors in the organization as is possible in the circumstances of any decision is clearly appropriate. In short, the HCU frame of reference demands that organizations do what needs to be done to ensure the achievement of market objectives, but takes very seriously the need to ensure that all actors understand and accept the technical and hence normatively neutral basis of decision-making.

The HCU policy model could be called 'soft control-oriented people management'. The only institutional structures that soft COPM really demands are permanent organizational hierarchy and the associated disciplinary structures. It may be that it is thought necessary to legislate to encourage or in some cases even to require individual and collective consultation structures, but these will not have decision-making powers. Beyond this, policy is about creating a situation in which the voices of professional managers are amplified and reinforced and the technocratic message of flexibility in the face of the demands of the market is widely accepted. Policies like the promotion of business education will be seen as appropriate. Policy development, particularly on worker protection measures, will be subject to strict 'business case' testing. If trade unions and individual and collective worker rights to freedom of association and collective bargaining did not already exist, it is difficult to see how they could be justified from the HCU perspective. Given that these rights do exist, HCU tends to see unionisation and collective bargaining as an institutional means of last resort for dealing with rare cases of organizational bad behaviour and/or as a vehicle for the articulation of employee voice in consultative processes. Measures to actively promote or encourage collective industrial relations are carefully avoided.

Where HCU is the dominant frame of reference, the epistemology of worker and organization behaviour demands orthodox economic analysis to capture the market pressures to which businesses are obliged to react. On the other hand, the HCU perspective suggests that we should expect a wide range of variation in how workers and businesses react to these pressures. One aspect of this involves the strategic choices of organizations and how these translate into approaches to coordination in the workplace, while the other is about the extent to which workers are persuaded that these choices represent effective market action. These questions are best approached from a qualitative perspective as action relies on socioculturally influenced perceptions of the work situation. Cognitive psychology, with its emphasis on perception, problem-solving and creativity, is also likely to be seen as an appropriate technique. Quantitative studies seeking causal relationships between management interventions, worker cognition and attitudes, and business performance outcomes would logically follow as a synthesis of the different sources of knowledge.

Bureaucratic Unitarism

Bureaucratic unitarism arises from the coincidence of a positively-evaluated economic system and a meaningless organizational system. The conceptual model here is the classical Weberian bureaucracy or the large 'corporatist' business on the Japanese or (historical) IBM/General Motors/General Electric model. The US welfare capitalist model is another example.

The economic imperatives that supply the goals of the organization are not thought of as technically complex and nuanced as they are from the HCU perspective, but as straightforward and unproblematic: efficiency, efficacy, continuous improvement of products, continuous increases in sales. That complying with these imperatives is the right thing to do is self-evident, not only from the perspective of the success of the business organization but from the perspective of the benefit to wider society of the availability of more and better and cheaper goods. The technical complexity and difficulty of organization lies not in reacting to market signals but in the design and continual improvement of an optimal system of work roles.

The task of management is to ensure that roles are carried out to the letter of their specification so as to maintain the integrity of the organizational system. The legitimacy of binding directives is a question of the formal sovereignty of the office-holder issuing the command. Workers accept the efficacy of the organizational system and will have a predisposition not to question appropriately authorised directives. Work relationships are impersonal and to the extent that they have substantive normative content in practice this makes little difference to the functioning of the organization. However, the positive evaluation of the economic system means that the aims of industry are closely associated with the well-being of the community and the nation.[1] The social value of continually improving economic performance lends its positive normative status to the otherwise meaningless 'cog-in-the-machine' work roles from which organizations are constructed.

The design of work roles is a question of administrative science and work-study and the economic system is not a significant point of reference in the day-to-day operation of the business. The maintenance of the system in a normatively positive state is achieved by the technical review of work roles and organizational structures. In contrast to high-commitment unitarism, in which the essential expertise or technical competence of office-holders relates to adapting the organization to the constantly evolving demands of the market, the technique of management in the bureaucratic unitarist frame of reference directly concerns the design of jobs and internal systems in the context of market imperatives that are stable and consistent. Work roles are well defined and structured into a hierarchy of grades. Salaries are attached to grades rather than related to individual performance and the reward for ability and effort is promotion. The principal dimension of variation in the design of roles and systems is the technology of the industry in question.

The IR policy model arising from the BU frame of reference is what we can call 'personnel administration'. Since work roles are unlikely to be intrinsically rewarding or meaningful, the maintenance of the organization in a viable state demands a focus on the extrinsic rewards of work. Organizations demand consistency, reliability and loyalty from their workers, to which the most important institutional counterpoints are good wages, security of employment and, as the first wave institutionalists argued, a degree of constitutionalisation of the work relationship in the form of the procedural justice of disciplinary and grievance mechanisms. Like the other unitarist frames of reference, there is nothing in the logic of the BU perspective that demands independent worker representation, but it may be recognised as having some technical value as a means of maintaining wages at an appropriate level, institutionalising routine conflict and so forth. Where it is accepted by management, its role is likely to be economistic, limited to those issues closest to pay setting and the effort bargain. Significant worker or union involvement in decision-making about organizational structures and job roles is not compatible with the strictly technical conception of these processes. The *duty* to bargain is not coherent with this frame of reference.

From within the BU frame of reference, the most appropriate sources of knowledge about worker and organization behaviour are behavioural psychology and production design and engineering. The maintenance of the organizational system in a stable functional state is not a normative question. Rather, it depends on the design of production systems, job tasks and coordination mechanisms that minimise the room for discretion via the close specification of roles and rational incentives. Organizations will function as intended to the extent that workers are able to perform their roles as designed. This puts a focus on problems such as monotony, fatigue and poor job-person fit as well as technical coordination issues like production line balancing. Research will be focused on issues like the impact of the use of psychometric testing prior to worker selection or attempting to relate particular types of organization structures to types of production technology.

Low Commitment Unitarism

Low commitment unitarism is the frame of reference from within which the work relationship has the minimum possible substantive normative content. Both the economic and organizational systems are seen as meaningless and only structural incentives, obligations and constraints have any consistent effect on worker behaviour. LCU maps onto the kind of approaches to management and employee relations that have been called 'hard' human resource management[2] or, as Sisson (1993) memorably put it, 'bleak house' industrial relations.

From within the LCU perspective, the organization and the market appear to actors as structures that are as concrete and as independent of human control as physical reality. The *imperative* nature of structural requirements is in sharp focus. The dominant feature of LCU is that managers have control and workers either passively comply with instructions and accept whatever wages are on offer or leave the organization. Actors do not recognise the possibility of making any kind of normative evaluation of structural demands or see it as a pointless exercise that will have no impact on the system.

The management of the organization is about technique and nothing more. The appropriate technique is in turn a question of finding adequate responses to system imperatives. Unlike HCU, it is not the case that a range of different types of work relationship are found within organizations that are internally legitimated on the basis of technique. Rather, the economic system penetrates into the interior of the organization, creating demands for the structuring of relationships via incentives and sanctions that cut through the social relations that might otherwise exist. Communicatively structured interaction is entirely excluded.

The LCU IR policy model, which we can call 'hard' COPM, is not so much a model as the absence of a model. What matters is maximising the ability of managers to control what happens within the business and to put in place whatever plans, strategies and modes of organization are thought to be appropriate in the current market circumstances. 'At will' employment is likely to be the default position, and remedies for breaches of contract by organizations are likely to be purely financial. Independent worker organization has no place whatsoever in this scheme. Although governments may be obliged because of international legal obligations to write respect for freedom of association and collective bargaining rights into the law, enforcement efforts will be superficial and formalistic. Resisting unionisation will be seen as normal and defensible organization behaviour and a blind eye will be turned to violations where possible. The legitimacy of trade union action will be publicly questioned on the grounds that it slows economic development and industrial conflict will be treated as a public order issue.

In terms of the epistemology of organization and workplace behaviour, orthodox labour market economics and the quantitative analysis of the impact of policy and strategy on competitiveness will be preferred and will be accurate to the extent that the LCU frame of reference is dominant.

Integrative Pluralism

Integrative pluralism is the frame of reference in which a negative evaluation of the economic system coexists with a positive evaluation of the organizational system. This perspective has been captured by Walton and McKersie as 'integrative bargaining' (1965), in the UK as 'good industrial relations' (TUC, 1971) and, more recently, 'social partnership' (NESF, 1997).

This perspective is based on the belief that the requirements of the economic system are negative in the sense that they represent a guide to the interests of the owners of capital only. Meeting these requirements is not a shared interest and they cannot be taken as neutral or in some sense technically required. As long as certain broad parameters of financial viability are respected, the governance of the organization is a matter of 'human arrangement'. The positive normative status of the organizational system arises not from shared substantive goals, but from labour and capital's recognition of their mutual dependence and their willingness to work together for their mutual benefit. The normative content of the work relationship is concerned with respecting commitments that have been freely entered into. Each participant in the work relationship *owes* the other the fulfilment of their side of the bargain in a broad and flexible sense and accepts that it is in their interest to ensure that their partner gets what they need from the relationship.

The directives of office-holders will be seen as legitimate to the extent that they remain within the pre-established parameters of the work relationship. Workers recognise the 'residual control rights' exercised on behalf of the organization by office-holders (managers). Nevertheless, they will not see it as their duty or responsibility to contribute to the organization beyond an agreed level. The lynchpin of the legitimacy of the organizational system is the substantive reality of this agreement. This is why collective rather than individual negotiation and agreement of the work relationship is appropriate in the vast majority of cases. The power imbalance between the individual worker and the organization is such that for all except the most exceptional workers there is little or no possibility that a negotiation could be genuine. At the same time, the process of bargaining is not conceived merely as an exercise in the mutual application of power. Rather, negotiators will be willing to attempt to understand the perspective of the other in order to be sure that the effort and engagement of the workers is used to its best advantage, and that financial and non-financial reward adequately reflects workers' contribution and the overall rewards of doing business. The collective work relationship is seen as a positive- rather than a zero-sum game. This in turn points to the appropriateness of participating in consultative structures like works councils alongside and in conjunction with bargaining structures.

The IP policy model, integrative collective IR, *demands* the independent collective representation of workers and the negotiation of the parameters of the work relationship. Collective industrial relations is not simply a choice that might reasonably be made by workers and organizations but an institution that is necessary to ensure that work relationships are genuinely agreed by the parties. In the terms I used in Chapter 2, the logic of the frame demands a strong institutionalisation of the conflict assumption. The IP model also implies that there should be institutional mechanisms to deal both with interests and rights disputes, that is, disagreement about the definition and redefinition of the limits of worker effort and engagement and the associated level of material reward (interests) and disagreement about whether some organizational or worker claim for conformity falls within the established limits or not (rights). The nature of these mechanisms should reflect not a legalistic logic, but a logic of good faith and willingness to compromise. Conciliation and voluntary arbitration are the models that fit best. Measures to encourage or require joint consultation or works councils are also coherent with the model, as long as there is a clear delimitation between issues that are subject to joint decision and those that are not.

The epistemology of workplace behaviour has a significant social-historical component because of the potential for the forms and goals of collective worker organization to vary. At the same time, the collective employment relationship is still a market relationship, the nature of which is heavily influenced by calculations of utility. Economic models can be useful, then, but exactly what the interaction between the potentially competing motivations of politics and culture and money will be is in the end an empirical question. The methods and techniques of institutional labour market economics (Kaufman, 2007, 2010) are the best available approach to developing knowledge in the area.

Adversarial Pluralism

Adversarial pluralism is the frame of reference arising as a consequence of the conjunction of a negative evaluation of the economic system and an organizational system perceived as meaningless. This version of pluralist industrial relations is realistic where the integrative version is idealistic and cynical where the other is optimistic. The bargains on which organizational life is built have no intrinsic value, simply serving the functional needs of a system in which two groups of economic actors compete for resources on the basis of their capacity to coerce each other. The needs of an economic system as carried by capital and its agents in management must be in equilibrium with the needs of the social system as carried by the trade unions. This vision of industrial relations is best captured in US style business unionism and the liberal pluralist models of the 1950s in which the avoidance of normative engagement on either side was deemed a critical advantage of the model.

As with the other frames in which the organizational system is viewed as meaningless, AP points to the importance of technique, but in this case the techniques of negotiation and collective bargaining. The substance of agreements is secondary to 'the art of the possible'. The balance of power is a concrete reality determined by factors largely beyond the control of the two groups, but taking the maximum advantage—or minimising the damage—of the particular configuration of forces at any given moment is a question of how well each side plays the hand it is dealt.

Relationships within organizations are a procedural game played with the aim of minimising the resources conceded to the other side while avoiding battles that cannot be won. This translates into minimal compliance with rules and close surveillance of the delivery of commitments made by the other side. There is nothing legitimate about rules or directives, merely the consequences attached to compliance or non-compliance. Industrial action is banalised and almost routine.

The IR policy model, distributive collective IR, is concerned above all with the institutionalisation and proceduralisation of conflict. Like integrative pluralism, adversarial pluralism demands the collective representation of workers but less to ensure fairness than to avoid anarchy. It recognises that there is no rational reason why workers would agree simply to fall in line with the demands of capital and that the only means to combine material reproduction with order is to ensure: (a) that there is the maximum possible clarity about what the exchange of work for money will involve; and (b) that the inevitable conflict about the terms of that exchange (interests disputes) and about whether those terms are being respected (rights disputes) is channelled and managed in such a way as to minimise economic and social disruption.

The epistemology of organization and worker behaviour in the adversarial pluralist context is largely undeveloped. In principle, what ought to be here is 'Dunlop but better'. This is best thought of as a kind of systematisation of the same basic approach applied in integrative pluralist contexts. IR systems models make sense in the AP context because they represent attempts to model the interaction of largely autonomous forces, and to connect the concrete reality of the balance of power to its institutional manifestation as the web of rules governing work. Rather than an institutionalist approach in which economic forces encounter an historically contingent set of normative practices, the IR systems approach conceptualises the capacities of organised labour on a much-reduced set of dimensions and attempts to predict outcomes on the basis of theoretical propositions about the interaction between forces—or at least, it would do if there had been any serious attempts to develop Dunlop's sketchy picture into a workable theory.

Anarcho-Capitalism

The interaction of a positive conception of the market and a negative conception of the organization is (something like) anarcho-capitalism, as proposed in slightly different versions by Murray Rothbard (1970, 2009) and David D. Friedman (1973). Sometimes also known as market anarchism, this frame of reference sees the firm and the state regulation that makes it possible as fundamentally and incorrigibly illegitimate. On the other hand, the market is welcomed as the only potential source of genuine agreement among truly free individuals. Anarcho-capitalists believe that the only institutional structure required is the guarantee of contractual rights arising from voluntary exchange relationships. As opposed to the more usual collectivist forms of anarchism that emphasise the nefarious nature of private property, anarcho-capitalism is premised on individual property rights.

Anarcho-Syndicalism/Workers' Control

The interaction of a negative view of the organization with the belief that the economy is meaningless is the most difficult of the frames of reference to characterise. The state and the hierarchical structures of the firm are instruments of oppression, but at the same time material reproduction demands a certain level of technical organization. As the anarchist activist and scholar Rudolf Rocker put it, the labour movement has a double purpose:

> 1. As the fighting organization of the workers against the employers to enforce the demands of the workers for the safeguarding and raising of their standard of living; 2. as the school for the intellectual training of the workers to make them acquainted with the technical management of production and economic life in general, so that when a revolutionary situation arises they will be capable of taking the socio-economic organism into their own hands and remaking it according to Socialist principles.
>
> (2004, p. 96)

The reason why the anarcho-syndicalist model does not seem to fit in this box is that anarchists would not normally propose systems of exchange and distribution based on markets. However, the problem of oppression they diagnose is almost certainly premised on the belief that the authority structures of the organization are designed to lock in the control of the owners of the means of production. They are unlikely to have considered the possibility that if we do not make this assumption there is no reason to believe that the economic system will necessarily be oppressive. If we allow this assumption, then we can characterise the ASWC frame of reference as a rejection of any kind of authority relationship, no matter how benign or accountable, on the basis of a belief in the capacity of autonomous, leaderless groups of workers to take collective charge of production. What is rejected in this frame of reference are both contractually and bureaucratically structured work relationships, not the idea of market exchange between collectives.

Revolutionary Anti-Capitalism

The final frame of reference involves the combination of negative evaluations of both the economic and organizational systems. This is revolutionary anti-capitalism, from the perspective of which there is nothing legitimate in the market economy, business organizations or the political-administrative structures that support them. The only possible solution is to dismantle the existing system and to replace it with some kind of planned economy. In the meantime, all workers can do is to organise themselves into revolutionary trade unions and work to disrupt and undermine capitalism wherever possible.

Table 6.1 The Characteristics of the Stable Frames of Reference

	Democratic unitarism	High commitment unitarism	Integrative pluralism	Bureaucratic unitarism	Low commitment unitarism	Adversarial pluralism
Conceptual model of the organization	The organization is a *self-governing community* of actors working together for their own collective benefit and that of the wider community. Their aim is to produce a good quality product or service and to sell it at a fair price. Action is coordinated on the basis of a substantive consensus among all organization members and/or via legitimate rules and binding directives issued by accountable office-holders.	The organization is a *technically-led community* of actors working together for their own collective benefit. Their aim is to respond to market opportunities in the most effective possible way. Action is coordinated on the basis of technically-legitimated rules and binding directives issued by appropriately qualified office-holders.	The organization is a *bargained community* made up of two mutually dependent groups of actors (capital and labour) that have freely agreed to work together with a view to pursuing their separate aims. Action is coordinated on the basis of agreed rules and binding directives issued by office-holders that remain with an agreed scope of 'residual control rights'.	The organization is a *technical-administrative action system* that fulfils a vital material reproduction function on behalf of society. Action is coordinated principally via the supervision of workers' fulfilment of fixed job roles designed to fit together into a production system.	The organization is an *economic action system* made up of individual actors responding to market incentives. Action is coordinated by a combination of labour market price signals and performance demands arising from within the organization.	The organization is a *bargained action system* that represents an arena for the strategic pursuit of group interests. Action is coordinated on the basis of rules and binding directives that embody a contingent and changing equilibrium between the economic power of capital and the social power of labour.

(Continued)

Table 6.1 Continued

	Democratic unitarism	High commitment unitarism	Integrative pluralism	Bureaucratic unitarism	Low commitment unitarism	Adversarial pluralism
Narrative of agency	Agency is exercised via participation in the definition and realisation of common goals. Since the design of work roles is consensual, there is unlikely to be any gap between work roles and work capacities. Discretionary effort is not a concept that makes sense.	Agency is exercised via respecting technically sound direction and leadership and participating whole-heartedly in any associated consultative processes. Worker discretionary effort in favour of the organization is appropriate where possible.	Agency is exercised via participation in the definition of group aims and in integrative bargaining processes as well as in ensuring that the overall exchange between the parties remains fair. Worker discretionary effort in favour of the organization is a betrayal of other workers.	Agency is exercised collectively via the social choice of achieving material reproduction using industrially and administratively effective organisational structures and systems. Within the organization, compliance *is* agency. Discretionary effort may upset the balance of the organizational system and is contraindicated.	Agency is not a concept that makes a great deal of sense. All the worker can do is respond to incentives, obligations and constraints.	Agency is exercised via participation in collective action aimed at establishing the parameters of the balance of power and in close surveillance of respect for the letter of collective contracts. The question of discretionary effort does not arise.
IR Policy model	Industrial democracy	Soft COPM	Integrative collective IR including collective consultation/works councils	Personnel administration	Hard COPM	Distributive (limited scope) collective IR

Worker discipline	Office-holders do not have a unilateral right to impose disciplinary measures on those to whom their authority extends. Rather, discipline is imposed on behalf of the organization by peer tribunals operating according to the principles of natural justice.	Discipline follows a 'coaching' or performance management logic, but the evaluation of performance is ultimately under the unilateral control of management.	Discipline is subject to agreed procedures in which workers are represented by their union. Trade unions accept the need for disciplinary measures in principle but unacceptable outcomes may ultimately be a cause of industrial action.	Disciplinary measures can be taken if appropriate procedure has been followed.	Disciplinary measures are taken on the unilateral decision of managers.	Managerial capacity to discipline workers depends on the balance of power. Unions will resist the imposition of disciplinary measures regardless of the substance of alleged infractions.
Logic of distribution of rewards between capital and labour	The division of returns between labour and capital is made on the basis of whatever criteria are agreed by the members of the organization.	The appropriate level of return on capital is determined by reference to financial markets. Wages are set by reference to the labour market but with the proviso that labour costs represent an 'investment in people' that may have organizationally specific returns that also need to be taken into account.	A substantively fair return on capital balanced with a substantively fair return to labour.	Labour costs are determined by technically necessary staffing needs. The return on capital is set by reference to the market within the scope left once labour costs have been met.	The return on capital is determined by the financial market and wage costs by labour market.	Distribution between capital and labour is based on the balance of power, that is, the capacity of the two groups for mutual coercion.

(Continued)

Table 6.1 Continued

	Democratic unitarism	High commitment unitarism	Integrative pluralism	Bureaucratic unitarism	Low commitment unitarism	Adversarial pluralism
Logic of distribution of rewards between different employees	The salaries of different workers are set according to whatever criteria are accepted as fair and reasonable by the members of the organization. The labour market may or may not be used as a reference point.	Individual salaries are based on market rates adjusted in the light of organization specific contributions like performance or specialised knowledge.	Pay relativities between different groups will reflect a compromise between organizational and collective worker priorities.	Workers are paid according to the hierarchical grade or rank of their job.	Salaries are set individually according to the labour market and the recruitment & retention needs of the business.	To the extent that unions are in a position to influence practice, salaries reflect custom & practice and the maintenance of existing relativities. To the extent that organizational priorities are dominant, market-focused needs like recruitment and turnover are most influential.
Epistemology of behaviour	Historical-qualitative analysis	Hermeneutic analysis and/or cognitive psychology combined with quantitative analyses to assess performance impacts	Institutional labour market economics	Administrative science and behavioural psychology	Neoclassical labour market economics	IR systems models

Conclusions: A New Synthesis

The new theory of industrial relations that I have proposed builds on the existing IR theoretical tradition and in particular on its determination to take both structure and agency seriously. As I argued in Chapter 3, what IR has so far failed to do is to develop the intuition that norms are as important as system requirements beyond the institutionalists' recognition that there may be sociocultural reasons why neoclassical labour economics does not work. We can think of the typologies proposed by Dunlop, Fox and Cox as efforts to do that on the basis of empirical observation. The more recent institutional turn represents a reasoned rejection of these older attempts at systematisation but offers little to replace them other than a renewed emphasis on the need for social-historical analysis.

What I have tried to show in this and the previous chapter is that we can arrive at a categorisation of IR contexts that are empirically recognisable and make intuitive sense if we start with the approach proposed by one of the most important social theorists of the 20th century, Jürgen Habermas. The nine frames of reference that NTIR proposes are *derived* from a reading of Habermas's *Theory of Communicative Action* which, while unconventional, remains faithful to his most basic theoretical propositions. At the same time, all of these ways of thinking about IR have been documented before, if not all by specialists in industrial relations. What NTIR allows us to do is to explain the empirically observable variation in ways of conceptualising work and work relationships on the basis of variation along two more fundamental dimensions, the economy and the organization. These dimensions are themselves very familiar to IR scholars.

There are two Habermasian elements in NTIR that represent distinctively new contributions. The first is Habermas's explanation for the apparent instability or lack of solid grounding for IR's explanatory theories and conceptual models. As I explain in Chapter 4, truth and legitimacy cannot be grounded in contexts governed by contractual-administrative rules in the same way that they can when action involves the natural world or moral and political choices. The judicial and ontological truth of the matter cannot be distinguished when what needs to be decided is based on observations of social action made from an external perspective using the 'counterintuitive methods of the social sciences'. The social world has no character other than that which our actions give it, but our actions are significantly determined by assumptions about the character of the social world. This is the circularity of action and action situation that can be stabilised by judiciously designed institutional structures.

The second Habermasian element in NTIR is the idea that neoclassical labour economics and Parsonian system theory *could* be true. NTIR introduces a dimension of passivity—agency in the face of structural demands that corresponds to the appropriateness of positivist as opposed to hermeneutic epistemologies of worker and organization behaviour. While

Habermas presents this as a sharp distinction between what he calls system and lifeworld, I have argued that the tendency to respond with passive compliance to structural imperatives as opposed to subjecting the demands of the market and organization to normative scrutiny and responding accordingly is a question of actors' frames of reference. Positivist analyses will be accurate to the extent that frames of reference validate unthinking compliance with market and organizational imperatives. This also means that adopting a communicative approach to system requirements will change the economic and organizational systems in a way that cannot be predicted but that will represent a reassertion of human autonomy.

Notes

1　This vision is particularly well captured in a short film called 'From Dawn to Sunset' produced for General Motors' Chevrolet division in the mid-1930s (Handy (Jam) Organization, 1937). With dramatic cinematography and portentous commentary, the film gives an account of a day in the life of the business, showing how the life and fortunes of the USA are intertwined with the industries in which thousands of workers 'serve' every day. There is a heavy emphasis on the efficiency of the techniques of organization and planning that give rise to the different job roles that add up to industrial production.
2　For a discussion of the origins and use of the terms 'hard' and 'soft' HRM, see Truss et al. (1997). I use the terms in the same sense in referring to the hard COPM and soft COPM policy models.

7   What Can We Do with NTIR? Implications for Research and Policy

In this final chapter, I want to discuss the implications of my argument for industrial relations research and, more particularly, industrial relations policy—although the two are, of course, very closely linked. In the first part of the chapter I discuss very briefly how the extended frames of reference approach could be tested and, if it proves to be a sufficiently accurate representation of actually existing intersubjective phenomena, used as a framework for the analysis of industrial relations contexts. In the second part, I discuss at a little more length how the critical ambitions of the theory can be realised via the development of IR policy that starts from the reality of existing industrial contexts but is oriented by the overarching goal of achieving democratic unitarism.

Research Implications of NTIR

As we saw in Chapter 3, Cox argues that the first task of any research effort focused on industrial relations must be to 'discern the historical structure of social reality' in which economic and organizational action takes place. This is accomplished by "the attempt to reconstruct the mental frameworks through which individuals and groups perceive their fields of action" (1996, p. 474) while ensuring that those frameworks are 'critically confronted' rather than passively accepted. The derivation of the frames of reference from Habermas's reading of Parsons's systems theory is only the first step towards accomplishing that task. The second is the attempt to find evidence: (a) that the frames of reference exist as operational mental frameworks based on the underlying cognitive and normative dimensions that the theory suggests they ought to have; and (b) that what actors actually do is coherent with the frames of reference from the perspective of which they see the world.

Confirming the Validity of the Extended Frames of Reference Approach

A range of ways this confirmatory research could be carried out come immediately to mind, from qualitative analysis of the transcripts of semi- or unstructured interviews through to self-completed attitude surveys.

However, one method looks especially appropriate. This is the approach usually known as 'Q methodology' (Brown, 1980).

Conventional approaches to attitude and opinion research use factor analysis to find patterns of correlations between variables, usually responses to a range of questions with 'likert scale' answers (strongly agree, agree, neither agree nor disagree and so on). These patterns of correlations are taken to be indicative of underlying, 'latent' psychological traits, dispositions or opinions. So, for example, responses to a series of questions about public policy might fall into two broad groups that could be interpreted as indicative of the innate conservatism or liberalism of subjects. The factor analysis thereby 'discovers' conservatism and liberalism as characteristics of individuals. By contrast, Q methodology inverts the logic of the analysis, identifying patterns of correlations of test *subjects* based on their responses to an exercise in sorting a series of 40–60 statements expressing subjective viewpoints on some issue.

Subjects are asked to sort the statements according to how closely they conform to their own perspective. The ranking is relative rather than absolute. Subjects are not asked whether and to what extent they agree or disagree with each statement, but to group the statements into categories according to how closely they conform with or contradict their own viewpoint. Because each statement is ranked in relation to all the others, each 'Q sort' represents a whole that should not be disaggregated into constituent components. The underlying assumption is that individuals who share a similar subjective 'take' on some aspect of the world will sort the statements in similar ways. As Watts & Stenner put it, "The method employs a by-person factor analysis in order to identify groups of participants who make sense of (and who hence Q 'sort') a pool of items in comparable ways. Nothing more complicated is at issue" (2005, p. 68).

Like other types of factor analysis, Q factor analysis can be exploratory or confirmatory. It can seek to investigate subjectivity without an *a priori* view of what is likely to be found, or it can aim to see if subjects hold theoretically expected patterns of opinions and beliefs (Sæbjørnsen et al., 2016). The difference between the two approaches lies in how the set of statements that subjects are asked to rank is developed. In exploratory analyses, a set of statements covering as wide as possible a range of opinions is drawn from texts, interviews, focus groups and so forth. In confirmatory or theoretically informed analyses, statements are created to embody a specific set of viewpoints based on a theory about the subjective viewpoints that actors hold. For our analysis of frames of reference the second approach would evidently be the more appropriate. Statements expressing viewpoints associated with the different specific frames of reference could be combined with statements expressing opinions about the value status of the economic and organizational systems themselves. A suggested set of statements is set out in appendix 1, together with a longer explanation of how Q methodology research is carried out.

The aim of research of this kind is not to characterise IR systems in terms of some kind of distribution of actors holding this or that frame of reference. In the first instance, the goal is simply to ask whether frames of reference are internally structured in the expected way. If our extended frames of reference approach is correct, then we ought to find that test subjects fall into groups whose Q sorts are coherent with the theory. So, an individual who ranks integrative pluralist statements as being close to her own viewpoint should also rank organization-positive and economy-negative statements highly. If we were consistently to find that this is not the case then this would be reason to question the basic NTIR approach.

On the assumption that we find that Q sorts *are* internally coherent, we can start to ask a series of questions relating frames of reference to structural situations on the one hand, and behaviour on the other. For example, we would expect there to be a reasonable level of consistency between subjects' Q sorts and their structural situation. It would be surprising if the Q sort of a senior executive in an aggressively anti-union business reflected a pluralist frame of reference, for example. Likewise, the responses of a production line worker in a non-unionised developing world garment factory might be expected to show evidence of low-commitment unitarism. This having been said, it is integral to NTIR to expect that dissonance between frames of reference and structural situations can and does occur. This dissonance is precisely that which Cox identified as once of the motors of change and transformation of IR systems. The senior executive might be new to the business and may have brought with her a pluralist outlook. She may be able to influence the actions of her business to be more accommodating to unions. Likewise, the production line worker may have been convinced by workers from other factories that the owners could easily afford a pay rise and that independent worker organization and action could be an effective means to force them to increase wages. This worker will start taking part in organising activities that might ultimately lead to unionisation. This is very likely to involve resisting structural forces like incentives to avoid union activity or sanctions for taking part in it.

What we would not expect to see, by contrast, is a basic lack of coherence between actors' frames of reference and their actions. For example, it makes no sense that a militant revolutionary trade unionist should see the world from the perspective of low-commitment unitarism or that a right-wing politician campaigning to ban strikes should be either type of pluralist. Finding a significant number of cases where this seems to be the case would probably demand a return to the drawing board.

Analysing IR Contexts Using NTIR

If we can establish that the frames of reference do indeed exist as mental constructs and affect action in the expected way, the normal starting point for any new analysis would be the characterisation of an IR context in terms of the frames of reference in use and the relationship between frames of reference, groups of actors and institutional structures. The IR context studied might be anything from a national economy or an entire industrial sector all the way through to an individual organization or workplace. It is only once this analysis is completed that we can move on to address more specific questions about appropriate types of IR policy, the likely outcome of new regulation and so forth. The analysis should also point to the most appropriate epistemological approach to take in analysing worker and organization behaviour.

Characterising an IR context demands that we find answers to questions such as the following:

- What frames of reference are the most prevalent and can we say that there is one which is dominant, shared across all social groups?
- If there is no dominant frame of reference, do differences in perspectives on IR reflect fractures between different social groups based on employment status, sector of employment, wealth, ethnicity, sex, education and so forth, or is the situation characterised by a more or less random fragmentation of subjective perspectives?
- What frame of reference best characterises the existing institutional structure of IR?
- Is the institutional structure of IR internally consistent, that is, to what extent does it constrain behaviour within limits that reflect a single frame of reference?
- Is there a significant 'hiatus' between the institutional structure and the dominant frame of reference (if any)?

I am not well qualified to say how best the first two of these questions could be answered. While Q methodology is an ideal means of verifying that actors are thinking in something like the way that NTIR predicts they will be, it is not a technique well adapted to the study of large numbers of subjects. Its originators would also argue that a sample of Q sorts should not be used as the basis for a probabilistic extrapolation to wider populations. Although I would be very happy to be shown to be wrong, I do not see how it could be possible to say, for example, that x% of the population is working with high-commitment unitarism while y% sees the world from the perspective of adversarial pluralism, or that women are more likely to be integrative pluralists than men. For this reason, I think historical-qualitative approaches such as that used by Cox would be among the most viable means to answer the questions above. A judicious blend of Q methodology studies, institutional analysis and the analysis of the content of arguments made in interviews and focus groups (see Cradden and Baccaro, 2013) ought to give a clear picture of the nature of each IR context. With this in hand, an appropriate epistemological and methodological approach could be chosen to investigate more specific questions.

What kind of research could follow from a characterisation of the IR context remains entirely open. As I see it, there is almost unlimited potential for studies relating different types of IR context and different dimensions of variation to outcome variables like productivity, pay levels, industrial action, poverty, inequality or innovation. The different dimensions of the IR context would lend themselves well to use as a framework for comparative analysis of national and sectoral IR systems, for example if used to structure a qualitative comparative analysis. A fascinating prospect is the comparison of two or more IR contexts, each characterised by a different single dominant frame of reference and a coherent institutional structure. These contexts would by definition all be stable and free of serious conflict, but what would be the difference in financial performance or worker engagement and satisfaction between a context characterised by high commitment unitarism and another where the dominant frame of reference is integrative pluralism? Is there a performance premium attributable to high- over low-commitment unitarism or integrative over adversarial pluralism?

One thing that is very clear, though, is that the logic of NTIR makes a nonsense of research questions framed as if it were possible to isolate a universal causal effect of specific institutional structures or policy measures relevant to the governance of work. Asking what impact collective bargaining has on productivity, for example, makes no sense whatsoever if no distinction is drawn between IR contexts on the basis of the subjective perspectives of the actors involved. There cannot be an 'average' effect of collective bargaining because it is not the same thing in one context as it is in another. The IR context changes the nature of a policy intervention; it cannot be 'controlled for' because it is theoretically relevant. Bargaining or consultative structures or employee involvement schemes *mean* something different to actors in different IR contexts. We cannot say that what is going on in one situation is the same as what is going on in another.

Nevertheless, it does make sense to attempt to isolate an effect of policy measures *within* different categories of IR context. While there are some differences between the UK and Irish IR systems, for example, the two situations are sufficiently similar that it would be surprising if a trade union recognition system like that used in the UK did not have a roughly similar impact in Ireland. The same prediction could not reasonably be made about, say, Myanmar.

Once we recognise that the different elements of IR systems (objective, subjective and institutional) cannot be treated in isolation from each other, we can start to think differently about our research questions. NTIR allows us to make a series of predictions not just about the nature of IR contexts under the different frames of reference, but about the effect of ideological and institutional coherence, opposition and transformation. I discuss these in the next section.

Stability and Change in IR Systems: Conflict, Cooperation and the Gravity of Normlessness

I argued above that one of Dunlop's more important insights, echoed in different ways by a number of other writers, is that there is a difference between anti-system conflict and conflict that is expected and routinised and, as such, does not challenge the basic policy parameters of the IR system. The dominant assumption of mainstream academic IR has been that only the pluralist frames of reference are an adequate basis for a stable IR system because the economic and organizational systems will necessarily give rise to requirements with which it is not in the interests of workers to comply. Avoiding anti-system conflict therefore demands an institutional structure in which some resolution of conflict on a requirement-by-requirement basis is possible. The only substantive question that remains is whether integrative as opposed to adversarial pluralism is a realistic ambition, that is, to what extent pluralist institutions can be compatible with the day-to-day cooperation that both arises from and gives rise to a sense of common ownership and purpose within business organizations. The problem with this approach, of course, is that it has some difficulty explaining the stability of the majority of IR systems in which there is a low level of worker representation.

By contrast, NTIR recognises that any of the six 'non-organization-negative' frames of reference could in principle form the basis of a stable IR system. Drawing on Cox's arguments relating change to 'actual or potential disjunctions' between the different aspects of the system, on Fox's arguments about the need for frames of reference to keep pace with social evolution and on our discussion of the weak institutionalisation of the conflict assumption in the ILO/common law policy model, we can say that the stability of IR systems is maximised when they are characterised by consensus, coherence and cognitive adequacy:

1. There is a *broad consensus* around a single frame of reference across different groups.

2. The institutional structure of IR:
    a) is *internally coherent* in the sense that it consistently reflects the conceptual logic of a single frame of reference;
    b) is *externally coherent* in the sense that it is in line with the intent of the system as articulated in the public narrative around industrial relations policy.

3. The dominant frame of reference represents an account of the objective aspects of work (the structural requirements of the system) that is *cognitively adequate* in the sense that it points to plans and strategies for organizational action that are sufficiently effective from the perspective of material reproduction while remaining in line with sociocultural values and expectations about work relationships.

Where all three conditions are in place, a level of cooperation sufficient to make running business organizations a viable proposition ought to be possible, whether spontaneously in the case of the unitarist frames or on the basis of a bargained agreement in the case of the two variants of pluralism. The greater the degree to which these conditions are *not* in place, the greater the potential for anti-system conflict.

Efforts to reform or transform IR systems can be parsed into those that aim to achieve or improve consensus around a particular frame of reference, those that aim to improve the internal and/or external institutional coherence of an existing system and those that aim transform an industrial relations system in the sense of changing the entire frame of reference around which it is constructed. If transformative change is to take hold, it demands that, regardless of where the impetus for change arises, the other aspects of the IR system be brought into line. For example, ideological change is unlikely to be transformative unless institutional change coherent with that shift is also implemented. NTIR also predicts that certain directions of transformation are likely to be easier than others, depending on the degree to which the substantive normative content of work relationships must increase. There is a tendency for relationships to degrade in the direction of less normative content. We discuss this further below.

Consensus, Fragmentation and Opposition

NTIR predicts that systems characterised by fragmented frames of reference will be prone to frequent but sporadic outbreaks of conflict that are unlikely to have a system-altering effect. There are two possibilities for change in fragmented systems. The first is institutional reform that sends a strong and unambiguous signal that a particular frame of reference is being adopted. The second is the emergence of an opposition movement that is able to articulate a strong, coherent narrative around a particular frame of reference along with demands for institutional reform consistent with it. The mobilisation of a critical mass of opposition to a system demands that enough actors accept a coherent alternative narrative. Whether such a mobilisation is possible depends on exactly the same factors as those that add up to system stability; the alternative vision must be internally coherent, in line with the zeitgeist and able to explain the current failures of the system as well as telling a convincing story about how they can be corrected.

An IR context in which different groups of actors are distinguishable by their different frames of reference but no one group is dominant will give rise to different outcomes than one in which there is a random fragmentation of different perspectives. Where there is variation by group, outcomes will depend on who sees the world from what perspective. This is something canvassed by Fox himself, who proposed that different patterns of IR would arise from the different possible combinations of frames of reference among workers and managers (Fox, 1974a). Depending on the empirical balance of power between groups, institutional structures may end up being internally incoherent, reflecting political compromise rather than a consistent institutionalisation of a single frame of reference. We discuss this possibility further below.

The character of an IR context in which there is a broad consensus around a single frame of reference will depend on which frame of reference it is. For this reason, we cannot say that stability is a characteristic that is desirable in and of itself. An IR system based on a widely shared low commitment unitarist perspective with the associated institutional structure of weak individual and collective worker rights could be viable or even competitive in purely financial terms at the same time as giving rise to low quality jobs and high levels of inequality. In these circumstances, introducing perspectives that challenge the LCU conception of work could well lead to instability and anti-system conflict, but it would be difficult to argue that this is not ultimately a good thing—despite governments in these circumstances having a tendency to react to the propagation of arguments for change as threats to economic development and public order.

Internal Institutional Coherence

Institutional structures are internally incoherent where they simultaneously embed contradictory principles derived from different frames of reference. There are a number of ways that this can happen. Perhaps the most obvious is that institutional structures are not the result of a policy-making process that proceeds smoothly from conception to execution based on a single, consistent set of ideas, but of compromises between competing groups that reflect an empirical balance of power. The ILO policy model is one example of this. As we saw in Chapters 2 and 3, the weak institutionalisation of the conflict assumption is the outcome of the historic political choices of representatives of workers and employers. Voluntarist types of collective IR, in which union organization and recognition take place largely on the initiative of workers themselves, make sense from a workers' organization perspective where the sociocultural context provides strong support for collective worker representation and action. The regulation of worker representation and trade union recognition is a risky business. The less formal regulation of trade union organization and action there is, the lower the chance that workers will have limits put on their empirical capacity to disrupt production to pursue whatever ends seem appropriate. Ensuring that worker representation remains voluntary also maximises the chances that trade unions will remain the sole legitimate voice of labour. The voluntarist model has been tolerated by employers because it preserves the possibility of resisting collective worker representation, no matter how distant a prospect that might have seemed in Europe or North America in the 1950s. Since the global policy turn against collective industrial relations in the 1980s, and now that the ILO's member states include developing economies in which there is little sociocultural knowledge of or support for trade unionism, employer representatives within the ILO have shifted from tolerance to a determined and tenacious insistence on the voluntarist model. The political vigilance of employers' representatives, and of the officials of the Bureau for Employers' Activities within the ILO secretariat, has been such that in its technical assistance programmes, the ILO can now only recommend to its constituents that they adopt the weakest possible formal institutionalisation of the conflict assumption, even though in the absence of strong social and political support for collective industrial relations, laws on freedom of association and union recognition are only one step away from useless (Cradden and Graz, 2015). The ILO cannot openly recommend a strong institutionalisation of the conflict assumption, even though in most developing economies the argument in favour of worker representation is particularly difficult to make at the workplace level. Neither has ILO been able to propose or sponsor the development of models of workplace collective representation that involve businesses that are not parties to the employment relationship but which potentially have significant influence over working conditions via the leverage that comes from being a large contractor. The result is a situation in which genuine collective representation of workers in the global manufacturing sector is exceptionally rare and seems likely to remain so. Despite this, workers' representatives within ILO have been unwilling to question the voluntarist model. For them, the possible alternative—some kind of mandatory worker representation—might put in question the unions' exclusive right to represent workers. As they see it, the risk that employers would dominate enterprise-based representation structures based on 'universal worker suffrage' is too high.

A second possible explanation for internal institutional incoherence is the gradual amendment and 'reform' of an institutional structure from the perspective of a different frame of reference from that within which it was originally designed. The common law system of industrial relations as it emerged first in the UK and then the USA was intended to recognise the social reality of industrial conflict and to provide a legal framework within which this potentially destabilising, anti-system conflict could be channelled and resolved via 'human arrangement'. Since the 1980s, however, legislation in the UK has made taking legal industrial action progressively more difficult, to the point at which it is only possible within a very narrow range of circumstances. The point of the successive amendments to the law has been to make it as easy as possible for businesses to prevent industrial action, something that is plainly inconsistent with the pluralist frames of reference. Not surprisingly, the policy arguments used to justify the 'reform' of strike regulation betray a determinedly unitarist orientation in which the demands of the market and competitiveness are presented as rigid imperatives and the overriding objective is the maximisation of managerial control (Cradden, 2004, 2014).

A third path to internal incoherence is that in which formal institutional structures remain unchanged, but come to be interpreted on the basis of principles that were no part of the original subjective backdrop to institutional design. As we saw in Chapter 2, this is what happened in the USA during the 1980s and 1990s. The NLRB began to interpret the existing law from the perspective of an overriding concern with the economic interests of employers and on the basis that workers' individual rights trumped their collective rights. The freedom *not* to associate gradually came to occupy centre stage. Successive rulings of the NLRB together with the increasingly aggressive political and legal strategies of employers have meant that from a simple administrative step intended to formalise the workers' choice of bargaining agent, union representation elections in the USA have become a veritable theatre of industrial war. Apart from the inevitable decline in bargaining coverage, one result of this has been that worker organization and representation is increasingly being carried out by groups that are not formally trade unions. Collective worker representation and action has moved out of the formal institutional structure, taking up the anti-system role that was originally played by the unions.

External Institutional Incoherence

Institutional structures (or proposals for institutional change) can be *externally* incoherent in the sense that although they are internally consistent, they do not reflect the frames of reference implied in the public policy narrative or the self-justifications of dominant groups. This will be the case when, to paraphrase Argyris and Schon (1992), 'espoused IR policy' is not is coherent with 'IR policy in use'. This can occur in two main situations. The first is where an attempt is being made to create a consensus around a narrative that would change the perception of existing institutional structures to the benefit of the group telling the story. The second is where system change is being sought via a change in the policy narrative alone in cases where institutional change is politically difficult to achieve because of the empirical balance of power between different groups with the capacity to prevent change.

The first situation tends to arise where dominant groups are seeking a normative justification for their own institutional position based on claims about how they will use the prerogatives the system accords them. For example, the widely espoused logic of high-commitment unitarism points clearly to the need for serious approaches to worker participation and involvement and the consistent choice of 'high road' skills and investment strategies. Nevertheless, the road to the high-performance workplace is littered with the abandoned shells of consultative structures and failed experiments in high involvement working practices.

The second situation can arise when attempts to change ways of thinking about problems are used as a substitute for tackling foreseeable political obstacles in the way of institutional change. In Ireland during the 1990s, for example, a system of national collective bargaining developed that self-consciously aimed to break with the adversarial tradition of negotiation without thereby falling into a naïve unitarism. The extension of this 'partnership' approach to collective relationships at the enterprise level was envisaged as a central part of the national agreement struck in 1996, 'Partnership 2000'. In this agreement, partnership was defined as

> an active relationship based on recognition of a common interest to secure the competitiveness, viability and prosperity of the enterprise. It involves a continuing commitment by employees to improvements in quality and efficiency; and the acceptance by employers of employees as stakeholders with rights and interests to be considered in the context of major decisions affecting their employment . . . [Partnership involves] the common ownership of the resolution of challenges, involving the direct participation of employees/representatives and an investment in their training, development and working environment.
>
> (Government of Ireland, 1996, paragraphs 9.8–9.9)

However, what the implementation of partnership at the firm level would involve in concrete terms was not specified, and it soon became clear that there was little agreement on the subject. A multipartite policy advisory body that included both worker and employer representation, the National Economic and Social Forum (NESF), was asked to produce a report on the subject. The NESF argued that partnership could be characterised exclusively neither as "functional interdependence, bargaining and deal-making" nor as "solidarity, inclusiveness and participation" (NESF, 1997 paragraph 4.1–4.2). Rather,

> [t]he partnership process combines these dimensions/conceptions. To fall entirely into the first could be to validate the claim that the process simply reflects the power of the traditional social partners. To adopt a naïve inclusivist view would risk reducing the process to a purely consultative one, in which all interests and groups merely voiced their views and demands.
>
> (ibid., paragraph 4.8)

The NESF went on to argue that partnership involved both of these dimensions at once together with a third, transcendent dimension they described as "deliberation, interaction, problem-solving and shared understanding". What emerges from this process are decisions that reflect both a balance between the interests of the parties to bargaining and a technical approach to the analysis of factual evidence. Reaching such a strategic consensus relies on all involved accepting that no one group or external expert is alone capable of defining the action situation—the underlying economic or social analysis in the context of which solutions to problems are sought—and that no part of the action situation is the 'possession' of any particular party.

Putting together the language of the 1996 national agreement and the NESF report, it is difficult to see how a coherent institutionalisation of the NESF model of partnership at the enterprise level could have been possible without a significant qualification of the authority of management, and a consequent reconceptualisation of its role and its relationship to the other groups who can claim an interest in the enterprise, particularly trade unions. What cannot logically be maintained is the unilateral right of managers to make all decisions on behalf of the enterprise. An obligation merely to consult with other stakeholders, or even an obligation to take account of their views before decisions are taken, is clearly insufficient to capture the point of partnership as a mode of policy-making. If policy is the outcome of a process whose character includes the idea of *negotiation*, then unilateral decision-making by any one party is excluded.

There was a brief moment, then, when Ireland's IR institutions teetered on the brink of what could have been a very radical reform. In the event, however, although the rhetoric of partnership was not abandoned, it was decided that no institutional reform or innovation was required. Whether or not the governance of work changed was left up to trade unions and businesses to decide. Experiments with partnership structures were carried out in a number of organizations, notably the public services, but none of these proved to be durable. By the time the entire national partnership structure collapsed, soon after the crash of 2008, it was already clear that there had been no significant diffusion of institutional innovation at the enterprise level (O'Dowd and Roche, 2009; Roche and Geary, 2006; Roche, 2007).

Stability and Cognitive Adequacy

IR systems are not just about ideas. They have to *do* something; to successfully fulfil a social and economic function. Whether any particular frame of reference can in practice be the basis of a stable IR system is ultimately an empirical question bound up with the historical specificities of each context. However, this does not mean that the incidence of different dominant frames of reference and the associated institutional structures is entirely random. Not just any frame of reference can be cognitively adequate in the face of any set of social and economic circumstances. For all that frames of reference and system requirements are intimately linked, the objective context of work can still change as a result of both endogenous system adaptation and factors that are exogenous to the IR system itself. Economic circumstances, for example, can change either as a result of 'regular' feedback processes or of unpredictable developments like technological innovation. Although we could argue about the degree to which sociocultural change is driven by system requirements, some of it at least remains autonomous, the result of processes that have to be characterised as communicatively structured and independent of system imperatives.

For example, NTIR predicts that a stable IR system is possible based on any of the six non-organization-negative frames of reference, but it also says that whether that stability is sustainable is an empirical question. It is perfectly possible to envisage a situation in which an IR system is characterised by widely-shared low commitment unitarism and an institutional structure consistent with it. But the pressures for change arising from sociocultural factors like those Fox identified as being at work in post-war Britain and from market factors like incentives to improve quality, productivity and innovation are very likely to disturb this equilibrium. This strongly suggests that the frames of reference that are better adapted to institutional and organizational adaptation seem likely to be more durable in the face of these internal and external pressures for change.

From this perspective, it is not surprising that the frame of reference that gives rise to the most rigid organizational structures, bureaucratic unitarism, is that which would probably be most difficult to find in current institutional and organizational practice. The logic underpinning the organization of production in large, bureaucratically-structured firms reflects the coincidence of a particular set of sociocultural circumstances and a particular stage of economic development in which the ability to maintain and expand the production of a relatively limited range of mass-market goods was paramount. Secular change in product markets demanded a move away from this focus on the constant improvement of a small number of well-established activities towards an increase in the adaptive capacities of firms. Early work like that of Lawrence and Lorsch (1967) on contingency theory, or later studies like Rosabeth Moss Kanter's *When Giants Learn to Dance* (1990), pointed to the importance of the capacity of firms to change what they do and how they do it and to the need to rework organizational structures to become more reactive or 'flexible' or 'nimble'. The need for this kind of adaptability is not compatible with the narrative of bureaucratic unitarism, undermining in particular the value of collectivism, loyalty and firm-specific skills and the logic of long-term employment relationships and internal career structures.

The frame of reference that gives rise to the next least adaptable of institutional and organizational structures is adversarial pluralism. Within this frame, substantive arguments for change have little purchase since what is possible in terms of organizational adaptation and innovation depends almost entirely on the empirical balance of power between capital and labour. Without taking a position on the substantive appropriateness or necessity of any specific type of change, we can still observe that there is absolutely no guarantee that the configuration of forces at any given historical moment will be such as to render any given organizational adaptation politically possible.

We can read the contemporary public policy argument about IR as being about whether an institutional approach based on integrative pluralism or one based on high-commitment unitarism would be the better alternative to the rudderless anomie of low-commitment unitarism. The disadvantages of LCU, logically enough, include low commitment on the part of workers, but also the minimal level of social control over economic activity that it affords together with the narrative of necessity that relieves those in control of organizations from bearing any real responsibility for what they do. As Altman (2002) has observed, however, it is not necessarily the case that high performance work practices and the associated higher levels of engagement and commitment on the part of workers will be financially advantageous for capital owners. Although there may not be any additional net costs, the benefits accrue principally to workers and societies. If these extra-organizational benefits are not included in what Altman calls the 'objective function' used by managers to reach decisions, then it is unlikely that the cost-benefit analysis will point clearly to the rationality of the 'high road' model.

By contrast, both high-commitment unitarism and integrative pluralism demand a normative effort and normative commitments that, to some extent at least, import generally valid values and objectives from beyond the organization. HCU implies that relationships within organizations have substantive, legitimisable normative content; that management involves real commitments to workers and hence to society. The logic and rhetoric of work relationships within the HCU frame of reference is that organizations will not break faith with workers by choosing the most rentable course of action, regardless of its impact on workers. However, HCU ultimately also accepts the logic of external market necessity that may force an organization's hand in certain circumstances. Making the commitments that HCU demands is therefore a risk. The dangers it poses are nicely reflected in this comment by a manager in the UK health service who had been involved in that most typical of high performance work practices, an employee involvement programme:

> I think if you're going to involve staff you have to carry through the things that are important to the staff and when you've already got a huge agenda for change which is government-driven, which may be at odds to what the staff think in some situations, then I think you've got big problems. And you know if you're just going to drive it according to government objectives then you're better off not involving the staff.
> (cited by Tailby et al., 2004, p. 416)

Replace the 'government-driven agenda for change' with the demands of the market and this comment could just as easily have come from the private sector. The holy grail of management in these circumstances is the ability to avoid blame by persuading workers that what the market demands, whatever that may be, is ultimately in their interest. Little wonder, then, that high-commitment approaches have become associated with manipulative styles of management and the tortured euphemism of corporate language attempting to portray even the most cynically self-serving strategic choices in positive terms.

Integrative pluralism is at an advantage here as, if we assume a strong institutionalisation as might have been envisaged on the basis of the Irish social partnership model, it *requires* employers to engage in joint and consultative decision-making rather than just suggesting that it is a good idea. The plans and strategies of management as these apply to the operation of production must be legitimisable in more than a formal sense. In some areas at least, substantive arguments about what activities are simultaneously good for the organization, its shareholders and its workers have to be settled before action can be taken. An equivalent guarantee is difficult to envisage as a part of an institutional structure based on high-commitment unitarism. The logic of that form of understanding demands that management retain the unilateral right to make decisions. This was the barrier that Irish social partnership failed to dismantle.

The Gravity of Normlessness: Dissensus and Low Commitment Unitarism

Habermas argues that while communicative action can and does occur within formal organizations, its validity basis is undermined. Managers know that they can draw a line under discussion and impose a course of action, regardless of whether that action is acceptable to other actors. As long as they can persuade themselves and those to whom they are accountable that some action is a *necessary* response to system requirements they are absolved from any need to justify it in normative terms. In practice, closing down the argument in this way gets easier the less consensus there is around the idea that organizational action *should* have substantive normative content.

This points to another possibility for the effective stability of IR systems, which is that there is no dominant frame of reference and no institutional coherence. As long as the existing institutional structure supports managerial hierarchy and the financial and non-financial incentives and sanctions that give it effect, a passive, non-normative stability can be maintained on the basis of material need and a certain level of despair about the possibility of change. This, of course, is precisely the formula for low-commitment unitarism, the frame of reference with the minimum possible normative content.

Low commitment unitarism is unique among the frames of reference in that it can 'survive' without argument or agreement. It is simply the default position in the absence of a consensus around any of the alternatives with higher levels of normative content. Low commitment unitarism is what is left when there is no agreement but also no will or capacity to agree; it is the anti-frame of reference. Those who suffer because of the system react either with a passivity borne of despair or by engaging in futile individual acts of anti-system behaviour that can never add up to concerted opposition.

The enormous advantage of low-commitment unitarism to managers— and I use the term advisedly to indicate that I am talking about office-holders in organizations where there are permanent managerial hierarchies with no accountability to workers—is precisely that employment relationships have minimal normative content. There is no need for managers to make excuses for hiring, firing and restructuring at will because all that counts is what the system demands. There is never any need to conciliate between values and profits; between returns to workers and returns to shareholders; between loyalty and opportunity. There is never any need, perhaps most notably, for managers to justify their own right to command in anything other than formal terms. As Milton Friedman put it in the title of his famous 1970 article for the *New York Times Magazine*, "The social responsibility of business is to increase its profits". If we adopt the perspective of low-commitment unitarism, the organizational arena is conveniently cleared of any political and ethical obstacles to compliance with system imperatives and managers can set about pursuing their individual objective of career success without fear of moral reproach.

That the easy fallback position of unilateral managerial prerogative exists means that there is an inherent tendency for the normative content of organizational action to degrade. American welfare capitalism crumbled during the great depression. Partnership forms of trade unionism in the UK and Ireland have disappeared. 'Productivity coalitions' in the USA have faded out of view. Employee involvement and participation initiatives are established and abandoned with depressing regularity. The lesson is that unless the institutional structure of the governance of work *requires* worker consent, then managers will sooner or later decide that they are 'obliged' to do something with which workers will not agree.

Conclusions, and Where to Next

The most important theoretical lesson that emerges from the discussion in this book is that industrial relations systems are chosen. The most important policy lesson is that it is very tempting to argue that they are not.

To start with the policy angle on theory, the trouble with accepting that it is possible to choose between substantively different institutional configurations of the governance of work is that the act of choosing one over another implies that there are reasons for that choice that are contingent; that could be otherwise. If those reasons are necessary, if they could *not* be otherwise, then an institutional configuration designed on the basis of those reasons is not a choice but merely a rational adaptation to the circumstances. To use a contemporary catchphrase, it is simply 'what works'. If this is the case, then opposition to it cannot be legitimate. Rather, it is irresponsible, self-defeating and wrong.

What I have argued, though, is that the nature of the structural circumstances of action is not fixed. It depends on what we believe about the nature of economic and organizational systems and the work relationships from which they are built. Institutional configurations of law and practice do not *recognise* facts and norms whose validity can be independently established, but *construct* social truth by stabilising the feedback relationship between beliefs about systems (frames of reference) and the outcomes of systems (the structures of the situation).

All this means that those who have a vested interest in the maintenance of a particular institutional configuration of the governance of work have a strong tendency to favour the positivist assumption that economic and organizational structures have fixed characteristics. What is more, they will tend to interpret the evidence in such a way as to support the maintenance of their preferred institutional configuration and to resist the gathering of evidence where there is a danger that it could be interpreted as support for a configuration they oppose.

This goes some way to explaining why, despite their disagreement about the governance of work, there is nevertheless an unholy alliance between the advocates of labour and of capital to deny the possibility of genuine choice in business decision-making. It is striking that both managers and trade unions seem to believe that business choices are effectively determined by the market. The difference is that business owners and managers want to minimise workers' capacity to resist these choices, while unions want to minimise the possibility that workers will accept them. Managers argue that workers might not understand the technical complexities of finance, marketing and production, or that they might be reluctant to take the hard decisions the market sometimes demands. Trade unions claim that if workers get directly involved in business decision-making they will simply be drawn into accepting the logic of the market and will achieve little more than the legitimation of their own oppression. Both sides assume that there are certain actions that business organizations *have* to take that are not good for workers. Neither accept that workers might be able to decide for themselves whether the substantive argument in favour of this or that course of action is a good one. The result is that the goal of developing institutional structures to support the making of informed decisions about organizational action on the basis of all of the relevant evidence and bearing in mind the aims and values of all the interested parties is simply not on the agenda. Instead, the partisans of labour and capital are engaged in a perpetual and unresolvable argument about whether market and organizational imperatives embody shared or merely partial interests. What ought to be clear by now is that there is no absolute sense in which the conflict or cooperation assumption is, a priori, closer to the truth.

This brings us to the theoretical angle on policy. IR policy is the basis on which IR institutions are designed. The logic of NTIR suggests that the best possible institutional configuration for the governance of work is that which maintains the possibility of reacting to system outcomes *as they actually are* rather than basing law and practice on a fixed assumption about what those outcomes will be. What I have argued is that an appropriate degree of social control over markets and organizations is only possible when structural requirements are treated not as rigid imperatives but as fallible guides to action to which a range of different responses are possible. If we accept that system requirements may be the outcome of abuses or mistakes elsewhere in the system then these should be corrected before they are retransmitted. Only then is the choice of response a genuine choice, in which the normative component of action is not hidden, but out in the open.

So, if some action that is apparently required by the system implies conduct on the part of the organization that would otherwise be considered wrong or some deal with a customer or supplier that is evidently unfair, then the organization's governance structure should make it possible for this action *not* to be taken. The model of social action is essentially the same as that behind the choice of, for example, a fair trade or organic product. Functionally equivalent products are available at a lower price, but the product is chosen because the lower price of the alternatives is recognised as the outcome of unfair market relationships. In most current contexts, however, organizational governance is directed towards ensuring that system requirements are taken at face value and implemented regardless of normative considerations.

Contrary to the opinion of orthodox economists and Parsonian systems theorists, I have argued that action in systemic contexts can and frequently does have a significant normative component. Where this is the case, we move away from a strategic yes/no response to system imperatives and towards communicatively structured forms of action coordination. As Habermas insists, communicatively structured action has an inherent connection to democracy. As we saw in Chapter 5, maintaining the legitimacy of a positively-evaluated system demands that all organization members should be entitled to participate in deciding what the requirements of the system are and how best to respond to them. It is certainly not impossible that the members of an organization could come to trust the judgement of an individual leader or group of leaders and to accept the legitimacy of their choices on the basis of this trust rather than actual, substantive good reasons. However, it is not enough simply to hope or to insist that managers will make legitimate choices while maintaining an institutional structure based on the permanent subordination of workers. Applying Habermas's formal pragmatics tells us that from the perspective of ordinary organization members, the absence of any opportunity to question a decision or the possibility that questioning be arbitrarily closed down is not compatible with the belief that office-holders *intend* to arrive at a legitimate decision.

Actors' beliefs about the intentions of office-holders have a real and serious impact on their behaviour. If actors suspect that office-holders in an organization may use their sanctioning capacity to impose a decision that would not otherwise be accepted, this puts a question mark over the rationality of unreserved cooperation. The logic of pluralist approaches is to contain cooperation with office-holders (managers) within tightly specified limits so as to prevent workers being obliged to act against their own best interests. Pluralist institutions thus create a certain space for cooperation but in so doing also limit it. This is why the capacities of individual actors can only be fully directed towards the realisation of organization goals when organizations are both democratic and unitarist. What is more, it is only under these circumstances, in which both ends and means are subject to positive democratic control, that it is reasonable to expect actors to devote themselves fully to the organization.

None of this is to say that democratic unitarism is likely to be a viable or appropriate choice of policy in every possible context. It depends entirely on the existing circumstances. However, there is every reason to believe that democratic unitarist institutions can and should be the ultimate goal of industrial relations development. In fact, democratic unitarism must be the endpoint of the critical approach to IR that aims to make capitalism a consensual form of life.

The question that remains is how to get there. We can think of this as a journey away from low commitment unitarism in which the normative content of the governance of work is gradually increased. Institutional reform should be used both to encourage different ways of thinking and as a barrier to what I have called the gravity of normlessness. The point is to oblige organizations to make decisions on the basis of substantive argument in a constantly increasing range of areas. I cannot emphasise enough that the starting point must be the definition of a range of aspects of the governance of work that are compulsorily subject to joint decision. Pay and basic worker safety are at the top of the list. For all that there are many managers and business owners in the world who are sincere in their wish to ensure that their workers have decent conditions, there are many more who are overwhelmed by the pressure of the system. Unfortunately, there are also many who simply do not care. In any case, in the face of the extensive evidence that is available about business practices, the argument that organizations will spontaneously make the right choices and do not need to be obliged to do so is risible. In the overwhelming majority of cases, businesses do not, will not and cannot choose to share power with their employees. Any approach to industrial relations reform that does not start by *requiring* each organization to agree basic terms and conditions with democratically elected representatives of its workforce is ultimately futile.

It seems to me that a logical sequence of reform would be to move from low commitment unitarism to adversarial pluralism, from there to integrative pluralism and from there to democratic unitarism. We can think of this as starting by introducing a degree of fairness to market relationships, and gradually moving from there to the development of democratic organizational relationships. The aim is to establish progressively increasing and irreversible worker rights at the same time as shifting from what would initially be a veto power over pay rates towards positive forms of participation and accountability and ultimately fully-fledged industrial democracy. The coordination of action within organizations would no longer be based on managerial hierarchy but on accountable office-holding.

Care would need to be taken in this process to ensure that institutional reform does not lock in certain types of thinking about work. For example, although it is critical that governments and capital owners understand the power of collective labour, maintaining a purely adversarial approach is not viable in the longer term. Somehow, we have to try to build the idea of progress towards participatory democracy into industrial relations development.

Ultimately, this will require radical changes to capitalism that I have not discussed here. Indeed, at the risk of overstretching the metaphor, there are two elephants in this book. One is the legal status of capital and the other is the liability of business organizations for their actions. An institutional structure coherent with democratic unitarism could not maintain the status quo in which the owners of a firm's capital have the ultimate right to control the business and in which the primary duty of the directors of the business is to the shareholders. No matter how much ownership rights are qualified or hedged around, business organizations remain someone's *property*. This has to change before democratic unitarism can be a reality. This is not to say that those who contribute capital rather than labour should have no say in running the firm. It is simply to say that they should not have it all. Power would have to be shared with workers on some basis that represented, for example, a fair reflection of the relative value of capital and labour to the organization together with the extent to which decision-making impacts on the life and livelihoods of the actors involved. This would necessarily involve an entirely new approach to company law including new regulations about how capital owners can behave, including some limitation on the right to withdraw their investment as a means of exercising leverage.

Legal reform would also have to involve the development of new concepts of liability, which is our second elephant. As things stand, workers are not responsible for the actions of their employers. Under a democratic unitarist institutional framework there would have to be some sense in which they were. If we are going to think of business organizations as the collective action of a group of individuals who each have an equal voice in decision-making, then we have to accept that all organization members share the ultimate responsibility for what the organization does, regardless of whether they contribute capital or labour. Obviously, the usual rules of natural justice would have to apply (immunity from liability for the actions of office-holders acting outside their legal competence, for decisions taken in good faith on the basis of fraudulently false information and so on) and the protections that currently apply to the owners of capital and that are intended to encourage investment by limiting liability could be extended to workers. Nevertheless, if workers who are genuinely and substantively in control participate in the making of decisions that run their businesses into the ground or that do damage to individuals, other organizations or the wider community then it is hard to think of any reason why they should be protected from that.

Yet, widening responsibility for the actions of businesses would surely also have a positive effect. It would mean that business stops being 'them' and starts being 'us'. We would no longer be able to tell ourselves that that capitalism is someone else's fault and that there is nothing we can do about it. In fact, control and responsibility are simply two sides of the same coin. If we do not want one, we cannot have the other. This is where we came in: the possibility of gaining control over our own societies and economies.

Democratic unitarism in itself will not save the world. Saving the world demands that we make the right decisions about the organization of production and about investment, marketing, logistics, innovation and sustainability. There is no guarantee that democratic organizations will succeed in any of this. As things stand, though, in most businesses these decisions are made with no regard whatsoever to whether they are the right ones. At best, they are just the decisions that have to be taken, nothing more than an adaptation to circumstances; at worst, they are expressions of what is best for whoever is deciding. Taking control means changing this. It means taking back the moral responsibility for what we do from the self-appointed few who in any case mostly shrug that responsibility off. Only we can save the world, but until the governance of work is democratic we are incapable even of deciding to save it.

Appendix
Outline of a Q Study of the Frames of Reference

The following short account of Q methodology draws on works by Brown (1980) and Watts and Stenner (2005).

Q methodology, or Q factor analysis, is a research technique specifically designed for the study of subjectivity. In a typical Q study, participants are presented with a set of cards, on each of which is printed a statement representing a subjective point of view. These statements are written in ordinary language, either by design or because they are real statements drawn from texts or interviews. Sorting the cards is generally a two-step procedure. In the first step, participants are asked to divide the cards into three piles, one containing the statements which are broadly in line with their own opinion, a second containing those to which they have no immediately clear reaction and a third containing those which are broadly out of line with their opinion. The second step involves refining the initial sort by reconsidering each statement and allocating them to finer degrees of proximity or distance to the subject's own point of view. (It is also possible to administer the sort electronically, usually by dragging and dropping statements into different areas of a computer or tablet screen). The sort is usually 'forced' into a normal distribution around a neutral middle category, with fewest statements in the 'most like my view' and 'least like my view' categories. Once a sort is completed, statements are accorded a numerical score according to their placement (for example, in a 5 category distribution, -2 for statements that are furthest from the subject's view through to +2 for statements that are nearest to it). A factor analysis is then carried out in which statements are treated as observations and test subjects as variables. The resulting factors represent complexes of relationships of agreement and disagreement between the different statements. Factor loadings represent how closely each subject's sort correlates with the idealised or typical sort that the factor expresses. A group of individuals with a similar loading on a factor can be taken to be expressing more or less the same point of view—to see the world in a similar way. In a study of the frames of reference, a researcher would then be in a position to see to what extent the views expressed by different groups of subjects resemble the views that we would expect actors with this or that frame of reference to express.

The set of statements to which subjects are asked to react, known as a 'concourse', can be derived either empirically or theoretically. Sæbjørnsen and her colleagues, for example, distinguish between 'naturalistic' and 'theoretical' Q sampling:

> *Naturalistic Q sampling* refers to processes of finding and gathering potential Q-set items, such as statements, from naturally occurring subjective viewpoints about the topic of interest expressed in newspapers, everyday conversations, interviews or the like. From a sample of such statements, a representative Q set may be derived using either a theoretically structured frame or the researchers' own judgements of representativeness. *Theoretical Q sampling* refers to processes that seek to find, build or construct statements based on some theory.
>
> (2016, p. 16)

A Q methodology study of the frames of reference would begin with the design of a set of statements, some of which are intended to reflect the logic of the specific frames of reference and others the more general positions in relation to the economic and organizational systems.

A Sample Concourse of Statements for a Q Study of the Frames of Reference

In an actual study, the statements would not be ordered as they are below, nor would there be any indication of the categories into which they fall. Rather, they would be presented to the subject in a random order. The concourse would be pilot tested with various different subjects to test for the comprehensibility of the different statements and refined if necessary before definitive testing is carried out.

Positive Market Evaluations

1. In principle, the market system is a very good one—certainly not just the 'least bad' economic system or the best we can do for the moment.
2. As long as the participants treat each other with respect and bargain in good faith then market transactions are win-win. No one loses in a fair deal.
3. The market gives back whatever is put into it. If you've got mutual respect, honesty and good faith going in at one end, you'll get fair outcomes coming out the other.
4. Trade is the best way out of poverty because it maintains people's self-respect and dignity.

Meaningless Market Evaluations

5. The market is not a good or a bad thing in itself. There's no inherent politics or morality to it.
6. There's no point trying to stop the rain from being wet or the sun from being hot. You just do whatever you need to do to stay dry or cool. It's the same with the market—you do whatever you need to do to stay competitive.
7. Businesses have to do certain things because if they don't they won't be able to compete. They don't have any choice about it.
8. Companies don't have a lot of room for manoeuvre in the market so if they put too much weight on behaving 'ethically' rather than doing the deals they need to do they could end up in trouble.

Negative Market Evaluations

9. Saying that the market 'demands' this or that action is really just saying that it would be in the interests of the bosses.
10. The economic interests of different groups in society will always conflict. It doesn't help anyone to pretend that they won't.
11. The market would be different if people were genuinely free to choose whether to enter a market relationship or not, but the idea that freedom of contract really exists is obviously nonsense.
12. You can't say that a deal is fair just because both partners sign the same piece of paper.

Positive Organizational Evaluations

13. Any organization should be a community in itself and should be based on trust and fellowship as much as on the pursuit of profits.
14. Organizations are nothing without the people that work in them, and you can't behave as if people are the same as machines or raw materials.
15. The relationships that people have with their colleagues at work are just as important as the relationships they have with their friends and neighbours.
16. People can't work together successfully unless they're united by something more than self-interest.

Meaningless Organizational Evaluations

17. Organizations exist because they're a good way to get things done, so professional relationships aren't about personalities or values but just about what the organization needs.
18. A lot of jobs aren't very interesting or challenging, but they need to be done.

19. Organizational design and decision-making is about finding the best way for the organization to achieve its goals, not about making people feel good.
20. You can't expect everyone who works for an organization to put their heart and soul into it. It needs to be clear exactly what they're expected to do, that's all.

Negative Organizational Evaluations

21. I think organizations are a problem in themselves. Once you've got that kind of hierarchy in place the people in charge will always find ways to bend things their own way.
22. It seems to me like management is mostly about maintaining control.
23. Employment law, HR departments, unions—none of it is about anything except keeping the ordinary workers in their place.
24. If workers want to carry on putting food on the table, they have to be who their employers want them to be, and to do what their employer tells them what to do in the way they tell them to do it.

Democratic Unitarism

25. I don't understand for a moment why workers wouldn't make good business decisions. They might not decide to move their factory to China, but since when is that a bad thing?
26. I think running a business decently is about doing the right thing, not just cutting whatever deals you can, and I don't see why it's only managers who get to decide what's right and what's wrong.
27. We'd all be a lot better off if managers were accountable to workers as well as shareholders.
28. If it's a good idea to do something then you should be able to convince people that it is. I don't see why you need to be able to force them into it.

High Commitment Unitarism

29. There's no one best way to organise a business—anything goes as long as everyone is happy and all the pieces fit together. All that counts is that the business does what the market wants. That's the part that won't move.
30. Working out how to be competitive is somewhere between a science and an art, but one thing that's for sure is that not everyone can do it. Managers don't get to be managers for nothing, so it just makes sense to be flexible and follow their lead.
31. I don't see how questioning the sincerity and competence of management helps anyone to be committed to the organization and engaged in their work.

32. You don't really get to choose what a business does—it's about keeping on top of what has to be done. If you've got a bunch of people who can work out what that is then everyone should do what they can to back them up.

Integrative Pluralism

33. If it's out in the open that workers' interests aren't always going to coincide with those of management then differences can be dealt with by honest bargaining, which makes building effective cooperation a lot easier.
34. I don't think anyone is under any illusion that the market environment will always be favourable to workers, which is why being up front about divergent interests is a much better basis for working together in a friendly and constructive way than any amount of faddish nonsense about shared vision or common values.
35. People need different things from the business they work in but everyone needs it to do well. There's nothing contradictory in trying to make sure that your partners get what they need as well as you.
36. Workers and businesses owe each other a good deal and shouldn't be mean when it comes to making good on it.

Bureaucratic Unitarism

37. Business is all about constant improvement: doing more for less. So in the end it's the processes that count—what people do and the way one job fits with the next. That's the difficult bit.
38. Everyone needs efficient businesses that produce decent stuff at a good price but you don't need people to put their heart and soul into what they do to get that.
39. The way I see it, work systems are about regularity and reliability. It's about getting the processes sorted out so you get it right every time. That's the way you make money.
40. If the system is designed properly then it won't need much adjusting once it's up and running. All this nonsense about flexibility actually gets in the way of that. Better to think carefully about whether anything really needs to change.

Low-Commitment Unitarism

41. Managers don't have any more choice about what they do than workers, so there's no point in blaming them. The system always wins in the end, and it's a lot less of a headache just to fall in line.
42. A strong economy is good for everyone, so we need to make sure that the people who have the skills to build that strength aren't prevented from applying those skills where they're needed.

43. Businesses have to do what they have to do. It's completely self-defeating to try to put limits on that.
44. Business decision-making is about staying focused on the bottom line. Maybe that's not good for everyone all of the time, but trying to pretend that companies can resist what the market wants isn't going to make it any better.

Adversarial Pluralism

45. The most important thing is making sure that economic and social forces balance out somehow. Unions are a way of channelling social forces in a way that businesses can understand and deal with by bargaining with labour, just like they bargain with suppliers and customers.
46. Collective bargaining about wages and conditions is nothing to do with politics and it's not about doing anyone any favours. It's just an effective way of dealing with one particular business issue.
47. Workers will always and should always unionise to fight for their rights, because if they don't they'll just end up paying for the privileges of the wealthy.
48. Exploitation is built into the system we live in, and thinking that managers will ever or can ever do anything to change that is naïve. Strong, combative unions are the only way to make a difference.

Anarcho-Capitalism

49. I don't see why anyone should work to someone else's plan or their way of seeing the world. No boss is going to look after your interests as well as you can yourself.
50. One person will always lose out if they are dealing with a business, but their voice will get totally lost in a union too. You can only cut a fair deal man-to-man.
51. I know best what I need, and you know best what you need. That's something we can work with. Problems only start when someone starts throwing their weight around and claiming to speak for other people just because they work together.
52. It's businesses that are the problem, not business. There's too much room for forcing people into line with things they wouldn't accept if they were bargaining on an equal footing.

Anarcho-Syndicalism/Workers' Control

53. Workers are perfectly capable of running a business the way it needs to be run. There's no need for bosses or chains of command or complicated collective agreements.
54. Maybe workers need to learn some stuff about marketing and doing the books, but what they don't need is some self-appointed bunch of school

prefects breathing down their necks telling them what to do and how to do it. They can work that out for ourselves.

55. The problem isn't markets, it's management. There will never be any justice as long as workers aren't completely in control of the businesses they work in.
56. Unions are just another obstacle in the way of workers really being in control of how a business runs.

Revolutionary Anti-Capitalism

57. It does not matter how much you hedge work about with rules and so-called protections, workers still lose out in the end. There is no way to fix it without taking back what the bosses have stolen off of workers over the centuries.
58. The unions are doing what they can, but I really don't think they're achieving anything except shoring up the system. The whole thing is going to have to come down before anything gets any better.
59. The point of getting organised isn't to put a measly couple of extra quid in people's pay packets. The point is to turn things upside down so workers don't have to go begging for what's theirs by right.
60. Everything about the way things are at the moment is wrong, so everything will have to change before anything can be right.

Bibliography

Abbott, K. (2006), "A Review of Employment Relations Theories and Their Application", *Problems & Perspectives in Management*, Vol. 4 No. 1, pp. 187–199.

Ackers, P. (2002), "Reframing Employment Relations: The Case for Neo-Pluralism", *Industrial Relations Journal*, Vol. 33 No. 1, pp. 2–19.

Ackers, P. (2014), "Rethinking the Employment Relationship: A Neo-Pluralist Critique of British Industrial Relations Orthodoxy", *The International Journal of Human Resource Management*, Vol. 25 No. 18, pp. 2608–2625.

Alston, P. (2004), "'Core Labour Standards' and the Transformation of the International Labour Rights Regime", *European Journal of International Law*, Vol. 15 No. 3, pp. 457–521.

Altman, M. (2002), "Economic Theory and the Challenge of Innovative Work Practices", *Economic & Industrial Democracy*, Vol. 23 No. 2, p. 271.

Andrini, S. (2004), "Max Weber's Sociology of Law as a Turning Point of His Methodological Approach", *International Review of Sociology*, Vol. 14 No. 2, pp. 143–150.

Anner, M. (2012), "Corporate Social Responsibility and Freedom of Association Rights: The Precarious Quest for Legitimacy and Control in Global Supply Chains", *Politics & Society*, Vol. 40 No. 4, pp. 609–644.

Argyris, C. and Schon, D.A. (1992), *Theory in Practice: Increasing Professional Effectiveness*, Hoboken: Wiley.

Barbet, D. (1991), "Retour sur la loi de 1884. La production des frontières du syndical et du politique", *Genèses*, Vol. 3 No. 1, pp. 5–30.

Barrientos, S. and Smith, S. (2007), "Do Workers Benefit from Ethical Trade? Assessing Codes of Labour Practice in Global Production Systems", *Third World Quarterly*, Vol. 28 No. 4, pp. 713–729.

Bellofiore, R. and Taylor, N. (2004), *The Constitution of Capital: Essays on Volume 1 of Marx's Capital*, Palgrave Macmillan, Basingstoke, UK.

Besson, S. (2005), *The Morality of Conflict: Reasonable Disagreement and the Law*, Hart, Oxford, UK.

Blain, A.N.J. and Gennard, J. (1970), "Industrial Relations Theory—A Critical Review", *British Journal of Industrial Relations*, Vol. 8 No. 3, pp. 389–407.

Blau, P.M. and Scott, W.R. (1962), *Formal Organizations: A Comparative Approach*, Stanford: Stanford University Press.

Bohman, J. (2016), "Critical Theory", in Zalta, E.N. (Ed.), *The Stanford Encyclopedia of Philosophy*, Fall 2016, available at: http://plato.stanford.edu/archives/fall2016/entries/critical-theory/ (accessed 27 October 2016).

Bourdieu, P. (2005), *The Social Structures of the Economy*, 1st ed., Polity, Cambridge, UK; Malden, MA.

Bray, M. and Wailes, N. (1997), "Institutionalism and Industrial Relations Theory", *Current Research in Industrial Relations: Proceedings of the 11th Annual AIRAANZ Conference, Brisbane*, AIRAANZ, available at: http://mngt.waikato. ac.nz/departments/Strategy%20and%20Human%20Resource%20Management/ Airaanz/old/conferce/pdf/bray%26wai.pdf (accessed 10 November 2014).

Brown, S.R. (1980), *Political Subjectivity: Applications of Q Methodology in Political Science*, Yale University Press, New Haven.

Bruce, K. and Nyland, C. (2011), "Elton Mayo and the Deification of Human Relations", *Organization Studies*, Vol. 32 No. 3, pp. 383–405.

Burchell, B., Sehnbruch, K., Piasna, A. and Agloni, N. (2014), "The Quality of Employment and Decent Work: Definitions, Methodologies, and Ongoing Debates", *Cambridge Journal of Economics*, Vol. 38 No. 2, pp. 459–477.

Burrell, G. and Morgan, G. (1979), *Sociological Paradigms and Organisational Analysis: Elements of the Sociology of Corporate Life*, Gower, Aldershot, UK.

Camic, C. (1991), "Introduction: Talcott Parsons before the Structure of Social Action", in *The Early Essays*, University of Chicago Press, Chicago.

Clarke, S. (1995), "Marx and the Market", available at: http://homepages.warwick. ac.uk/~syrbe/pubs/LAMARKW.pdf (accessed 10 May 2017).

Comstock, P. and Fox, M.B. (1994), "Employer Tactics and Labor Law Reform", in Friedman, S., Hurd, R.W., Oswald, R.A. and Seeber, R.L. (Eds.), *Restoring the Promise of American Labor Law*, Cornell University Press, Ithaca, NY.

Cox, R.W. (1971), "Approaches to a Futurology of Industrial Relations", *Bulletin of the International Institute for Labour Studies*, Vol. 8, pp. 139–164.

Cox, R.W. (1987), *Production, Power and World Order: Social Forces in the Making of History*, Columbia University Press, New York, NY.

Cox, R.W. (1996), "Labour and Hegemony", in Cox, R.W. and Sinclair, T.J. (Eds.), *Approaches to World Order*, Cambridge University Press, Cambridge.

Cox, R.W. (2013), *Universal Foreigner: The Individual and the World*, World Scientific Publishing Company, Singapore.

Cox, R.W. and Harrod, J. (1972), *Future Industrial Relations: An Interim Report*, International Institute for Labour Studies, available at: www.ilo.org/public/ libdoc/ilo/1972/72B09_778.pdf.

Cradden, C.G. (2004), *Beyond Pluralism: Reconciling the British Industrial Relations Tradition and Habermas' Theory of Communicative Action*, European University Institute, Fiesole.

Cradden, C.G. (2005), *Repoliticizing Managment: A Theory of Corporate Legitimacy*, London: Ashgate.

Cradden, C.G. (2014), *Neoliberal Industrial Relations Policy in the UK: How the Labour Movement Lost the Argument*, London: Palgrave Macmillan.

Cradden, C.G. and Baccaro, L. (2013), "Suffrage without Citizenship? Deliberating about the Boundaries of the Demos in Geneva", in Arjomand, S.A. and Reis, E.P. (Eds.), *Worlds of Difference*, Sage, London.

Cradden, C.G. and Graz, J.-C. (2015), "Transnational Private Authority, Regulatory Space and Workers' Collective Competences: Bringing Local Contexts and Worker Agency Back In", *Travaux de Sciences Politiques*, No. 62.

Cradden, C.G. and Graz, J.-C. (2016), "Is Transnational Private Regulation Potentially an Effective Means of Promoting Collective Industrial Relations?", *Global Labour Journal*, Vol. 7 No. 1, available at: https://escarpmentpress.org/ globallabour/article/view/2353 (accessed 11 April 2016).

Cradden, C.G., Graz, J.-C. and Pamingle, L. (2015), "Governance by Contract? The Impact of the International Finance Corporation's Social Conditionality on Worker Organization and Social Dialogue", Swiss Network for International

Studies, available at: www.snis.ch/system/files/3296_final_wp_governancebycontract_ final_working_paper_1.pdf.

Dahrendorf, R. (1959), *Class and Class Conflict in Industrial Society*, Stanford: Stanford University Press.

Dimmock, S.J. and Sethi, A.S. (1986), "The Role of Ideology and Power in Systems Theory: Some Fundamental Shortcomings", *Relations Industrielles*, Vol. 41 No. 4, p. 738.

Dunlop, J.T. (1993), *Industrial Relations Systems*, Boston: Harvard Business School Press.

Egels-Zandén, N. and Merk, J. (2014), "Private Regulation and Trade Union Rights: Why Codes of Conduct Have Limited Impact on Trade Union Rights", *Journal of Business Ethics*, Vol. 123 No. 3, pp. 461–473.

Finkin, M.W. and Mundlak, G. (2015), *Comparative Labor Law*, Edward Elgar Publishing, Cheltenham, UK.

Fischer, F. and Gottweis, H. (2012), "The Argumentative Turn Revisited", in *The Argumentative Turn Revisited: Public Policy as Communicative Practice*, Kindle ed., Duke University Press, Durham, NC.

Flanders, A. (1975), *Management and Unions: The Theory and Reform of Industrial Relations*, Faber and Faber, London.

Fox, A. (1966), *Industrial Sociology and Industrial Relations*, HMSO, London.

Fox, A. (1971), *A Sociology of Work in Industry*, Collier-MacMillan, London.

Fox, A. (1974a), *Beyond Contract: Work, Power and Trust Relations*, Faber & Faber, London.

Fox, A. (1974b), *Man Mismanagement*, Hutchinson, London.

Fox, A. (1986), *History and Heritage: The Social Origins of the British Industrial Relations System*, Allen & Unwin, London.

Fox, A. (2004), *A Very Late Development: An Autobiography*, 2nd ed., British Universities Industrial Relations Association Keele, UK.

Fransen, L. (2013), "Global Companies and the Private Regulation of Global Labor Standards", in Mikler, J. (Ed.), *The Handbook of Global Companies*, Wiley-Blackwell, Chichester, UK.

Friedman, D.D. (1973), *The Machinery of Freedom: Guide to a Radical Capitalism*, Harper & Row, New York, NY.

Geare, A.J. (1977), "The Field of Study of Industrial Relations", *Journal of Industrial Relations*, Vol. 19 No. 3, pp. 274–285.

Gernigon, B., Odero, A. and Guido, H. (2000), *Collective Bargaining: ILO Standards and the Principles of the Supervisory Bodies*, International Labour Office, Geneva.

Godard, J. (2004), "The New Institutionalism, Capitalist Diversity, and Industrial Relations", in Kaufman, B.E. (Ed.), *Theoretical Perspectives on Work and the Employment Relationship*, Industrial Relations Research Association, Champaign, IL.

Gonce, R.A. (2002), "John R. Commons's 'Five Big Years': 1899–1904", *American Journal of Economics and Sociology*, Vol. 61 No. 4, pp. 755–777.

Gourevitch, P., Martin, A., Ross, G., Allen, C., Bornstein, S. and Markovits, A. (1985), *Unions and Economic Crisis Britain, West Germany and Sweden*, George Allen & Unwin, London.

Government of Ireland. (1996), *Partnership 2000 for Inclusion Employment and Competitiveness*, Stationery Office, Dublin, IE.

Granovetter, M. (2002), "A Theoretical Agenda for Economic Sociology", in Guillen, M., Collins, R., England, P. and Meyer, M. (Eds.), *New Directions in Economic Sociology*, Russel Sage Foundation, New York, NY.

Green, D. and Shapiro, I. (1996), *Pathologies of Rational Choice Theory: A Critique of Applications in Political Science*, Yale University Press, New Haven.

Greenhalgh, Trisha, and Jill Russell. (2009), "Evidence-Based Policymaking: A Critique." *Perspectives in Biology and Medicine* Vol 52 No 2, pp. 304–318.

Gross, J.A. (1994), "The Demise of National Labor Policy: A Question of Social Justice", in Friedman, S., Hurd, R.W., Oswald, R.A. and Seeber, R.L. (Eds.), *Restoring the Promise of American Labor Law*, Cornell University Press, Ithaca, NY.

Haas, P.M. (2015), *Epistemic Communities, Constructivism, and International Environmental Politics*, London and New York: Routledge.

Habermas, J. (1984), *The Theory of Communicative Action: V1 Reason and the Rationalization of Society*, Polity, Cambridge, UK.

Habermas, J. (1987), *The Theory of Communicative Action: V2 Life World and System a Critique of Functionalist Reason*, Polity, Cambridge, UK.

Habermas, J. (1996), *Between Facts and Norms: Contributions to a Discourse Theory of Law and Democracy*, The MIT Press, Cambridge, MA.

Habermas, J. (1998), *On the Pragmatics of Communication,* edited by Maeve Cooke, The MIT Press, Cambridge, MA.

Handy (Jam) Organization. (1937), *From Dawn to Sunset (Part I)*, available at: http://archive.org/details/FromDawn1937.

Harrod, J. (2008), "The International Labour Organisation and the World Labour Force: From 'Peoples of the World' to 'Informal Sector' | Corporatism | Trade Union", *Scribd*, available at: www.scribd.com/document/2389635/The-International-Labour-Organisation-and-the-World-Labour-Force-From-Peoples-of-the-World-to-Informal-Sector (accessed 6 June 2017).

Hayek, F.A.V. (1986), "The Moral Imperative of the Market", in Harris, R., Anderson, M.J. and Seldon, A. (Eds.), *The Unfinished Agenda: Essays on the Political Economy of Government Policy in Honour of Arthur Seldon*, Institute of Economic Affairs, London.

Howe, G., Howell, D., Joseph, K. and Prior, J. (1977), "The Right Approach to the Economy: Outline of an Economic Strategy for the Next Conservative Government", Conservative Party, London.

Hyman, R. (1978), "Pluralism, Procedural Consensus and Collective Bargaining", *British Journal of Industrial Relations*, Vol. 16 No. 1, pp. 16–40.

Hyman, R. (1995), "Industrial Relations in Europe: Theory and Practice", *European Journal of Industrial Relations*, Vol. 1 No. 1, pp. 17–46.

Hyman, R. (2001a), *Understanding European Trade Unionism: Between Market, Class and Society*, Boston: Sage.

Hyman, R. (2001b), "The Europeanisation—Or the Erosion—Of Industrial Relations?", *Industrial Relations Journal*, Vol. 32 No. 4, p. 280.

Hyman, R. (2004), "Is Industrial Relations Theory Always Ethnocentric?", in Kaufman, B.E. (Ed.), *Theoretical Perspectives on Work and the Employment Relationship*, Industrial Relations Research Association, Champaign, IL.

ILO. (1924), *International Labour Conference 1924: Record of Proceedings*, International Labour Office, Geneva.

ILO. (1995), *International Labour Conference 1994: Record of Proceedings*, International Labour Office, Geneva.

ILO. (1997), "The ILO, Standard Setting and Globalization (Report of the Director-General to the 1997 ILC)", International Labour Office, Geneva.

ILO. (1998), "Overview of Global Developments and Office Activities Concerning Codes of Conduct, Social Labelling and Other Private Sector Initiatives Addressing Labour Issues (GB.273/WP/SDL/1)", International Labour Office, Geneva.

ILO. (2012a), *Conference Committee on the Application of Standards: Extracts from the Record of Proceedings*, Geneva.

ILO. (2012b), *General Survey on the Fundamental Conventions Concerning Rights at Work in Light of the ILO Declaration on Social Justice for a Fair Globalization, 2008: International Labour Conference, 101st Session, 2012; Third Item on the Agenda; Information and Reports on the Application of Conventions and Recommendations; Report of the Committee of Experts on the Application of Conventions and Recommendations (Articles 19, 22 and 35 of the Constitution)*, International Labour Office, Geneva.

ILO. (2013), *Towards the ILO Centenary: Realities, Renewal and Tripartite Commitment: Report of the Director-General: International Labour Conference, 102nd Session, 2013*, International Labour Office, Geneva.

ILO. (2015), *The Standards Initiative—Appendix I Outcome of the Tripartite Meeting on the Freedom of Association and Protection of the Right to Organise Convention, 1948 (No. 87), in Relation to the Right to Strike and the Modalities and Practices of Strike Action at National Level*, International Labour Office, Geneva.

Jacoby, S.M. (1998), *Modern Manors: Welfare Capitalism since the New Deal*, Princeton University Press, Princeton, NJ.

Jami, I. and Achin, C. (2017), "Le travail, cet impensé de la gauche", *Mouvements*, No. 89, pp. 165–177.

Joas, H. and Knöbl, W. (2009), *Social Theory: Twenty Introductory Lectures*, translated by Skinner, A., 1st ed., Cambridge University Press, Cambridge.

Kahn, W.A. (1990), "Psychological Conditions of Personal Engagement and Disengagement at Work", *Academy of Management Journal*, Vol. 33 No. 4, pp. 692–724.

Kannankulam, J. and Georgi, F. (2014), "Varieties of Capitalism or Varieties of Relationships of Forces? Outlines of a Historical Materialist Policy Analysis", *Capital & Class*, Vol. 38 No. 1, pp. 59–71.

Kanter, R.M. (1990), *When Giants Learn to Dance*, Simon and Schuster, New York, NY.

Kaufman, B.E. (2003), "John R. Commons and the Wisconsin School on Industrial Relations Strategy and Policy", *Industrial and Labor Relations Review*, Vol. 57 No. 1, p. 3.

Kaufman, B.E. (Ed.). (2004a), *Theoretical Perspectives on Work and the Employment Relationship*, Industrial Relations Research Association, Champaign, IL.

Kaufman, B.E. (2004b), *The Global Evolution of Industrial Relations: Events, Ideas and the IIRA*, International Labour Organization, Geneva.

Kaufman, B.E. (2004c), "Employment Relations and the Employment Relations System: A Guide to Theorizing", in Kaufman, B.E. (Ed.), *Theoretical Perspectives on Work and the Employment Relationship*, Industrial Relations Research Association, Champaign, IL.

Kaufman, B.E. (2007), "The Core Principle and Fundamental Theorem of Industrial Relations", *International Journal of Comparative Labour Law and Industrial Relations*, Vol. 23 No. 1, pp. 5–33.

Kaufman, B.E. (2008), "Paradigms in Industrial Relations: Original, Modern and Versions In-Between", *British Journal of Industrial Relations*, Vol. 46 No. 2, pp. 314–339.

Kaufman, B.E. (2010), "The Theoretical Foundation of Industrial Relations and Its Implications for Labor Economics and Human Resource Management", *Industrial and Labor Relations Review*, Vol 64 No. 1, pp. 74–108.

Kaufman, B.E. (2014), "History of the British Industrial Relations Field Reconsidered: Getting from the Webbs to the New Employment Relations Paradigm", *British Journal of Industrial Relations*, Vol. 52 No. 1, pp. 1–31.

Kerr, C. (1964), *Labor and Management in Industrial Society*, Doubleday, Garden City, NY.

Kerr, C., Dunlop, J.T., Harbison, F.H. and Myers, C.A. (1973), *Industrialism and Industrial Man: The Problems of Labour and Management in Economic Growth: With a Postscript*, New York: Penguin Books.

Korpi, W. (2006), "Power Resources and Employer-Centered Approaches in Explanations of Welfare States and Varieties of Capitalism: Protagonists, Consenters, and Antagonists", *World Politics*, Vol. 58, pp. 167–206.

Lawrence, P.R. and Lorsch, J.W. (1967), "Differentiation and Integration in Complex Organizations", *Administrative Science Quarterly*, Vol. 12 No. 1, pp. 1–47.

Legge, K. (1995), *Human Resource Management: Rhetorics and Realities*, New York: Macmillan Business.

Marsden, D. (2004), "Employment Systems: Workplace HRM Strategies and Labor Institutions", in Kaufman, B.E. (Ed.), *Theoretical Perspectives on Work and the Employment Relationship*, Industrial Relations Research Association, Champaign, IL.

Marx, K. and Engels, F. (2010), *Karl Marx, Frederick Engels*, Volume 35, Lawrence & Wishart Electric Book, London, available at: http://site.ebrary.com/id/10502167 (accessed 5 January 2017).

Maslach, C., Schaufeli, W.B. and Leiter, M.P. (2001), "Job Burnout", *Annual Review of Psychology*, Vol. 52 No. 1, p. 397.

Maupain, F. (2009), "New Foundation or New Facade? The ILO and the 2008 Declaration on Social Justice for a Fair Globalization", *European Journal of International Law*, Vol. 20 No. 3, pp. 823–852.

Maupain, F. (2013), *The Future of the International Labour Organization in the Global Economy*, Bloomsbury Publishing, London.

Meardi, G. and Marginson, P. (2014), "Global Labour Governance: Potential and Limits of an Emerging Perspective", *Work, Employment & Society*, Vol. 28 No. 4, pp. 651–662.

Mercier, H. and Landemore, H. (2012), "Reasoning Is for Arguing: Understanding the Successes and Failures of Deliberation", *Political Psychology*, Vol. 33 No. 2, pp. 243–258.

Mercier, H. and Sperber, D. (2011), "Why Do Humans Reason? Arguments for an Argumentative Theory", *Behavioral and Brain Sciences*, Vol. 34, pp. 57–111.

Michelson, G. and Wescott, M. (2001), "Heading into Orbit? Braham Dabscheck and Industrial Relations Theory", *The Journal of Industrial Relations*, Vol. 43 No. 3, pp. 308–329.

Mouzelis, N. (1997), "Social and System Integration: Lockwood, Habermas, Giddens", *Sociology*, Vol. 31 No. 1, pp. 111–119.

Muller-Jentsch, W. (2004), "Theoretical Approaches to Industrial Relations", in Kaufman, B.E. (Ed.), *Theoretical Perspectives on Work and the Employment Relationship*, Industrial Relations Research Association, Champaign, IL.

NESF. (1997), *A Framework for Partnership: Enriching Strategic Consensus through Participation*, National Economic and Social Forum, Dublin.

O'Dowd, J. and Roche, W.K. (2009), "Partnership Structures and Agendas and Managers' Assessments of Stakeholder Outcomes", *Industrial Relations Journal*, Vol. 40 No. 1, pp. 17–39.

Parsons, T. (1949), *The Structure of Social Action: A Study in Social Theory with Special Reference to a Group of Recent European Writers*, 2nd ed., The Free Press, Glencoe, IL.

Perkmann, M. (1998), "Social Integration and System Integration: Reconsidering the Classical Distinction", *Sociology*, Vol. 32 No. 3, pp. 491–507.

Phelan, Edward. "The Contribution of the ILO to Peace." *International Labour Review* 59, no. 6 (1949).

Piore, M.J. and Safford, S. (2006), "Changing Regimes of Workplace Governance, Shifting Axes of Social Mobilization, and the Challenge to Industrial Relations Theory", *Industrial Relations*, Vol. 45 No. 3, pp. 299–325.

Quiggin, J. (2012), *Zombie Economics: How Dead Ideas Still Walk among Us*, With a New chapter by the author ed., Princeton University Press, Princeton, NJ.

Redman, P.T. and Wilkinson, P.A. (2008), *Contemporary Human Resource Management: Text and Cases*, 3rd ed., Financial Times/Prentice Hall, Harlow, UK.

Rittich, K. (2003), "Core Labor Rights and Labor Market Flexibility: Two Paths Entwined", in International Bureaus of the Permanent Court of Arbitration, *Labor Law beyond Borders: ADR and the Internationalization of Labor Dispute Settlement*, Kluwer Law International, Netherlands, pp. 157–208.

Roche, B. and Geary, J. (2006), *Partnership at Work: The Quest for Radical Organizational Change*, London and New York: Routledge.

Roche, W.K. (1986), "Systems Analysis and Industrial Relations: Double Paradox in the Development of American and British Industrial Relations Theory", *Economic and Industrial Democracy*, Vol. 7 No. 1, pp. 3–28.

Roche, W.K. (2007), "Social Partnership and Workplace Regimes in Ireland", *Industrial Relations Journal*, Vol. 38 No. 3, pp. 188–209.

Rocker, R. (2004), *Anarcho-Syndicalism: Theory and Practice*, AK Press, Oakland, CA.

Rodgers, G., Lee, E., Swepston, L. and Van Daele, J. (2009), *The International Labour Organization and the Quest for Social Justice, 1919–2009*, International Labour Office, Geneva.

Rose, M.E. (1978), *Industrial Behaviour: Theoretical Development since Taylor*, New York: Penguin.

Rose, M.E. (2008), *Employment Relations*, 3rd ed., Financial Times/Prentice Hall, Harlow, UK.

Rothbard, M.N. (1970), *Power & Market: Government and the Economy*, Ludwig von Mises Institute, Auburn, AL.

Rothbard, M.N. (2009), *Man, Economy, and State, Scholar's Edition*, Ludwig von Mises Institute, Auburn, AL.

Sæbjørnsen, S.E.N., Ellingsen, I.T., Good, J.M.M. and Ødegård, A. (2016), "Combining a Naturalistic and Theoretical Q Sample Approach: An Empirical Research Illustration", *Operant Subjectivity*, Vol. 38 No. 2, pp. 15–32.

Saks, A.M. (2006), "Antecedents and Consequences of Employee Engagement", *Journal of Managerial Psychology*, Vol. 21 No. 7, pp. 600–619.

Sayer, A. (2004), "Moral Economy", Dept. of Sociology, University of Lancaster, available at: www.lancs.ac.uk/fass/sociology/papers/sayer-moral-economy.pdf (accessed 25 August 2010).

Schiller, R.E. (1999), "From Group Rights to Individual Liberties: Post-War Labor Law, Liberalism, and the Waning of Union Strength", *Berkeley Journal of Employment and Labor Law*, Vol. 20, p. 1.

Sen, A.K. (1977), "Rational Fools: A Critique of the Behavioral Foundations of Economic Theory", *Philosophy & Public Affairs*, Vol. 6 No. 4 pp. 317–344.

Simon, H.A. (2013), *Administrative Behavior*, 4th ed., New York: Simon and Schuster.

Sisson, K. (1993), "In Search of HRM", *British Journal of Industrial Relations*, Vol. 31 No. 2, pp. 201–210.

Sisson, K. (2007), "Revitalising industrial relations: Making the most of the 'institutional turn'", *Warwick Papers in Industrial Relations*, No. 85, available at: www.mbsportal.bl.uk/secure/subjareas/hrmemplyrelat/wubs/irruwp/116446wpir_85.pdf (accessed 10 November 2014).

Sisson, K. (2008), "Putting the record straight: Industrial relations and the employment relationship", *Warwick Papers in Industrial Relations*, No. 88, available at: www.mbsportal.bl.uk/secure/subjareas/hrmemplyrelat/wubs/irruwp/116449wpir_88.pdf (accessed 10 November 2014).

Strauss, Anselm Leonard. (2008). *Continual Permutations of Action*. Aldine Transaction.

Tailby, S., Richardson, M., Stewart, P., Danford, A. and Upchurch, M. (2004), "Partnership at Work and Worker Participation: An NHS Case Study", *Industrial Relations Journal*, Vol. 35 No. 5, pp. 403–418.

Thompson, J. (1994), "Ideology and Modern Culture", in Mommsen, W. (Ed.), *The Polity Reader in Social Theory*, 1 ed., Polity, Cambridge, England.

Thompson, P. and Newsome, K. (2004), "Labor Process Theory, Work, and the Employment Relation", in Kaufman, B.E. (Ed.), *Theoretical Perspectives on Work and the Employment Relationship*, Industrial Relations Research Association, Champaign, IL.

Toit, Andries du. "Making Sense of 'Evidence': Notes on the Discursive Politics of Research and Pro-Poor Policy Making (Working Paper 21)." Institute for Poverty, Land and Agrarian Studies, University of the Western Cape, 2012. http://www.plaas.org.za/sites/default/files/publications-pdf/PLAAS_WorkingPaper 21dutoit_0.pdf.

Tosstorff, R. (2013), *Workers' Resistance against Nazi Germany at the International Labour Conference 1933*, International Labour Office, Geneva.

Truss, C., Gratton, L., Hope-Hailey, V., McGovern, P. and Stiles, P. (1997), "Soft and Hard Models of Human Resource Management: A Reappraisal", *Journal of Management Studies*, Vol. 34 No. 1, pp. 53–73.

TUC. (1971), *Good Industrial Relations*, TUC, London.

TUC. (1977), *Industrial Democracy*, New ed., TUC, London.

Tucker, E. (2014), "Can Worker Voice Strike Back? Law and the Decline and Uncertain Future of Strikes", in Bogg, A. and Novitz, T. (Eds.), *Voices at Work: Continuity and Change in the Common Law World*, Oxford University Press, Oxford.

Walton, R.E. and McKersie, R.B. (1965), *A Behavioral Theory of Labor Negotiations: An Analysis of a Social Interaction System*, Cornell University Press, Ithaca, NY.

Watts, S. and Stenner, P. (2005), "Doing Q Methodology: Theory, Method and Interpretation", *Qualitative Research in Psychology*, Vol. 2 No. 1, pp. 67–91.

Webb, B. and Webb, S. (1902), *Industrial Democracy*, 2nd ed., Longman, Green & Co, London.

Weber, M. (1978), *Economy and Society: An Outline of Interpretive Sociology*, edited by Roth, G. and Wittich, C., University of California Press, Berkeley, CA.

Weiss, M. and Schmidt, M. (2008), *Labour Law and Industrial Relations in Germany*, Kluwer Law International, Alphen aan den Rijn, NL.

Wilton, N. (2010), *An Introduction to Human Resource Management*, Pap/Psc., Sage Publications Ltd, London.

Wood, S.J., Wagner, A., Armstrong, E.G.A., Goodman, J.F.B. and Davis, J.E. (1975), "The 'Industrial Relations System' Concept as a Basis for Theory in Industrial Relations", *British Journal of Industrial Relations,* Vol. 13 No. 3, pp. 291–308.

Index

'abstract economics' 53–54
Ackers, P. 9
adversarial pluralism 158–159, 193
agency 49–51, 93–95, 98–99, 101, 133–136
American Federation of Labor 22
anarcho-capitalism 159, 193
anarcho-syndicalism/workers' control 160, 193
arguments 110–111
Austin, J.L. 102, 139
authority: abandoning authority assumption 11–15; 'authority relations' 68–71; hierarchy 130–131; legal 12–14; post-traditional forms of 17–21; relationships and organizational systems 130–131

Bergson, H. 97
Bohman, J. 95
Bourdieu, P. 100, 138–139
Bruce, K. 25, 57
bureaucratic unitarism 154–155, 192
Burrell, G. 23

Camic, C. 98
capital 6–7, 12, 29–30, 58, 186
capitalism 6, 14–16, 22–25, 52–53, 61, 76, 85, 89, 141, 187
classical organization theory, 99
Clegg, H. 67
cognitive adequacy 178–181
collective bargaining: adversarial pluralism 158, 193; collective worker representation and 32–33, 35–45, 119; empirical case for 95; employer hostility and resistance to 26, 29–30; high commitment unitarism 153; ideological backdrop to 97–98; impact on productivity 171; individual bargaining and 114; institutionalism and 52–54; institutions and 82; in Ireland 177; low-commitment unitarism 156; narratives of agency 135; as panacea 74; systems-industrialisation approach 63–64; unitarist frames of reference 136
collective industrial relations (CIR): business case for 41–44; in COPM world 30–36; decline of 27–28; golden age of 25–27; political advantages of 26–27; political aspect to 19–20; postwar policy consensus around 27
collective worker representation: tyranny of the business case 40–44; weak institutionalisation of the conflict assumption 36–40
Committee of Experts on the Application of Conventions and Recommendations (CEACR) 33–36
common law systems 27, 37–38, 44–46, 149, 172, 175
Commons, J.R. 24, 55–56
communicative action 101–103
communism 19, 23, 26
compliance 68–71
Conference Committee on the Application of Standards (CCAS) 35
conflict assumption: frame of reference and 67–68; internal institutional coherence and 174–176; IR policy and 19–20; origins of conflict 49–51; reasonableness of conflict 44–46; theoretical framework that avoids 14–15; weak institutionalisation of 36–40

consensual capitalism 6–7, 14, 96, 123, 185
consensus 8, 173–174
contestation 109–110
contracts 56, 96–97, 123
contractual-administrative rules: ontological truth and 111–112; stabilising money and power steering 112–115
control 12–13
control-oriented people management: CIR in 30–36; 'hard' 156; as manifesto and technique for managers 23; political aspect to 20; return of 27–30
cooperation assumption 14–15, 19–21, 23–25, 40–41, 67–68
Cox, R. 9, 20, 66, 77–85, 88–91, 97, 139, 148–149, 172

Dahrendorf, R. 13
democratic imperative 131–132
democratic unitarism 150–152, 187, 191
dissensus 181–182
Dunlop, J.T. 58–61, 65–66, 75, 79, 86, 88, 138
Durkheim, E. 94, 96–97, 102
Durkheimian sociology 25

'economic nationalism' 3
'economic patriotism' 3
employment relationship 12–13, 68–69, 71–72, 74, 76
exchange 96–97, 123–126, 128

Fayol, H. 23
Fischer, F. 119
Flanders, A. 67, 129
formal pragmatics 102, 115, 119–120
formal rules 103–105, 108–109, 114
Fox, A. 14, 21, 49, 66–71, 75–77, 86, 89, 97, 145
frames of reference: concept of 75–76; conceptual models of organization 136–137; content of 132–133; epistemology of worker and organizational behavior implied in 137; Fox and 66–77; IR policy models 136–137; meaningless organizational evaluations 190–191; meaningless systems 122; negative economic systems 123–128;

negatively-evaluated systems 121–122; negative market evaluations 190; negative organizational systems 128–131; normative choice and social systems 122–123; NTIR 144–147, 149–166; outline of Q study of 188–194; pluralist 71–74, 76–77; positive economic systems 123–128; positively evaluated systems 120–121; positively evaluated systems and democratic imperative 131–132; positive market evaluations 189; positive organizational evaluations 190; positive organizational systems 128–131; radical 73–74, 76–77; systems from action perspective 118–120; theoretical significance of 137–140; unitarist 71–72
Friedman, D.D. 159
Friedman, M. 29, 124

General Agreement on Tariffs and Trade (GATT) 31
'generalized values' 96
Georgi, F. 149
Godard, J. 86–87
Gompers, S. 22
Gottweis, H. 119
Granovetter, M. 100
grounded theory 100–101

Habermas, J. 18, 93, 99, 101–105, 115–116, 119, 123, 138–139, 165
Harrod, J. 79
Hayek, F. 14, 124
high commitment unitarism 152–153, 191–192
Hyman, R. 50, 63, 97

industrialisation theory 26–27, 56–58, 61–65, 79
industrial relations (IR): analysing IR contexts using NTIR 169–171; Anglo-American tradition 9; contemporary significance of 1; focus for 9–11; normative and analytic orientations 6–11; stability and change in systems 172–173
industrial relations policy: approaches arising from cooperation assumption 23–25; basic types of 19–20; conceptual models of the organization and 136–137; impact

of Second World War on 25–27; international policy in context of neoliberalism 30–36; post-traditional forms of authority at work 17–21; systems thinking and 94–95; on trade unions 28–29
industrial relations theory: Cox and social relations of production 77–83, 88–91; development of theory and preoccupations 51–91; Dunlop and the systems turn 58–61; end of IR history 83–85; first wave of institutionalism 52–56; Fox and frames of reference 66–71; Fox's legacy 75–77, 88–91; industrialisation theory and end of IR history 61–65; manifesto for 15–16; pluralism 71–74; possibility of 50–51; post-institutionalist 88–91; return of institutionalism 85–88; second wave institutionalists 56–58; systems-industrialisation model 61–66; unitarism 71–73
institutional coherence: external 176–178; internal 174–176
institutionalism 52–56, 85–88, 115–117
institutional structures 82, 87–88, 147–149, 174–178
integrative pluralism 156–158, 192
international financial institutions (IFIs) 30
International Institute for Labour Studies (IILS) 78
International Labour Organization (ILO) 17, 18–19, 22–23, 31–36, 62
international standards 8–9

Jacoby, S.M. 24
judicial truth 107, 113

Kannankulam, J. 149
Kaufman, B.E. 24, 51, 78
Kerr, C. 57–58, 86
knowledge 107–109
Korpi, W. 7, 28

labour 6–8, 56, 58
labour economics 7
labour movements 7–8, 25, 29–30
Labour Party 3, 5
language philosophy 139
legal authority 12–13

legal legitimacy 10
legal reform 186
legitimacy 10–11, 68, 72, 77, 103–109
liability 186
lifeworld 100–101
Linhart, D. 5, 7–8
low-commitment unitarism 155–156, 181–182, 192–193
Luhmann, N. 99, 139

management 23–25, 56–57, 76, 90, 154–155
market anarchism 159
markets: constraints of 5; impact on business decision-making 85; 'interests of capital' conception of 13–14; management and 76; negative organizational systems in market context 128–131; positive organizational systems in market context 128–131; 'price signals' conception of 14–15; relationships of forces and 90; SRP and 80–81; views of 13–14, 19–20
Marshall, A. 53
Marx, K. 6–7, 61, 99, 102, 129
Maslach, C. 135
Maupain, F. 22
Mayo, E. 25, 57, 61
McCarthy, T. 103
meaningless market evaluations 190–191
meaningless organizational evaluations 190–191
meaningless systems 122
Mill, J.S. 97
monetarist economics 29
money 112–115
Morgan, G. 23
Morse, D. 77–78
Mouzelis, N. 116

National Labor Relations Act 23
necessity 94–95
negative economic systems 123–128
negatively-evaluated systems 121–122
negative market evaluations 190
negative organizational evaluations 191
negative organizational systems 128–131
neoclassical economic paradigm 29–30
neoclassical economic theory 54–55
neoliberalism 30–36

new theory of industrial relations (NTIR): analysing IR contexts Using 169–171; implications for policy 182–187; implications for research 167–182; overview 141–143
normative choice 122–123
normative evaluation 133–136
norms 68–71
Nyland, C. 25, 57

ontological truth 107, 111–112, 113
organizations: authority relationships and organizational systems 130–131; behavior 137; constraints of 5; goals 129–130; hierarchy 11–12; industrial relations policy conceptual models of 136–137; meaningless organizational evaluations 190–191; negative organizational evaluations 191; positive organizational evaluations 190; ownership 12–13, 186

Parsons, T. 58–60, 66, 95–100, 101, 138–139, 165
passivity 135
Perkmann, M. 118
Piore, M.J. 86
pluralism 71–74, 76–77
'pluralistic industrialism' 58
Polanyi, K. 99
political-administrative systems 59, 98
populist right 3–4
positive economic systems 123–128
positive law 103–105
positively evaluated systems 120–121, 131–132
positive market evaluations 189
positive organizational evaluations 190
positive organizational systems 128–131
positivism 93–95
power 65, 74, 79, 110–111
power steering 112–115
procedural legitimacy 10, 14, 106
procedural rules 64, 106
production: ethics of 81–82; reorganisations of 5–6; revolutionisation of 13; social relations of 66, 77–83; systems 8

Q methodology: 168–169, 188–189

'radical anti-intellectualist positivism' 96
radical frame of reference 73–74, 76–77
radical left 2, 3–4
radical right 2
Reagan, R. 29
reform 21–23
resistance 68–71
revision 109–110
revolution 21–23
revolutionary anti-capitalism 160
Roche, W.K. 58, 61
Rothbard, M. 159
rules: contractual-administrative 111–115; formal 103–105, 108–109, 114; industrialisation theory and 56–58; procedural 64, 106; social structure of 76; systems 65–66

Safford, S. 86
Sayer, A. 99
Searle, J. 102, 139
Sisson, K. 50, 51, 87
social relations of production (SRP) 66, 77–83
social systems 122–123
Spencer, H. 94, 96
stability 178–181
structure 49–51, 93–95, 101
substantive legitimacy 10–11, 14, 16, 106, 111, 124
supply-side economics 29
systems: from action perspective 118–120; common law 27, 37–38, 44–46, 149, 172, 175; democratic imperative and positively evaluated 131–132; meaningless 122; negative economic 123–128; negatively-evaluated 121–122; negative organizational systems in market context 128–131; normative choice and social 122–123; political-administrative 59, 98; positive economic 123–128; positively evaluated 120–121; positive organizational systems in market context 128–131; systems-industrialisation model 61–66
systems-industrialisation model 61–66
systems intuition 94, 95–100
systems thinking 93–101

Taylor, F. 23
Taylorism 56
Thatcher, M. 29
trade unions 2, 5, 7–8, 21–22, 26–28, 52–55
truth 107–109
truth gaps 109–110

unitarism 71–72
utilitarianism 66, 96–97

values 96
voluntarism 64
von Mises, L. 14

'wage fund' theory 53
warranted belief 106
Webb, B. 2, 52–55, 61

Webb, S. 2, 52–55, 61
Weber, M. 10, 96, 99, 102, 107, 108, 110
welfare capitalism 23–25, 182
work: consensual social relations and 6–7; as denial rather than an affirmation of workers' true social identity 73; employer-employee relationship 12; frames of reference and 71–72; governance of 10, 11, 19; institutionalism and 52–55; market economy and 6–7; objective requirements and benefits of 143–144; post-traditional forms of authority at 17–21; structure vs. agency at 49–51
worker behavior 137
worker engagement 133–136
World Trade Organization (WTO) 31

For Product Safety Concerns and Information please contact our EU
representative GPSR@taylorandfrancis.com
Taylor & Francis Verlag GmbH, Kaufingerstraße 24, 80331 München, Germany